Explaining Music

EXPLAINING MUSIC

Essays and Explorations

by Leonard B. Meyer

UNIVERSITY OF CALIFORNIA PRESS
BERKELEY, LOS ANGELES, LONDON 1973

University of California Press
Berkeley and Los Angeles, California

University of California Press, Ltd.
London, England

Copyright © 1973, by
The Regents of the University of California

ISBN: 0-520-02216-5

Library of Congress Catalog Card Number: 73-187749
Printed in the United States of America

Designed by Dave Comstock

The Ernest Bloch Professorship of Music and the Ernest Bloch Lectures were established at the University of California in 1962 in order to bring distinguished figures in music to the Berkeley campus from time to time. Made possible by the Jacob and Rosa Stern Musical Fund, the professorship was founded in memory Ernest Bloch (1880–1959), Professor of Music at Berkeley from 1940 to 1959.

THE ERNEST BLOCH PROFESSORS

1964	RALPH KIRKPATRICK
1965–66	WINTON DEAN
1966–67	ROGER SESSIONS
1968–69	GERALD ABRAHAM
1971	LEONARD B. MEYER
1972	EDWARD T. CONE

To my brother Dan

Preface

This book is concerned with the criticism of music. As I intend the term, criticism seeks to explain how the structure and process of a particular composition are related to the competent listener's comprehension of it. In other words, the role of the music critic is similar to that of the literary critic. And just as the literary critic need not explicitly consider questions of value—exhibit the greatness of *King Lear*, or demonstrate the brilliance of *Middlemarch*—but is content for these to remain implicit in his analysis of the ways in which plot and character, setting and diction shape our understanding of and response to literature, so the music critic need not expressly inquire about the excellence of the compositions he chooses to discuss.

Values are, of course, always latent in what the critic does—in his account of the ways musical relationships affect the listener's understanding of and response to particular musical works, and also in his choice of works to analyze. But the critic does not, I think, begin with aesthetic principles and arrive at critical judgments. Quite the opposite. He begins with his own responses—his cognitive-affective sense of whether a composition is convincing and exciting, intriguing and entertaining. Then he attempts to find rational grounds for his judgment.

Moreover, since he deals for the most part with works by acknowledged masters, it seems a bit pretentious for the critic to take as his main task an examination of the virtues of compositions by Bach or Beethoven, Haydn or Handel. To do so is probably also circular, and perhaps somewhat disingenuous. For the works of such masters are in some sense the initial basis for his stylistic standards and his criteria of value. In short, the critic does not come to praise masterpieces, but to explicate and illuminate them: to understand and explain, that is, how the various sorts of tonal relationships in a particular composition are understood and enjoyed by experienced sensitive listeners.

Every explanation must be in terms of some general principle. And to a considerable extent, the reasons and arguments used by the critic come from the theory of music. Because genuine music theorists, such as Heinrich Schenker, are few and far between—most so-called theorists are teachers of the grammar and syntax of music—music theory is at present rather rudimentary. Consequently, the critic must at times assume the role of theorist. He must engage in the formulation of general hypotheses and principles which relate events within compositions to one another. In the course of this book, I have not infrequently had to assume such a role, and, as a result, the book is theoretical as well as critical.

The relationships among events within musical compositions—even seemingly simple ones—are frequently surprisingly complex and subtle. The analyses explaining them are, accordingly, often complicated and involved. I have not sought to simplify the difficult, or to gloss over intricate inter-actions with plausible generalities and vague poetic appeals. Rather I have tried to make my analyses as precise and specific as my abilities and the subject allow. And while I take no particular pleasure in long and sometimes difficult discussion, I know of no other way of doing justice to the wonder of music and the miracle of human intelligence which makes and compre-hends it.

This brings me to a question traditionally answered in prefaces: namely, to whom is this book addressed? Frankly, I'm not sure. Sometimes in those moments of doubt and depression that come when one is near to finishing, I have felt that it is addressed mostly to its author—though I hope not. I would like to believe that a wide range of readers seriously interested in music, in aesthetics, and in criticism will find the problems I have grappled with not only important and challenging, but even amusing.

Writing the preface to a book is always both a sad occasion and a happy one. Sad, because the fun is in the search, not the solution; in the problem, not the proposition; in the formulation, not the finishing. Sad, too, because the author knows better than anyone else that his book is going to press with all its imperfections on its head. Specifically, I am acutely aware of all that has been left undone: of theoretical problems not solved successfully, of particular passages not adequately explained, and of examples not used whose analysis would have illustrated yet another fascinating aspect of musical structure. I can only console myself with the thought that the only perfect book is a book *imagined*—not one actually written. For to write is to fix what is in flux and to pigeonhole the particular. But, as I argue in Chapter I, there is no alternative. To explain and explore is necessarily to compromise and misrepresent the rich individuality of the specific musical pattern.

The occasion is a happy one because, for all its joys and rewards, writing is somewhat frightening and, in the final stages, when discovering has reached a temporary end, the task tends to be onerous. But, above all, the occasion is a happy one because it is an opportunity to acknowledge the help and encouragement of friends, colleagues, and students.

This book grew out of a set of five public lectures given at the University of California at Berkeley. I am grateful to the faculty of the Department of Music at Berkeley for inviting me to serve as Ernest Bloch Professor during the winter and spring of 1971, and for the cordial kindness they showed me while I was their colleague. In particular, I extend my affectionate thanks to Professor Daniel Heartz, who encouraged me when I was depressed and calmed me when I was uptight about delivering public lectures. I am also indebted to Helen Farnsworth, who not only made sure that I got the materials and equipment I needed, but read and corrected portions of this manuscript. Jane Wilkinson prepared the musical examples for publication.

The first part of this book—the Essays—are basically the same as four of the lectures given at Berkeley. The second part—Explorations—which began as the fifth lecture—has obviously been much expanded. But even thus expanded it is a kind of compromise.

Some two years ago my colleague, Professor Edward E. Lowinsky, urged me to write a book about melody. I thought about it and began work on such a book, but found that the task was beyond my capability. The second part of this book, which attempts to explore some aspects of tonal melody, however, is the result of Professor Lowinsky's suggestion. It may be mistaken in part or in parcel. But whatever its value—and, needless to say, I believe it to be interesting and inventive—it is offered to him as a sort of separate Festschrift, a token of respect and affection.

Parts of this book have been read and criticized by a number of scholars. All have my heartfelt thanks. Professors Monroe Beardsley and Forest

Hansen, who saw an early draft of Chapter I together with part of the chapter which closes the book, made several important suggestions. Professor William Thomson's criticisms of Chapter III were specially careful and cogent. Professor Barbara H. Smith read the first part of the book. In addition to her specific comments and corrections, I have benefited enormously both from her writings and from the general discussions we have had about works of art and related matters. Professor Janet Levy read most of this book, and, again, it is not merely her perceptive and specific criticisms that merit grateful acknowledgment, but the serious and sympathetic talks we have had about particular compositions, and about the theory and history of music.

Like most teachers, I am specially indebted to my students, whose probing questions and enthusiastic skepticism have been a source of continuing delight and constant learning. Though I cannot name them all, one in particular must be mentioned. Eugene Narmour, who now teaches at the University of Pennsylvania, has been working on the analysis of tonal melody, too. The last part of this book owes a very considerable debt to our many discussions.

While I was working on this book—and particularly in the difficult beginning stages—Zita Cogan assumed many administrative chores which were properly mine. Her devotion and concern merit much more than perfunctory acknowledgment.

Finally, what can I say (that has not been said time and time again by other authors in similar circumstances) about Lee's help? That she was patient, understanding and forebearing? She was all of these. That she saw relatively little of California because I wanted to work and that, on our return to Chicago, we neglected our friends because I was trying to finish this book? That, too, is the case. And what is her reward? Only the customary connubial thanks—and the prospect of proofreading!

L. B. M.

Contents

Part One
ESSAYS

CHAPTER I

On the Nature and Limits of Critical Analysis

I.

Experienced naively—without any psychological predispositions or cultural preconceptions whatsoever—the world, as William James observed, is a buzzing, booming confusion of discrete, unrelated sense impressions. It is "full of sound and fury. . . ." One may, of course, try to experience existence in this way: unmediated by concepts, classes, or relationships. And a number of artists and writers—for example, John Cage, Norman O. Brown, and Alain Robbe-Grillet—have urged such mindless innocence upon us. So, too, have some members of the hippy-drug subculture. In the *Electric Kool-Aid Acid Test*, Tom Wolfe gives us this viewpoint unadulterated:

> That baby sees the world with a completeness that you and I will never know again. His doors of perception have not yet been closed. He still experiences the moment he lives in. The inevitable bullshit hasn't constipated his cerebral cortex yet. He still sees the world as it really is, while we sit here, left with only a dim historical version of it manufactured for us by words and official bullshit, and so forth and so on.

But Wolfe's world of scatological romanticism, reminding us of Wordsworth's *Ode*, cannot be understood. It has neither process nor form, meaning nor value. Like the world of Benji in Faulkner's *The Sound and the Fury*, "It is a tale told by an idiot . . . signifying nothing." It merely exists.

To understand the world, we must abstract from the ineffable uniqueness of stimuli by selecting and grouping, classifying and analyzing. We must attend to some features of an object, person, or process rather than others—distinguishing (from some particular point of view) the essential from the accidental, the intrinsic from the incidental. The intelligible present is not an isolated instant in time, but, as Whitehead put it: "What we perceive as the present is the vivid fringe of memory tinged with anticipation." A meaningful, a humanly viable world must be ordered and patterned into relationships of some sort. This is the case not only in everyday existence, but in the arts and sciences as well.

The order thus discerned—whether in nature, culture, or art—is not, however, arbitrary or fictitious. The processes and forms, patterns and principles discovered by scientists, social scientists, and humanists are derived, directly or indirectly, from existent events that are really *there* in the world. They are not arbitrary figments of subjective imagination. The similarities between events, the orderliness of processes, and the hierarchic structuring of relationships are just as real as the differences between events, the features which are disordered, and the absence of relationship. The critic does not, like God, bring order out of chaos. Rather, like the scientist, though with important differences, the critic seeks to reveal and explain an order already present in some work of art—an order perhaps not previously observed, or observed only partially or inaccurately.

Because it abstracts, classifies, and conceptualizes, criticism is often disparaged on the ground that it distorts the complex richness of the individual aesthetic experience—its special savor and indescribable affective quality. In a strict sense, this charge cannot, I think, be refuted. A specific musical experience which combines the perception of musical events with the subjective peculiarities of an individual human psyche at a specific moment in its history, *is* unique. Criticism cannot fully know or explain that experience. Nor is it concerned to do so. For criticism endeavors to understand and explain the relationships among and between musical events, not the responses of individual listeners. Those we must leave to the shamans of the middle-class—the psychoanalysts.

However, though the individual's particular experience is unique and perhaps unknowable, the perceptions which shape that experience are not so. Whenever it goes beyond the mere sensing of incoming stimuli, listening is necessarily analytical—abstracting, classifying, and organizing musical stimuli into patterns, processes, and relationships. As soon as one perceives the tone of, say, an oboe, is aware of octave identity, or groups tones into motives and motives into phrases, one has abstracted—has ignored a myriad of attributes present in the series of stimuli. Awareness virtually compels conceptualization. Our perception of the splendor of a sunset or of the subtle nuances of a lovely theme are inseparable from our knowledge of the event as being a sunset or a theme.

In his novel, *End of the Road,* John Barth has put this much better than I can. His hero, Jacob Horner, a writer, exclaims: "Articulation! There, by Joe, was *my* absolute, if I could be said to have one. . . . To turn experience into speech—that is, to classify, to conceptualize, to grammarize, to syntactify it—is always a betrayal of experience, a falsification of it; but only so betrayed can it be dealt with at all, and only in so dealing with it did I ever feel a man alive and kicking." And just as the artist in presenting *a* reality in words, visual materials, or musical tones in this sense distorts his and our experience of existence, so criticism in its turn necessarily falsifies the experience of the art work. But only so betrayed, to paraphrase Barth, can works of art be understood or discussed at all. Only a totally mystical experience is entirely nonanalytic, and it cannot be conceptualized or even adequately described—since the act of description is itself a distortion. Those who seek to savor the singularity of their own psyches must, therefore, abandon all hope of rational discourse or intelligible communication. The only valid response to unmediated experience is silence. As Tom Lehrer has said: "If you can't communicate, the least you can do is shut up!"

Conceptual analysis, then, is not just something done by stuffy, arid academics. It takes place whenever anyone attends intelligently to the world. It is the only way in which we can cope with the buzzing, booming confusion which everywhere surrounds us. On the other hand, particularly in an academic context such as this, it is well to remember that we tend to teach and study those aspects of experience that most easily lend themselves to abstraction and syntactification. There are, however, other, more elusive forces shaping any rich human experience. For instance, pace and timing (how long a particular sort of event should continue, and how different sorts of events should follow one another) are, I think, of central importance in both music and literature. But I know of no adequate study of these aspects of temporal experience. Thus, even though we reject Macbeth's picture of the world, we should take Hamlet's caution seriously: "There are more things in heaven and earth, Horatio,/Than are dreamt of in your philosophy."

It is also often objected that criticism or analysis is coldly intellectual and inhumanly detached, fragmenting what is really one and conceptualizing what should be felt. With regard to the first, one can only answer that *good* criticism separates where separation is warranted by the musical structure and unites wherever the musical organization permits. Because music is hierarchic—tones combining to form motives, motives phrases, and so on—what is separated on one level becomes unified on the next. Only in the music of transcendentalism—the music of Cage, Earl Brown, Pousseur, etc.—is there complete homogeneity and nondifferentiation. And such music cannot be analyzed, only described.

With regard to the assertion that criticism conceptualizes what should be felt and is, therefore, somehow inhuman, two observations seem pertinent. First, the charge rests upon a doubtful dichotomy: namely, that which separates mind and body, and intellect from affect. Our emotional responses to the world are invariably linked to cognitive patternings. Conceptualization precedes and qualifies affective experience. Turning to William James again: he reminds us that a grizzly bear securely confined behind bars elicits one response—perhaps one of amused empathy; the same bear escaped and running toward us, quite another—anxious antipathy. And the difference lies in our conceptual understanding of the situation. Second, there are reasonable grounds for believing that the musical processes and structures explicitly conceptualized in criticism are those which evoke affective responses in sensitive and experienced listeners.

To conclude the first part of this chapter, I dispute vehemently the notion that an intellectual response to works of art, and to the world in general, is inhuman or undesirable. Quite the opposite. The arts, philosophy, and history, as well as the sciences and social sciences, are valuable and relevant because they are entertaining. Not in the sense of the Ed Sullivan show —it diverts. But in the sense that T. S. Eliot had in mind when he said that poetry is superior amusement. For to entertain ideas—to see pattern and structure in the world—and to be entertained *by* ideas is both the most human and the most humane condition to which man can aspire.

2.

Criticism (or critical analysis) must be distinguished from style analysis. For these disciplines, though complementary, involve different viewpoints, methods, and goals.

Critical analysis seeks to understand and explain what is idiosyncratic about a particular composition: how is this piece different from all other pieces—even those in the same style and of the same genre? It is concerned with the implications of this specific motive or process, the function and structure of this specific harmonic progression, the relationship between this particular slow introduction and the Allegro which follows it, the reason why there is a *sforzando* on this note or why this theme is interrupted at this particular point. In short, criticism tries to discover the secret of the singular—to explain in what ways the patterns and processes peculiar to a particular work are related to one another and to the hierarchic structure of which they form a part.

Style analysis, on the other hand, is normative. It is concerned with discovering and describing those attributes of a composition which are common to a group of works—usually ones which are similar in style, form, or genre. It asks, for instance, about the characteristic features of late Baroque music —its typical textures, harmonic procedures, and formal organization; or it inquires into the features common to diverse movements in sonata form or different types of operas. Style analysis, in its pure form, ignores the idiosyncratic in favor of generalization and typology. Consequently statistical methods are as a rule more appropriate in style analysis than in criticism. For style analysis, a particular composition is an instance of a technique, a form, or a genre.

In describing and classifying typical processes and schemata, style analysis discloses and defines those probabilities—those rhythmic, melodic, harmonic, and textural relationships—which are characteristic of the music of a particular period, a form, or a genre.[1] Here style analysis shades into what is commonly called music theory. For harmony and counterpoint, too, are normative and probabilistic. To take an obvious example, a progression from the dominant to the tonic is normative and probable in the harmonic practice of the eighteenth century, as is indicated by the fact that it is called an authentic cadence. A motion from the dominant to the submediant is less probable, and is said to be deceptive. Indeed, what has traditionally been called music theory is by and large the translation of the normative practice of some style period into a set of syntactical rules for writing exercises in that style.

But a significant distinction must, I believe, be made between the essentially inductive norms of style analysis and an authentic theory of music. Briefly, a real theory of music endeavors, where possible, to discover the

---

[1] We need not consciously classify in order to understand what is normative. We can and do learn the norms of a style—get to know its typical procedures and schema —through listening and performing, just as we do when we learn a language or any other kind of cultural behavior.

principles governing the formation of the typical procedures and schemata described in style analysis. Let me give a simple example of what I have in mind. In books on counterpoint there is generally a rule which states that after a skip, a melody should normally move by step in the opposite direction. This rule is a generalization from sixteenth-century practice. It describes a practice, but it does not explain why the practice makes sense or why it was developed in the first place. Suppose a student were to ask: "Why does this melody of Palestrina descend in stepwise fashion after an upward skip of a sixth?" We might answer: "Well, that was the rule," or "That's what composers writing at the time usually did." But this is clearly circular reasoning, since Palestrina's music was part of the data used in deriving the rule. So the student—probably he is an *undergraduate*—presses us further, asking: "Why did Palestrina follow this practice?" Here we would have to answer him with a general law of some sort. We might, for instance, cite the Gestalt law of completeness, which asserts that the human mind, searching for stable shapes, wants patterns to be as complete as possible. A skip is a kind of incompleteness: the listener is aware of the gap between the first pitch and the second, and "wants" the gap to be filled in, which stepwise motion in the opposite direction does. This "law" of melody is presumably not style-bound, but applies to the music of Beethoven or that of south India, as well as the music of the sixteenth century—though what represents a satisfactory filling of a gap will depend upon the repertory of tones prevalent in the modes of a style.[2]

One might, of course, attempt to generalize still further, asking why the mind searches for stable shapes. And one might explain that because human behavior is not for the most part genetically determined, men must envisage the consequences of choices in order to know how to act in the present; and they can envisage and choose only in terms of patterns and processes which are regular and relatively complete. But I doubt that the explanation of musical practice needs to be pushed back this far. As a rule we are, I think, satisfied with the least inclusive law which will account for the events described.[3] To put the matter in another way: we endeavor to

[2] The melodic style of contemporary pointillists is not an exception to this "law," because the relationships among intervallic events in, say, a piece by Webern are not processive but formal.

[3] As Mario Bunge has pointed out: "*Every system and every event can be accounted for (described, explained or predicted, as the case may be) primarily in terms of its own levels and the adjoining levels. . . .* For example, most historical events

go beyond descriptive or statistical norms to the simplest explanation which takes the form of a general principle. The goal of music theory is to discover such principles.

It is not, however, the goal of critical analysis to do so. Critical analysis uses the laws formulated by music theory—and, as we shall see, the normative categories of style analysis—in order to explain how and why the particular events within a specific composition are related to one another. Theory gives us the general principles governing, say, the processes of melodic implication and closure, while criticism is concerned with the ways in which those principles are actualized—or perhaps evaded—in the case of a specific motive, theme, or section in a particular work.

A description, no matter how detailed and elaborate, is not an explanation. A catalogue of successive pitches (e.g., observing that "the melody begins on D, skips up to B♭, and then moves down to A which is trilled . . ."), the labeling of chords (as C major, F major, etc.), or a listing of dominant instrumental timbres—none of these constitute a critical analysis of a composition.

I do not intend to suggest that descriptive discourse is not relevant—even necessary—in critical analysis. To be so, however, it must be used in conjunction with a viable theory about how the various parameters of music —melody, rhythm, timbre, harmony, and the like—function; that is, how they give rise to patterns and relationships. For instance, given an hypothesis about the psychological functioning of structural melodic gaps, it is meaningful to observe that "the melody begins on D, skips up to B♭ . . ." and so on. Similarly given an hypothesis about the role and function of ornaments in melodic-rhythmic processes, it becomes significant to describe a note as bearing a trill—usually giving some reason why it does so. But in the absence of a background of theory which relates events to one another, description, even when disguised in a cloak of obscure technical jargon, explains nothing.

3.

Even when not explicitly stated, general hypotheses are invariably implicit in critical analysis. Often such hypotheses are of a common-sense

---

can be accounted for without resorting to physics and chemistry, but they cannot be properly understood without some behavioral science." "The Metaphysics, Epistemology and Methodology of Levels," in Whyte, Wilson, and Wilson, eds., *Hierarchic Structures* (New York: Elsevier, 1969), p. 24.

variety. For example, near the end of the second theme of the Finale of
Mozart's Symphony No. 39 an interruption, followed by a digression, takes
place.

Example 1

Had the consequent phrase been regular it would have been as follows:

Example 2

That is, the major mode would have remained and the melody and harmony of the cadence would have been:

Example 3

And this cadence exactly is presented at the end of the digression (Example 4).

Now this interruption might be explained by pointing out that the second theme employs the same motivic material as the first, and both are antecedent-consequent phrase structures. Moreover, the form and process of the second theme are particularly patent and predictable. Therefore, had the consequent phrase closed in the expected way, the whole theme would have seemed obvious and anticlimactic. One could, of course, formulate a general law covering the case: what is too predictable is uninteresting and is, as a rule, avoided. But this is scarcely necessary. Indeed, because common sense lets us take the proposition for granted, as a kind of cultural *donné*, the explicit statement seems artificial and pretentious.

This is not to suggest that one should not try to build a more refined and comprehensive theory of music. But because specific musical events are the result of nonrecurring concatenations of conditions and variables, no set of general laws can adequately explain the particular relationships embodied in an actual composition. In other words, no matter how refined and inclusive the laws of music theory become, their use in the explanation of

Example 4

particular musical events will have to depend in part upon the *ad hoc* hypotheses of common sense.

Here an analogy might be helpful. Let us liken music theory to a written score, the critic to the interpreter-performer of that score, and the tradition of performance to common-sense hypotheses. Just as any symbolic notation, if it is to be useful, can specify only a part of what is to be presented in a performance, so music theory can formulate only some of the hypotheses needed in the analysis of a particular composition. To put the matter the other way around: a score which contained *all* of the information communicated by a particular performance—every nuance of duration, pitch, dynamics, timbre, etc.—would not only be unreadable, but would take years to write down and months to decipher. Similarly a theory which covered every possible interaction of all possible variables would be useless because it would lack precisely what any theory must have—namely, generality. For the performer, the composer's score constitutes a more or less definite set of directions which suggests a particular interpretation; and in parallel fashion, the explicit formulations of music theory suggest possible explanations of particular musical events to the critic. Just as the performer's actualization of a score is controlled in part by the stylistic tradition of performance practice, so the critic's use of music theory depends in part upon the common-sense tradition of his culture. If performance traditions may be considered as a kind of unwritten notation, then common sense may be regarded as unformulated theory.

Because this point is of crucial importance for criticism, I should like to emphasize it by stating it in another way. In the *Ghost in the Machine*, Arthur Koestler points out that every skill—for our purposes: composition, performance, and listening as well—has a fixed aspect and a variable one:

> The former is determined by its canon, the 'rules of the game', which lend it its characteristic pattern—whether the game is making a spider's web, constructing a bird's nest, ice-skating, or playing chess. But the rules permit a certain variety by alternative choices: the web can be suspended from three or four points of atttachment, the nest can be adjusted to the angle of the fork in the branch, the chess-player has a vast choice among permissible moves. These choices, having been left open by the rules, depend upon the lie of the land, the local environment in which the holon operates—they are a matter of strategy, guided by feedbacks. Put in a different way, the fixed code of rules determines the permissible moves, flexible strategy determines the choice of the actual moves among the permissible ones. The larger the number of alternative choices, the more complex and flexible the skill.[4]

[4] *The Ghost in the Machine* (New York: Macmillan, 1968), p. 105. A "holon" is a more or less separable entity or event that forms part of a hierarchic structure. For instance, a motive would be a holon on a low level; a theme would be one on a

In music, psychological constants such as the principles of pattern organization, the syntax of particular styles, and typical schemata such as triadic holons constitute the *rules of the game*. Their actualization as specific musical events is the realization of what Koestler calls *flexible strategy*. For any given musical repertory the "rules" determine the kinds of patterns that can be employed in a composition. They are the province of style criticism. Strategies, which are variable and nonrecurring, give rise to particular instances of some general type or class. The task of critical analysis is to explain why a general rule was actualized in the way it was. For instance, in the example from Mozart's Symphony No. 39, the rules of the game tell us that the theme belongs to the characteristic pattern called "antecedent-consequent phrase." The strategy to be explained is the particular realization of this normative pattern. Because rules do not determine strategies, common-sense reasons are necessary to explain specific musical events. They bridge the gap between rule and strategy. And because common-sense reasons are necessarily *ad hoc*, criticism is, and will always be, an art—not a science.

The reasons used to explain a particular musical event will, then, be of two different sorts: rule reasons, derived from style analysis and music theory, which will tend to be constant, and strategy reasons which will be of the *ad hoc*, common-sense variety. Because they depend upon particular circumstances, strategy reasons are generally eclectic. Sometimes they will be drawn from established disciplines such as acoustics or psychology; at other times they will be based upon common sense. Rule reasons, too, at least for the present, will from time to time be eclectic. This, because music theory is still rudimentary and style analysis only somewhat less so.

Not only will criticism tend to be eclectic, but some aspects of music may for a time simply be inexplicable. Fortunately, however, explanation need not be exhaustive and absolutely certain in order to be illuminating. Were complete information and incontrovertible theory a prerequisite for understanding, science, for example, would never have even begun.

4.

Even though critical analyses are seldom comprehensive, all too often they will seem unduly arduous and protracted. This is because there is invariably a disparity between the speed and ease with which music is experienced and understood, and the length and complexity of the discussion

higher level. Essentially the same point is made by Herbert A. Simon in *The Sciences of the Artificial* (Cambridge: M.I.T. Press, 1969), Chapter 2, particularly pp. 23–31.

needed to explain why and how it is experienced and understood. A simple
melody of, say, sixteen measures, which takes less than a minute to perform,
may require several pages—five or six minutes worth—of explanation. Many
students and discerning listeners find this disparity incongruous and discon-
certing. And the critic frequently feels the same way. But this "Disparity
Effect" is by no means confined to criticism; it holds true for every explanation in every discipline: in the sciences and social sciences, as well as in the
humanities. A solar eclipse may last little more than an hour; a student disturbance less than a day. But explaining these events may require extended
and intricate discussion.

Take riding a bicycle, for instance. Why a bicycle is relatively stable and
hence ridable has been considered by a number of scientists—most recently
by David E. H. Jones. Jones begins his discussion as follows: "Almost every-
one can ride a bicycle, yet apparently no one knows how they do it. I believe that the trick contains much unrecognized subtlety . . ."[5] Why a
bicycle is stable proves to be a subtle problem involving questions of gravity,
geometry, centrifugal force, gyroscopic action, and so on. But Jones's
seven-page article, detailed and complex though it is, is an account only of
the *theory* of bike-riding—of the rule reasons for stability.

Suppose, however, that the series of events in an actual bicycle ride was
to be explained. Taking into consideration not only Jones's theory of stability, but specific features of the terrain (hills, curves, road surface, etc.) and
information about the rider (his weight, muscular strength, experience, and
so on), analysis would seek to explain precisely what happened on the ride—
how and why the rider shifted his weight, turned the wheel, changed gears,
and modified his speed in order to follow the specific course taken. It is this
sort of particular musical event-series which the critic attempts to explain.
Considering that even a simple melody is at least as complex an event as a
short bike ride, it is scarcely surprising that explanations in criticism are
usually longer and more involved than one might wish.

Jones's statement calls attention to another important consideration.
Just as one can ride a bicycle without knowing how a bicycle really works, so
experienced listeners can respond sensitively to music without knowing anything about what makes music work: without knowing about the theory or
history of music. Because it involves attending to and comprehending tonal
relationships, understanding music is, I have argued, necessarily cognitive
and analytical. But it does not follow from this that understanding depends

[5] "The Stability of the Bicycle," *Physics Today*, XXIII, 4 (April, 1970), 34.

upon knowledge of theory or information about means and techniques. We can perceive and comprehend actions and relationships—musical as well as nonmusical—without the explicit conceptualization necessary for explanation.

Zealous listeners are sometimes heard to protest that they "love" music, but don't understand it. This is, of course, absurd People seldom like what they do not understand. Quite the opposite. Because it threatens a deep need for psychic security, men generally detest and reject what seems incomprehensible. Witness the hostility which contemporary music so often excites in audiences accustomed to the syntax and structure of tonal music.

What listeners mean when they say that they don't understand music is that they can't read it, name syntactic processes, classify formal procedures, or otherwise explain how music works. Like many theatergoers in ancient Greece or Elizabethan England, they are illiterate, but they are by no means ignorant.[6] Luckily, understanding does not depend upon literacy or upon theoretical knowledge. If it did, the audiences for the plays of Aeschylus and Shakespeare, or for the music of Bach and Brahms, would have been very small indeed.

Understanding and enjoying a Bach fugue or a Brahms sonata does not involve knowing about—conceptualizing—cadences, contrapuntal devices, bridge passages, and the like, any more than being entertained by *Hamlet* involves knowing about syntactic functions, prosodic devices, or dramatic means. Understanding music, to paraphrase what Bertrand Russell has said of language, is not a matter of knowing the technical terms of music theory, but of habits correctly acquired in oneself and rightly presumed in others. Listening to music intelligently is more like knowing how to ride a bicycle than knowing why a bicycle is ridable.

[6] And this may be true of creative artists as well as of audiences. For instance, Albert B. Lord's account of the singing of epics in Yugoslavia indicates that conceptualization and classificatory knowledge are not necessary for the composition of oral poetry: "Man without writing thinks in terms of sound groups and not in words, and the two do not necessarily coincide. When asked what a word is, he will reply that he does not know, or he will give a sound group which may vary in length from what we call a word to an entire line of poetry, or even an entire song. . . . When a singer is pressed then to say what a line is, he, whose chief claim to fame is that he traffics in lines of poetry, will be entirely baffled by the question; or he will say that since he has been dictating and has seen his utterances being written down, he has discovered what a line is, although he did not know it as such before, because he had never gone to school." *The Singer of Tales* (Cambridge: Harvard University Press, 1960), p. 25.

This is not to contend that education cannot enhance understanding and hence appreciation and enjoyment. By calling attention to patterns and relationships which might otherwise have been missed, it refines the aural imagination and increases the sensitivity of the cognitive ear. And to this enterprise, critical analysis can certainly make an important contribution. But education is not its primary goal. The primary goal of criticism is *explanation* for its own sake. Because music fascinates, excites, and moves us, we want to explain, if only imperfectly, in what ways the events within a particular composition are related to one another and how such relationships shape musical experience. Though knowledge about the theory and history of music are not a prerequisite for sensitive understanding, they are a necessary basis for explanation.

Criticism depends not only upon knowledge, nonmusical as well as musical, but upon such elusive qualities as general intelligence—the ability to perceive the propriety of some reasons and the irrelevance of others—and, most important of all, musical experience and sensitivity. For the critic begins by sensing or guessing how a musical event "works"—how it fits together and functions. Michael Polanyi's observation that "the study of an organ must begin with an attempt to guess what it is for and how it works"[7] applies to the study of a musical composition as well. Once a work or passage is understood in this almost intuitive way, the critic will begin to analyze its structure. He will attempt to discover what kind of patterning underlies it, and hence which rule reasons are appropriate for its analysis; what sorts of implications are suggested by its melodic, rhythmic, and harmonic organization, and whether and how these are actualized; how the event is structured hierarchically, and in what ways the several levels of the hierarchy are related to one another.

The answers to questions such as these are not always obvious at first. Repeated playing and listening may be required. Because the several parameters do not necessarily move in congruent fashion (with the result that harmony, melody, rhythm, and so on may each yield a different pattern of organization), it will at times be helpful to analyze the parameters separately in order to study their interrelationships. Often it is illuminating to "normalize" a passage—rewrite it in a simpler, archetypal form—in order to understand how the composer has modified a traditional schema. Always it is important to discover which tones or harmonies are structurally essential and which are ornamental. When employing such techniques—which are

[7] *Personal Knowledge* (Chicago: University of Chicago Press, 1958), p. 360.

not modes of explanation, but methods for disclosing how a musical event functions—the critic's "ear," his musicality, must guide analysis. It must accept or reject a linear abstraction, an harmonic reduction, or a rhythmic analysis. His ear keeps the critic honest. Without its control, theory or style analysis tends to become a Procrustean bed to which the practice of composers is made to conform.

Because its reasons are often *ad hoc* and its explanations eclectic, criticism may at times seem somewhat improvisatory. But this does not mean that it is arbitrary or illogical. Different sorts of arguments from a variety of sources may be employed, but they must be applied *objectively:* rules and techniques, arguments and evidence must be used in the same way in each analysis; and, though not systematized, reasons must be consistent with one another. Criticism must obviously be musically persuasive, but this is not enough. For what finally convinces is aural cogency combined with logical coherence. Because it must be scrupulous in reasoning, but flexible in strategy, criticism might well be called the *delicate discipline.*

5.

Looked at from another point of view, criticism attempts to understand and explain the choices made by a composer in a particular work. In order to do so, the critic must be aware of the options available to the composer at each point in the composition, and he must be able to estimate (in a general way) what the probable consequences of alternative decisions would be. The critic must have not only a viable theoretical framework, but equally important a sensitive feeling for the style.

Style analysis is therefore necessary to and relevant for criticism. A particular melody, harmonic progression, or formal procedure is almost always understood in terms of the normative type or schema of which it is an exemplification. As Morris Cohen points out, "The absolutely unique, that which has no element in common with anything else, is indescribable, since all description and all analysis are in terms of predicates, class concepts, or repeatable relations." [8] For instance, a listener who has not learned—through cultural experience, not necessarily through classroom instruction—the stylistic syntax of tonal harmony will not be able to appreciate the deviant delay of a deceptive cadence. Similarly, without a sense of the normative procedures of a classical rondo with its more or less regular returns of the main

[8] *The Meaning of Human History* (LaSalle, Illinois: Open Court, 1947), p. 84.

theme, much of the delightful play present in, say, the Finale of Haydn's Symphony No. 102 would be missed.

Style analysis is necessary for criticism not only because particulars are invariably understood in the light of classes and norms, but because such typologies suggest how the passage or event being considered will probably "work." And, as noted earlier, analysis of an event must begin with some sort of hypothesis about its function. Polanyi's observation is akin to William Dray's contention (made in connection with the study of history) that "explaining what a thing is . . . is just not the same enterprise at all as explaining why it . . . happened." [9] A part of a composition without patent and closed melodic shapes and characterized by rapidly shifting harmonic motion is more understandable when conceived of as a "development section," just as an historical period marked by disturbance and turmoil can be better comprehended as a "revolution." Moreover, to classify an event is to call attention to the way it functions and to promote a heuristic attitude with respect to events within it. The classification of the Mozart theme discussed earlier as an antecedent-consequent type led us to look for the missing normative cadence and, in this case, to find it.

To understand a composer's choices is to envisage the psychological-stylistic alternatives open to him at a particular point in a composition. For this reason, particularly in the short run, our guesses about implications and continuations may often be partly or wholly mistaken. Ends are generally more accurately envisaged than means. And the predictable route which suggests itself to the critic will not as a rule be the one chosen by the composer. Their invention is both more subtle and more adventurous than ours —which is why they, and not we, are creators. That our guesses may be mistaken does not, however, gainsay the importance of considering possible alternatives. For our understanding of what the composer *actually* did is significantly dependent upon our understanding of what he *might* have done.

(From an aesthetic point of view this is crucial. For it makes clear that musical enjoyment lies as much, if not more, in the *act* of traveling as in the *fact* of arriving. What delights and moves us, as we listen to a composition, are the changing landscapes, the turns in the road revealing unexpected vistas, and the surprise of delectable detours encountered *en route* to goals of relative repose.)

[9] " 'Explaining What' in History," in Patrick Gardiner, ed., *Theories of History* (Glencoe, Illinois: The Free Press, 1962), pp. 403–408.

But even in the long run, our most confident surmises about routes and goals may prove wrong. This is because, given the particular style within which he works, the composer is a *free agent*. He invents and shapes his initial musical substance—his themes, harmonic progressions, textures, and the like. These have implications for subsequent events. But they do not *determine* those events. This for two main reasons.

First of all, the implications—the possible consequences of a musical event, of a motive, phrase, or even section—are always plural. A musical event implies a number of alternative actualizations. What the composer does is to discover the possibilities implicit in his own musical ideas. In Stravinsky's words, "Step by step, link by link, it will be granted [the composer] to discover the work." [10] The quality of his compositions depends both upon his ability to discern or, if you will, to invent such implications, and upon his artistic judgment in selecting interesting and fruitful ones for his composition.

Determinism is a mistaken notion applied to works of art not only because implications are plural, but also because, within the style he employs, the composer may at any particular point in a piece be absolutely arbitrary. That is, he may invent and use a musical idea or relationship which has nothing to do with—was in no way implied by or dependent upon—preceding events in the piece. Though he is free at any point in a work to do as he likes, a responsible composer will subsequently take such an arbitrary act into account. That is, the relationship between antecedent events and the arbitrary one will, taken together, have consequences later in the composition. For instance, the interruption of the consequent phrase in Mozart's Symphony No. 39 cannot (as far as I can see) be inferred from anything that preceded it. It is simply a decision—though the critic can suggest, as I tried to do, why it is not an unreasonable one. The interruption is acceptable for a number of reasons. One of these is that it is subsequently seen to have important consequences—particularly in the development section.

All of this suggests that the notion of "inevitability" in music must not be taken literally, but in a Pickwickian sense. The series of events in a piece of music is not *actually* inevitable. If it were, music would be as uninteresting and dull as detergent commercials. Rather a piece of music must seem *in retrospect* to have fitted together—to have been "right." A good composi-

[10] Igor Stranvinsky, *Poetics of Music*, trans. by A. Knodel and I. Dahl (Cambridge: Harvard University Press, 1947), p. 50.

tion makes us feel the uncertainty of the improbable, even while convincing us of its propriety. It confronts us with the capricious and cons us into believing it was necessary.

If the goal of criticism is to understand and explain the musical decisions made by composers, then ideas about music expressed by the composer himself, or by critics and theorists close to his time, should be particularly relevant for the present-day critic. They are, but with important qualifications. Such information is just as relevant, but not one whit more so, as statements made by other protagonists in history—by kings and philosophers, generals and social reformers, tradesmen and theologians—about their beliefs, motives, and goals. They may be reliable and pertinent, or they may be biased, incomplete, and misleading. Just as the political or social historian evaluates the asserted beliefs and views of an historical figure in the light of his actual actions (and vice verse), so the critic must evaluate the statements of composers or theorists in the light of the compositional practice to which they refer.

Such documentation may provide fruitful avenues for criticism and analysis. Thus, as Leonard Ratner has shown, the views of eighteenth-century composers and theorists about sonata form help us to understand the practice of the period. On the other hand, ideas and theories from the past must, when contradicted by the practice of the past as we see it, be rejected or modified by present-day theory and criticism. In Donald Jay Grout's words: "the correspondence of theory and practice is no more exact for medieval modal melodies than for any other type of actual music in any period." [11] Most often, however, differences between the views of composers and theorists of the past and critics and theorists of the present are ones of emphasis. For example, most critics today would explain Bach's Brandenburg Concertos or the Well-Tempered Clavier largely in terms of syntactic processes and formal organization, rather than in terms of the doctrine of affec-

[11] *A History of Music* (New York: W.W. Norton, 1960), p. 53. Lawrence Gushee makes a similar point when, in a review of a translation of Gafurius' *Practica Musicae*, he writes: "But what are we to make of the fact that most of Gafurius' fourth book described proportions which are not encountered in the written music of the time? Was Gafurius intoxicated by the spirit of systematization, mating the arithmetic theory of proportions inherited from Classical Antiquity with the principles of mensural music developed during the 13th and 14th centuries? . . . But apart from sensitizing students to the importance of rhythmic relationships and of understanding the original form of notation of a work—such sensitivity would also arise from a study of the works themselves—I cannot see many insights accruing from the study of Gafurius." *Journal of Music Theory*, XIV, 1 (Spring, 1970), 129–130.

tions, a form of explanation which would probably have been favored in Bach's own time. Finally a somewhat general observation. Because they have a very special relationship to, and technical interest in, their art, composers are often inaccurate reporters of what they do and not unbiased judges of the work of others.

The preceding discussion calls attention to the fact that there is a significant difference between the concern of the critic or theorist who attempts to use present-day knowledge about man to explain the art of music, and the concern of the historian of theory or of criticism who seeks to account for the sequences of theories and critical viewpoints about music. The distinction, analogous to that between a scientist and a historian of science, has not always been recognized by musicologists. For them theory in particular has meant explaining what past treatises have said about music—usually music close to the time the treatise was written. Such studies are undoubtedly important; but they are essentially historical, not theoretical.

The task of the theorist is different. Using as his primary data the music itself, together with his own stylistic experience and whatever can be ascertained about performance tradition, he attempts to construct hypotheses about the ways musical events—melodic, rhythmic, harmonic, textural, etc. —are related to one another. In so doing, he may refine existing hypotheses, devise quite new ones, or borrow concepts and methods from other disciplines such as linguistics, psychology, or systems analysis. His theory may be corroborated by treatises written at the time that the music he is concerned with was composed, and this will constitute supporting evidence. But the absence of historical corroboration will not necessarily prove the newly formulated theory mistaken. For theories are confirmed or disconfirmed in terms of their internal integrity, their agreement with the body of cultural beliefs and theories of which they are a part, and according to whether, when dispassionately employed, they correspond to and can explain the facts— which in this case are musical, not historical. The validity of the theories of Schenker or Kurth, for example, do not depend upon whether Beethoven or Wagner, or the theorists contemporary with them, held similar views about the nature of musical processes and structures.

And in fact it must be thus. For, at least until our topsy-turvy century, practice almost always preceded theory. And whether theory follows by a day, a decade, or a century, it is necessarily a hypothetical construct—not an absolute, eternal truth.

It is important that "understanding the choices made by composers" does not mean knowing what actually went on in the composer's mind when he wrote a particular work. Probably neither he, nor we, will ever know his mental processes as they actually occurred. Even when a composer was conscious of making a decision—when his habit of craft was not immediately adequate to the problem at hand—choice may have been largely intuitive. After considerable thought, trial and error experimentation, and just plain daydreaming, the right solution may have appeared, as it were, out of the blue—often when least expected. The result seems clear and "logical," but the route followed in reaching it may well have been veiled and circuitous. In other words, just as there is a difference between the logical steps through which a scientific argument is presented and the act of scientific discovery which may have been the result of unconscious processes, owing something to training, to disposition, to the current state of the discipline, and frequently quite a bit to chance; so there is a difference between the coherence and consistency of a completed composition and the composer's creative processes which depend upon a combination of training, tradition, personality, and, again, plain luck.[12] In short, the critic attempts to understand not the history of the decisions which resulted in a composition, but the "logical" alternatives presented to the composer given the structure of a particular set of musical circumstances. He is, to paraphrase Aristotle, concerned with what might be called the poetry of creative choice, not its history.

This point is especially relevant because there has of late been a salutary interest on the part of historians as well as theorists in the sketches, drafts, and autographs of composers—that is, in how they went about writing music. And while sketches and notebooks may be revealing, they should not be confused with the finished work.[13] Equally important is the fact that the changes made by composers from sketches to draft to finished work can be understood and explained only in the light of some theoretical-critical viewpoint. To discover and classify the compositional stages followed and changes made by Bach or Beethoven is to describe their compositional pro-

[12] For an account of these aspects of the creative process, see Arthur Koestler, *The Creative Act* (New York: Dell, 1967), Part II and particularly Chapters 5–10. Koestler is, I think, mistaken when he disparages the positivists' account of scientific reasoning and explanation. He argues that it misrepresents the nature of the creative act. True. But the positivists are concerned to understand the structure of scientific arguments, not the genesis of the insights which led to them.

[13] See the discussion at the end of Chapter 3 of the theme of the Trio from Beethoven's "Eroica" Symphony.

cedures, not to explain their compositional thinking. We can explain why a composer changed a passage as he did—put a *sforzando* on this note, modified a melody in this way, or altered a modulatory scheme in a particular fashion—only if we have a theory about the nature of musical relationships.

6.

I should like to close by briefly considering the limits and hazards of critical analysis. Clearly just as the punishment must, according to a famous Oriental potentate, fit the crime, so an analytic method or theory must be appropriate to the style of the composition being studied. It is pointless to analyze, say, a work by Machaut or one by Boulez in terms of techniques developed by Heinrich Schenker for the analysis of tonal music. In this respect critical methods must be *ex*clusive.

Given this important limitation, however, critical analysis should in general be as *in*clusive as possible. That is, *all* the methods, theories, and techniques which are relevant to and will illuminate the composition being considered should be brought to bear. In analyzing a Beethoven sonata, for instance, a number of techniques and theoretical approaches are appropriate: conventional harmonic analysis, motivic derivation (judiciously employed), the methods developed by Schenker, theories having to do with the ethos and character of music, and so on. *Which* analytic means are used will depend not only upon what kind of relationship is being considered, but also upon the hierarchic level being analyzed. For instance, conventional harmonic analysis is appropriate to the study of the lowest level of harmonic progression, while the techniques of Schenker are relevant to the understanding of higher levels—the middleground and background.

But no matter how inclusive and detailed a critical analysis is, it is seldom exhaustive, and it is never definitive. It is seldom exhaustive because most pieces of serious music are complex. Consequently it is almost always possible to discover relationships not previously observed. The critical analysis of a particular work is never definitive because the theory of music and those of related disciplines such as psychology are likely to change. And because it is partly dependent upon such theories, analytic criticism will probably change too.

This should not, however, be cause for despair. For though criticism is neither exhaustive nor definitive, it does not follow (any more than it does in the fields of chemistry or biology, psychology or philosophy) that valid and valuable insights are impossible—that criticism can explain nothing about music and our experience of it. On the other hand, the inchoate state of music theory and style analysis, together with the need for specially sensitive judgments in the explanation of particular instances (strategies), make criticism not merely a delicate, but a hazardous discipline.

The desire for certitude and permanence is both deep and abiding. Consequently style analysis, chronological studies, and paleography tend to be more attractive to most members of the academic establishment than theory, criticism, and history. For, insofar as style analysis merely describes and classifies, and history merely authenticates or arranges data in chronological order, their observations and results appear to be certain and secure. They will stand the test of time, except, of course, when newly discovered information makes it necessary to revise existing norms or chronologies—a possibility which diminishes as the accumulation of data grows. Theories and critical analysis, on the other hand, are fallible, debatable and provisional; and so are those histories which attempt to explain why a series of events happened as it did. Theories are rejected or revised, histories are rewritten, and criticisms are not definitive.

Disheartened and perhaps dismayed by the speculative uncertainties of theory, criticism and, one should add, history as distinct from chronicle, too many humanists, particularly those in music, have tended to follow the well-worn path of safe scholarship. But to choose prospective certainty over present insight is both mistaken and misguided. It is mistaken because the search for final, definitive answers is an unattainable goal for those disciplines concerned with understanding and explanation. For, since the future is open and influential, it can change our understanding both of past compositions and of past historical events. It is misguided—paradoxically so—because the enduring monuments of scholarship, which have shaped men's minds and beliefs, far from being cautious and circumspect, have been those which illuminated a relationship, a work of art, or a past epoch through a bold, encompassing hypothesis. Though in all probability they will subsequently be revised, or even rejected, such works and theories endure because they are exciting and seminal: they lead to new discoveries and further formulations, and thereby continue to affect language, thought, and behavior.

CHAPTER II

Critical Analysis and Performance: The Theme of Mozart's A-Major Piano Sonata

PRELUDE

Though the patterning of tonal music will be the specific concern of this book, one or two general observations need to be made at the outset. The first is that the existence of both similarity and difference between musical events is a necessary condition for patterning of any sort. Since the concept of pattern includes the notion of regularity and orderliness, patterning is incompatible with complete heterogeneity. What is less obvious, but equally important, is that total uniformity also tends to preclude patterning.

A note or a harmony repeated without any change in dynamics, duration, or timbre is not a pattern. Like the ticking of a clock it is not *dis*-ordered, rather it is *un*ordered. Even a motive (which is itself a pattern) will not, if repeated exactly, create implicative patterning on the next hierarchic level. What ordering there is will be formal, not processive. Similarly, the patterns produced by completely uniform changes will be unsatisfactory. For instance, chromatic and whole-tone scales or exactly uniform melodic and harmonic sequences, though they give rise to very regular low-level relationships, establish no points of relative stability and closure. The series of events is so undifferentiated that it is potentially endless and, in this sense, unordered and abortive. If a repeated event is entirely formal, then a uniform series of changes is exclusively processive (see Chapter IV). Viable patterns fall somewhere between these extremes. They involve both form and process.

In general, the more clearly and completely shaped a pattern is—the more patent its order on a number of hierarchic levels—the more specific and compelling its implications will be. A single tone, for instance, is not a pattern. Even within a particular musical style, it might be followed by an indefinitely large number of alternative continuations—many of which would to all intents and purposes be equally probable. As tones are added, durational relationships established, and other parameters specified, the relational ordering—the pattern—becomes apparent, and implications are defined. In other words, as an event unfolds in time, the probability of some modes of continuation and closure increases relative to others. Delays—digressions, extensions, and the like—occur toward the end of patterns both because they are most effective when specific goals are in view [1] and because the clearer and more probable the mode of continuation, the greater the need for the heightened interest provided by delay or deviation.

Musical patterns arise within and are governed by the grammar of a specific style. In the case of the music considered in this book, the style is that of Western tonal music from about 1650 to, roughly, 1910. Just as literary criticism broadly speaking takes the syntax of a particular language for granted, so an understanding of the grammar and syntax of tonal music is assumed in what follows. To do otherwise would be to attempt an entirely different task—that of explaining not particular musical relationships, but how and why tonality works. For instance, the relative melodic stabilities of the tonic, fifth, and third of the scale, as well as the tendency of other tones to move toward these in more or less specific ways, are not explained. Familiarity with the syntax of tonal harmony is also taken for granted—presuming that there is agreement about which progressions are strongly implicative and which are less so, which triads are relatively stable and which tend to be mobile and on-going, and so on.

I must also assume that the concepts of rhythmic structure and syntax which Grosvenor W. Cooper and I developed are either understood or can be grasped, as particular examples are analyzed.[2] In our book, rhythmic relationships were analyzed as *patterns* in which a stable accent and one or more weak beats were grouped together in different ways. Though the terminology of prosody was employed, our fundamental concern was with the nature and basis of temporal patternings seen as the result of the interaction

[1] Indeed, delay entails the notion of goals-in-view.
[2] See *The Rhythmic Structure of Music* (Chicago: University of Chicago Press, 1960).

of all parameters of music—melodic, harmonic, dynamic—as well as durational relationships.

More specifically. End-accented groups—iambs (◡ —) and anapests (◡ ◡ —) —are generally speaking more stable and closed than either middle-accented amphibrachs (◡ — ◡) or beginning-accented trochees (— ◡) and dactlyls (— ◡ ◡). Like other aspects of tonal music, rhythm is hierarchically structured: lower-level, foreground patterns combine with one another in various ways to form more extended rhythmic groupings. The groupings on the several levels are indicated by brackets (⌣—⌣) beneath the accent and weak beat signs. Overlapping brackets (⌣⌣⌣) mean that a group is joined by a pivot. Finally, a rhythmic event at first understood to be accented may, in retrospect, be understood to be mobile and weak. The converse of this occurs, but only infrequently. In the analyses, such changes are shown by putting the retrospective function underneath the initial one. For instance, the symbol, ‿ , means that an event first considered to be accented is subsequently thought of as being mobile and on-going.

Throughout this book musical relationships are characterized as being more or less "probable." Since the term probability is used in a number of different ways, its meaning here should be made as clear as possible. First of all, the term is not used to refer to mathematical probability, which is numerically measurable and involves the axioms of the probability calculus. Mathematical probability, as Bertrand Russell observes, "has to do always with classes, not with single cases except where they can be considered merely as instances." [3] Nor, on the other hand, is implicative probability subjective. For there is clearly considerable agreement among competent listeners about stylistic probability: for instance, that in tonal melody, a motion from C to E will more prabably be followed by G or D than by A♭ or B. Rather implicative probability is more like what Russell calls "credibility" which "is objective in the sense that it is the degree of credence that a *rational* man will give." [4] Or, in my terms, it is the strength of implication as understood by a competent listener.

There is, however, a problem—though fortunately it is essentially theoretical rather than practical. It is that of the influence of frequency

---

[3] *Human Knowledge: Its Scope and Limits* (New York: Clarion Books, 1948), p. 343. For this reason, as noted in Chapter I (p. 7), statistical methods are appropriate for style analysis, but only indirectly (through the relevance of style analysis) for criticism.

[4] *Ibid.,* p. 343.

upon probability estimates. On the one hand, the history of music seems to show that a change in the frequency with which, say, a particular chord progression occurs in the literature of music does affect the listener's sense of harmonic probability. On the other hand, we are not simply products of Pavlovian conditioning, as an essentially statistical theory of pattern comprehension would imply. Since I have considered this point elsewhere,[5] let me only restate my judgment that implicative probabilities, though influenced by frequency at times, arise out of and are significantly the result of fundamental modes of human perception and cognition—dispositions and proclivities having to do with the ways in which the human nervous system process and patterns sense-experience.

I.

In Chapter I, I argued that analysis is something which happens whenever one attends intelligently to the world. Whenever stimuli are grouped, ordered, and related into coherent patterns and processes, analysis has taken place. The performance of a piece of music is, therefore, the actualization of an analytic act—even though such analysis may have been intuitive and unsystematic. For what a performer *does* is to make the relationships and patterns potential in the composer's score clear to the mind and ear of the experienced listener. Conversely, as Edward Cone has pointed out "Active listening is, after all, a kind of vicarious performance . . ."[6]

Just as analysis is implicit in what the performer does, so every critical analysis is a more or less precise indication of how the work being analyzed should be performed. By explaining the processive and formal relationships of a composition, analysis suggests how phrases, progressions, rhythms, and higher-level structures should be shaped and articulated by the performer. At times such relationships may be equivocal either because the patterning itself is so or because several different groupings are implied simultaneously. In such cases alternative analyses will be possible. But such alternative interpretations, and the performances to which they give rise, will be complementary rather than contradictory.

In this chapter I hope to show how critical analysis and performance are related to one another. Because there can be a number of viable interpretations of a particular composition and because decisions among them may

---

[5] *Music, the Arts and Ideas* (Chicago: University of Chicago Press, 1967), pp. 19–20, 260.

[6] *Musical Form and Performance* (New York: W. W. Norton, 1968), p. 21.

depend upon the taste, temperament, and training of the critic or the performer, perhaps the best—the least ambiguous—way to deal with these matters is to consider an interpretation which I think is definitely wrong, and try to show why it is so.

In the Peters edition of Mozart's Piano Sonatas, edited by Louis Köhler and Adolf Ruthardt, the Theme of the first movement of the A-Major Sonata is phrased as shown in Example 5.

Example 5

According to the most recent authoritative edition of the sonatas, done by Nathan Broder, Mozart phrased the Theme as shown in Example 6.

Example 6

In my judgment the phrasing in the Peters edition is downright wrong. The question is: what is wrong with it? What reasons can one give for preferring Mozart's phrasing?

One might content oneself by arguing from authority, saying: "Well, that's the way the composer wrote it." But such an argument would not help us in making phrasing decisions in Bach's music—where such marks are few and far between. Nor does it tell us why Mozart's marking makes musical sense, while Köhler's and Ruthardt's phrasing does not.

At first blush the difference between the two versions seems slight. After all, the notes, durations, and harmonies remain the same. But the rhythms of the two are different. Consider the low-level rhythmic analysis of Mozart's phrasing (Example 7A) and that in the Peters edition (Example 7B):

Example 7

In Mozart's version, the lowest level (1) consists of a series of trochees, except for the final group which is pivoted and forms a compound event. The groups stay within the measure, as indicated, even on the second rhythmic level (2). The phrasing in the Peters Edition, on the other hand makes the weak eighth-notes, particularly those at the end of each measure, function as upbeats. The units are primarily iambic—though complexly so. The second level (2), too, is rather irregular and lacks symmetry; particularly, one is in doubt about how to group the three iambs in the middle of the phrase.

Here a general reservation about Köhler's and Ruthardt's aberrant phrasing should be voiced. Its asymmetric irregularity seems at odds with the basic simplicity of the tune and the harmony. Moreover, variations are to be based upon this theme, and since complexity will probably come later in the movement, its propriety is at least doubtful here. Somehow, too, the rather strong upbeats of the aberrant version lack refinement and nuance. Next to the subtle cool of Mozart's phrasing, they seem blatant and gratuitously emphatic.

The aberrant version "sounds" obvious because in a sense it is more "natural." Let me explain. When short and long notes follow one another, the short notes tend to be heard as upbeats to the longer ones which follow, rather than as weak afterbeats. For instance, a series of notes of equal duration in duple meter tend to be heard as trochees:

This effect will be particularly clear if a slight stress is placed upon each main beat. If every weak beat is now shortened relative to its accent, the weak beats will begin to group with the notes which follow rather than with those which precede:

And if these triplets are made into dotted eighths and sixteenths, the effect is even more striking:

For this reason, the eighth-notes following quarter-notes in a ⁶⁄₈ meter tend to function as upbeats (anacruses).

This is also the case in Mozart's Theme. The E at the end of the first measure and the D at the end of the second have a tendency to act as upbeats. The same is true of the weak beats on A and B in the third measure. The ambiguity of the E—the possibility of hearing it either as the weak beat of a trochee (   ) or as the upbeat of an iamb (   )—is easily tested. For instance, if the E at the end of measure 1 is followed by conjunct motion, as in Example 8, then the final eighth-note of the measure is perceived as an unequivocal anacrusis. Pitch proximity allows the potential mobility of the final eighth-note to be actualized. Notice that durational

Example 8

relationships and harmony are the same as in Mozart's Theme. The eighth-note E in Mozart's Theme acts as the weak part of a trochee rather than as an upbeat because pitch disjunction (the skip of a fourth) tends to prevent rhythmic grouping across the barline and because the sequential repetition of the melodic pattern in measure 2 makes it clear that the first measure is a separate, integral musical event.

The potential mobility of the last eighth-note of measure 1 is also shown in the fact that its function is easily influenced by prior organization. Thus if the theme is made to begin with an upbeat, E, as in Example 9, then the E at the end of measure 1 and the D at the end of measure 2 will tend to group with the notes which follow them, as anacruses. This is the case because once a particular mode of organization, such as a rhythmic grouping, is established, it tends to be continued as a way of patterning until counter-vailing events take place. And for this reason, the weak beats in measure 3 (of Example 9) were also probably felt to be anacruses.

Example 9

But an even more modest change will show that the E at the end of measure 1 is a potential upbeat. For if the sixteenth-note D in the first measure, and the C♯ in the second, are deleted, as in Example 10, the groups tend to be heard as end-accented—as iambic. Observe that though these sixteenth-notes seem to be merely decorative, they perform an important

Example 10

musical function. Consequently conscientious analysis will consider each note and duration as well as every nuance of dynamics and phrasing to be syntactically significant unless shown to be otherwise.

The sixteenth-note D is crucial because it makes the first group into a *closed* trochee—that is, it prevents the weak eighth-note C♯ from acting as an upbeat to the E. More specifically: the sixteenth-note not only links the two C♯'s as a changing note, but because of its brevity, it functions as a kind of low-level upbeat; as a result, the following eighth-note is perceived as the *end*, rather than as the beginning, of a group. Let me illustrate this point with a somewhat simple-minded example.

Because it is quite uniform and regular, the tune in Example 11 can be grouped in different ways. It can be performed as a dactyl, as in 11A, as

Example 11

an anapest (11B), or as an amphibrach (11C). What changes in each case is the way in which the weak beats are grouped with the accent. But if the first note is dotted and the second is made into a sixteenth (as in Example 11D), then the final weak beat is tied to the preceding accent and cannot function as an anacrusis.

Now this is precisely what the sixteenth-note, D, in Mozart's Theme does: it prevents the following weak beat, the C♯ from functioning as an anacrusis to the E. Once this trochaic grouping is established—and reinforced in the second measure—it acts as a model for subsequent groups until measure 4. As indicated in Example 7A, the weak third beat (the two sixteenths) in measure 4 acts as a pivot linking the two C♯'s. The sixteenths are heard with the preceding quarter-note C♯ because of the previously established trochaic grouping, and they act as upbeat to the following C♯ both because they are separated from the preceding C♯ by a skip and because they move to the second C♯ by more rapid, conjunct motion. Were the phrasing of the Peters edition, shown in Example 7B, followed, no pivoting would take place because the previously established iambic pattern, far from linking the C♯ and E of measure 4, would separate them. The result, as we will see, would be an asymmetrical, awkward phrase structure.

Like the antecedent phrase, the consequent begins with trochaic groups. But, as indicated in Example 12, the organization is 'modified in measure 7. The eighth-note B serves as a pivot linking A and C♯, so that it is *almost* an upbeat—though an internal one. The final eight-note, D, however, is a

Example 12

strong, unambiguous anacrusis. This anacrustic function is emphasized by the skip in the base from A down to the D which precedes the conjunct motion across the barline, by the thickening of the chord sonority, and, above all, by the *sforzando* which the weak beat bears. Indeed, the *sforzando* marking makes sense because it makes clear that the final eighth-note of the ⁶⁄₈ measure has at last become an upbeat.

This perhaps needs some clarification. It is often thought that dynamic markings—*sforzando*, *forte-piano*, *crescendo*, and the like—essentially act to define the character and mood of a composition. Surely they do so. But they have an even more important syntactic function: they serve to articulate and shape patterns and formal structures. When it comes on a weak beat, as it does in measure 7 of Mozart's Theme a *sforzando* serves as a rule to make it clear that the weak beat is an anacrusis.[7] For example, in the

---

[7] In metered tonal music, a *sforzando* does not as a rule make a weak beat into an accented one. The added stress serves to articulate a grouping, but does not change the metric functions of the beats. When a *sforzando* comes on an accent, it often makes the accent function as the beginning of a rhythmic pattern and ties subsequent weak beats to the accent. This is what the *sforzandi* in measures 11 and 12 of Mozart's Theme do (see Example 17). These and other matters having to do with the articulation of rhythmic patterns are discussed in Grosvenor W. Cooper and Leonard B. Meyer, *The Rhythmic Structure of Music* (Chicago: University of Chicago Press, 1960), Chapters I–III.

Example 13

fourth movement of Beethoven's Fifth Symphony, the anacrustic groupings are to a considerable degree dependent upon the series of *sforzandi* (Example 13). Observing, incidentally, that orchestration too helps to make the syntactic patterning clear.

Returning to Mozart's Theme: the decisive upbeat at the end of measure 7 is the realization of a potential which was latent, *but not actualized*, in the preceding weak beats. When it finally arrives, the clear anacrusis is experienced as a kind of achievement—a psychic satisfaction. Were the groupings unambiguously anacrustic from the outset, as called for by the phrasing in the Peters edition, the emphatic upbeat at the end of measure 7 would be anticlimactic, and the *sforzando* which enforces it would be redundant—without syntactic significance. These remarks suggest that the performer must take considerable care not to stress the weak beats in the first six measures—either by dynamic emphasis or by slightly lengthening them. For if he does so, they will tend to be perceived as *actual*, rather than potential, upbeats.

If the E at the end of the first measure is understood as a potential upbeat, then the interval from E to B across the barline must be an unrealized perfect fourth. That is, if the structure of the first two rhythmic levels is trochaic, then (as shown in the analysis in Example 14) the melodic motion within each measure will be heard as a rising third, and the motion between measures will be a conjunct descent from C♯ to A. Consequently the

Example 14

fourths—from E to B and from D to A—are *not* perceived as active syntactic connections. The relationship is potential. It remains to be actualized.

However, not until the first variation are the fourths heard as syntactically explicit events. *There* they become aural actualities. And when they do so, the upbeats latent in the first measures of the theme are also actualized. Once again the phrasing in the Peters edition misconstrues and distorts the musical meaning of the theme. The fourth relationship must be kept potential in the Theme if its actualization in the first variation is to be interesting and significant (Example 15).

Example 15

These observations call attention to a more general and perhaps more serious shortcoming of the aberrant phrasing. Namely, to emphasize the connection between weak eighth-notes and the accented quarter-notes, which follow, is to direct perception to low-level, foreground events at the expense of higher-level structural relationships. Thus, if the E is heard as directly connected to the B, the importance of the larger motions from C♯ to B to A on accents and from E to D to C♯ on weak beats tends to be obscured. This difference is indicated, perhaps in a somewhat exaggerated way, in the analyses in Example 16. Note, incidentally, that the structural importance of

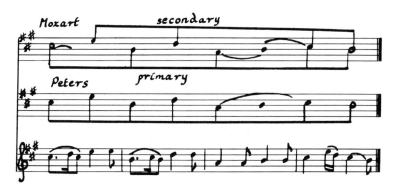

Example 16

the C♯ and the B in measure 4 is the result not only of their harmonization as a $\frac{6\text{-}5}{4\text{-}3}$ semicadence, but also of the fact that the primary melodic line (C♯-B-A) and the secondary melodic line (E-D) converge on these pitches.

The structure of Mozart's Theme, though hierarchically complex, is at the same time exceptionally clear, at least when performed as Mozart phrased it. This structure is shown in Example 17. In measures 1 and 2 the rhythmic groups are as we have seen, trochaic on the first two levels. On the third

Example 17

level, measure 1 is initially heard as accented, but is understood as being weak when grouped in retrospect with the second measure. That is, both measures function as anacrustic events leading to measures 3 and 4. Thus the organization of the whole antecedent phrase is, as indicated over Example 17, m-m'-n or, in eighth-note values, 6+6+12. Such patterns, whose proportions are 1+1+2, are called *bar-forms*. Notice that measures 3 and 4 are

a miniature version of this kind of structure. The first trochee of measure
3 which is on A, is initially heard as accented; it combines with the following trochee on B, and both function as anacruses to measure 4 which is a
single pivoted group. In other words, the two halves of measure 3 (p and p′)
are to measure 4 (q), as the first two measures (m and m′) are to the third
and fourth measures (n). Measures 3 and 4 are a bar-form with the proportions 3+3+6.

If this elegant parallelism of structure is to be projected in performance,
the prevailing rhythm must be trochaic. If it is iambic, measure 4 will fail to
form a single pivoted group, and the bar-form in measures 3 and 4 will be
obscured. This is what happens when the Theme is played as Köhler and
Ruthardt have phrased it. The hierarchic organization of the phrase, as well
as its formal parallelism, is destroyed—as can be seen by comparing a diagram of Mozart's groupings

$$\frac{m(6) \ - \ m'(6) \ - \qquad n(12)}{p(3)\text{-}p'(3)\text{-}q(6)}$$

with the aberrant one (Example 18):

Example 18

Like the antecedent phrase, the consequent is also a bar-form, m-m′-n′, on
level 3. But no miniature bar-form arises in measures 7 and 8, as was the case
in measures 3 and 4, because at this point the prevalent trochaic rhythm is
decisively broken, and the upbeat grouping, potential in the preceding
measures, is actualized.

2.

The influence of tempo and dynamics must be considered in any discussion of performance. Tempo is generally thought to be important because it affects the character and mood of the music. A fast tempo is gay
or energetic, a slow one is sad or contemplative. The performer presumably
senses the ethos of a composition and then decides upon an appropriate
tempo. Though this seems circular—for character is made dependent upon
tempo and choice of tempo upon imagined character—there is no doubt

something to it. But tempo and dynamics (including foreground accentuation) are even more important because of the subtle influence they may have on phrasing—on the syntactic sense and formal structure of the composition projected in performance. Mozart's Theme provides an almost ideal illustration of this interaction between tempo and dynamics, on the one hand, and phrasing on the other.

I have argued that Mozart's Theme should be performed in such a way that the groups are basically trochaic—that is, with patterns beginning on the accent and ending on the weak beat. Yet they must be equivocally so. The tendency for weak beats to become upbeats must be a felt potential—until the D in measure 7, an unequivocal anacrusis marking the end of the antecedent-consequent phrase.

If the tempo is too fast, the weak beats will be strongly tied to the accents which precede them, and will, as a result, not be felt as potential upbeats. This is the case because, generally speaking, the faster the tempo, the greater the tendency to emphasize metric accents—that is, to play downbeats louder than weak beats. And stress on accents tends to create unambiguously beginning-accented rhythmic groups. On the other hand, if the tempo is too slow, the weak eighth-notes will almost certainly be perceived as upbeats. This is so because, though grouping is mostly a matter of relative duration, absolute duration can also be influential. As the absolute amount of time between the sounding of an accented quarter-note and an unaccented eighth-note increases, the tendency of the eighth-note to function as an anacrusis grows.

It is possible, however, to play the theme quite slowly, yet still phrase it correctly. To do so, great care must be taken in the articulation of dynamics. The weak beats must receive no stress. For just as the *sforzando* on the D in measure 7 emphasized its upbeat character, so even a slight stress on an equivocal weak beat will tend to make it function as an anacrusis. Nor should the duration of the final eighth-note be lengthened. Rather its duration should, if anything, be cut slightly, creating a tiny break between measures. These modes of projecting trochaic groups are somewhat crudely indicated in Example 19.

Example 19

There is also a danger, if the tempo is too slow, that in order to project the correct rhythmic groups undue stress will be placed on the beginning of each measure, with the result that the theme will seem too obvious and assertive.

In short, though Mozart's Theme is syntactically simple and structurally clear, a good performance requires great technical control and interpretative finesse. Tempo and dynamics must so complement one another that a delicate ambiguity of rhythm is felt by the listener. And all this is lost, if the phrasing in the Peters edition is followed.

If a slow tempo tends to produce iambic groupings, then a performer phrasing as in the Peters edition might play the Theme more slowly than one following Mozart's markings. The hypothesis is difficult to confirm directly because there is no way of knowing which pianists, if any, use this edition in performance. But the hypothesis can be checked indirectly. For this kind of phrasing appears in a work based upon Mozart's Theme. As Example 20 shows, Köhler and Ruthardt's phrasing is very similar to that which Max Reger uses in his Variations and Fugue on a Theme of Mozart.

Example 20

Indeed, the Peters edition phrasing may be taken from Reger—a thought which suggests the desirability of using primary sources. The only recording of this work I have been able to find is by Eduard van Beinum conducting the Amsterdam Concertgebouw Orchestra. Despite the metronome marking in the score, the performance tempo is $\downarrow. = 28$!

Looking at Reger's phrasing, I wondered why an excellent musician—and Reger was that, whatever you may think of his compositions—should have made what I considered to be an unmusical mistake. Or was I perhaps wrong? Then I had one of those happy "inspirations" for which one thanks the Goddess Fortuna. I recalled that the great German musicologist, Hugo

Riemann, had a theory that all music was essentially anacrustic—even though the upbeats might be suppressed. I checked for a possible connection, and there in old, reliable *Grove's Dictionary*, I learned that: ". . . in 1890 young Reger went to [Riemann] as a pupil, following him the next year to Wiesbaden and soon becoming a teacher in the same conservatoire as his master." [8] But the gifts of Goddesses generally have their price—their uncomfortable side—as this did for me. For the moral of the story of Reger's aberrant phrasing would seem to be: "Cultivate a taste for speculative theory, but season it with a soupçon of saline skepticism."

[8] *Grove's Dictionary of Music and Musicians*, Fifth Edition, Eric Blom ed. (New York: St. Martin's Press, 1954), Vol. IV, p. 346.

CHAPTER III

Conformant Relationships

I.

By conformant relationships I mean simply those in which one (more or less) identifiable, discrete musical event is related to another such event by similarity. Consider, for instance, the following folk tune (Example 21).

Example 21

The first measure forms a clearly identifiable motive or event (m), which is rhythmically closed and intervallically coherent.[1] The second measure (m′) repeats this motive at a lower pitch level. The conformant relationship between the events is unmistakable because two of the primary pattern-forming parameters—pitch and rhythm—form a succession of similar events and because few other parameters (for instance, timbre, dynamics, register, etc.) are varied. Measure 4 (m″) is related to measure 1, but less patently so. For in this case rhythm conforms, but pitch does not—except for the fact that the first note, G, is the same. The last two quarter-notes of

[1] That is, both notes can be understood as belonging to a single harmony.

measure 7 and the first beats of measure 8 are also related to the opening motive by conformance (m‴). This time, though pitch relationships are identical, rhythm is varied. For even though the durational relationships are the same—♩♩♩—the quarter-notes now have an anacrustic function, as indicated in the analysis under the example.

That measures 5–8 are a varied repetition of measures 1–4, and measures 13–16 an exact repetition of measures 5–8, is worth noting because it calls attention to two facts of some importance. First, it indicates that, like many other musical relationships, conformant ones are often hierarchically structured. That is, not only may low-level events like motives be related through conformance, but themes and sections may be so too. Indeed, strophic forms, such as a theme and variations, depend for their coherence primarily upon the perception of conformant relationships.

Secondly, it should be observed that though measures 13–16 are an exaction repetition of 5–8 *from a structural point of view*, they are quite different from a *functional point of view*. Because they come *after* a less stable section (marked B in the example), they now function to promote closure—they constitute an arrival and at the same time a return. This change can easily be tested by playing over the first half of the tune. No matter how often it is played it will not end—even though the notes of A′ are literally the same as those of A″—unless the middle part of the tune precedes A″.

Not all conformant relationhips are as obvious as those thus far mentioned. For instance, measures 10 and 12 of the folk tune might be analyzed as varied retrogrades of measures 2 and 1 respectively, with the interval of a third filled in. But the relationship, if perceived at all, is subliminal: we are not really aware of it. Their latent similarity is masked by manifest differences. Not only is their direction reversed (rising rather than falling), but their identity as separable motives is weakened because they are parts of larger events begun by the repeated notes which precede them. Even more important, their function is changed. The opening motives (m and m′) are experienced as part of a stable statement, while their "retrogrades" (m^r and m′^{r}) are understood as parts of less stable groups which lead us back to the tune.

Finally, this conformant relationship is attenuated because the retrogrades are separated in time from the motives they may be said to vary. Had each variant followed its model motive immediately (as shown in Example 22A), the relationship would have been apparent.

Example 22

Notice, however, that not only has the function of the retrogrades (m^r and m'^r) changed—they are now part of the relatively stable portion of the tune—but so have the morphological lengths out of which the tune is constructed. For though it can be subdivided, the first *complete* event is now two measures long—and so, of course, is the second event. This change in morphological length is shown by the fact that in comparison with the first four measures of Example 21, these four measures seem incomplete—not even a phrase. More music is required: as illustrated in part B of Example 22, at least four measures are needed for the phrase to reach closure.

Our awareness of conformance depends not only upon the proximity between the variant and its model, but also, as suggested earlier, upon the degree of similarity between them. That is, the more all the parameters are duplicated in model and variant, the stronger the conformant relationship. This is specially the case with the primary pattern-forming parameters of pitch, duration, and harmony. For instance, a motive can be changed in register, dynamics, tempo, and instrumentation and still be recognizably the same. But if time and pitch relationships are significantly altered, either separately or together, conformant relationships tend to be masked. To take an uncomplicated example: though the final movement of Mozart's Clarinet Quintet (Example 23B) begins with the same melodic (23B') and even rhythmic structure as the folk tune we have been discussing, the conformant relationships between measures 1 and 2 of the Mozart work are less patent than

Example 23

those of the folk tune simply because the first two beats of the second measure are varied.

Or perhaps not so "simply." For the motion to the F♯ not only somewhat disguises the motivic repetition, but it creates implications not present in the basic descending step-motion common to both tunes. As indicated in part A of Example 23, the motion from D to F♯ as part of a triad implies the possibility of the high A as a goal.[2] At least partly for this reason, the middle part of Mozart's Theme (Ex. 29B) exploits the upper perfect fourth of the A-octave (emphasizing G♯)—as well as the lower perfect fifth—and the melody closes on a high A in measure 16, while the folk tune is bound, so to speak, to the lower fifth. Had the motivic repetition been disguised as shown in Example 23C, we would have been more aware of the conformant relationship between the first two measures—not only because motive and variant are more alike, but also because no alternative implications would have drawn our attention away from the similarity between the measures. And had the motive been varied as in 23C, the high A which closes the first part of the melody would have been less "called for" and might have come as a slight surprise.

Often secondary parameters, such as dynamics, register, and timbre, help to disguise what might otherwise have been a rather obvious conformant relationship. This occurs, for instance, at the beginning of the exposition section of the first movement of Haydn's "Surprise" Symphony. The melodic-temporal pattern of measure 20 is continued in somewhat varied form in measures 21 and 22. This can be seen from the analysis over Example 24. But this similarity is virtually masked by the abrupt change in dynamics, orchestration, register, and low-level ornamental motion (i.e., the sixteenth-notes), and, most important of all, the change in rhythmic grouping.

Example 24

<hr />

[2] For a discussion of implication, see Part II of this book. In the analyses, an arrow is used as a sign of implication. When the implied event is separated from the generating pattern, the arrow is broken: generating pattern ——————→ >—————— goal.

One of the reasons for this "masking effect" is, I suspect, that the similarity between events is not merely one of syntax and form, but one of character—of ethos. And in this example, the lyrical-playful character of the first measures is so different from the assertive character of later measures that we are only partially aware of their motivic similarity.

In addition to temporal proximity and similarity of structure and character, our perception of conformant relationships depends upon the individuality of the model event. Other things being equal, the more striking its melodic, rhythmic, or harmonic profile, the more easily it will be recognized when varied and in diverse contexts. The phrase "other things being equal" must, however, be taken seriously. For we can perceive conformant relationships only if we can remember the model to which subsequent events are to be related. And to a considerable extent memory—musical, linguistic, or other—depends upon the presence of a constant and consistent syntax and of relatively regular patterns which often become the basis for archetypal schemata. The linear descending motion of falling thirds—the motion which begins both the folk tune and Mozart's theme—is both simple and regular. But in neither of these melodies is the schema given a particularly individual profile.

Essentially the same schema, though in the minor mode, is used as the motto which opens Beethoven's Fifth Symphony. There, however, the famous upbeat rhythm gives the pattern a very striking identity (Example 25A).

Example 25

As the music unfolds, we hear the motto undergo a myriad of transformations. It acts as the basis for the remainder of the first theme group (Example 25B), leads to the second key area which it announces (Example

25C), and then acts as an accompaniment motive for the lyrical portion of the second theme. In the first movement it is ubiquitous: in the theme groups, the development section, and the codas. The special rhythm and repeated notes of the motto are so vivid that there is no doubt about its recurrence in the Scherzo (Example 25D)—though Beethoven is careful to mark the return by preceding it with a *ritardando*, and a *fermata*. Nor is there any difficulty in recognizing the repetition of the Scherzo-version of the motto when it occurs just before the recapitulation in the Finale of the Symphony.

The preceding discussion might be summarized in a formula such as:

$$\frac{\text{Strength of}}{\text{perceived conformance}} = \frac{\text{regularity of pattern (schemata)} \cdot \text{individuality of profile} \cdot \text{similarity of patterning}}{\text{variety of intervening events} \cdot \text{temporal distance between events}}$$

In other words, the greater the variety of intervening events and the greater the separation in time between two comparable events, the more patent the shape of the model must be if a conformant relationship is to be perceived. Or, to put the matter the other way around: the more regular and individual the pattern (and, of course, the more alike events are in interval, rhythm, etc.), the greater can be the temporal separation between model and variant and the greater the variety of intervening motives, with the conformant relationship still recognizable. Perhaps it is partly for this reason that, as symphonic movements tend to grow in scope and length during the nineteenth century, there is a correlative tendency for composers to invent motives and melodies which fulfill these conditions.

As we listen to the first movement of Beethoven's Fifth Symphony, the varied repetitions—the successive modifications—of the motto are heard, generally speaking, as a more or less continuous process of transformation. When the varied version of the motto occurs in the Scherzo and the Finale, however, it is heard not as having "gradually evolved" from immediately preceding events (as was, for instance, the case with the beginning of the second theme in the first movement), but rather as a return to something which had been stated earlier. There is, in other words, an important distinction between *repetition* and *return*, and there is a related distinction between processive and formal conformant relationships.

Returns of a motive or theme almost always serve to articulate structural units—emphasizing points of departure or of arrival. This is perhaps their most significant function—and in works of any complexity it is an important one. Though return contributes to the impression of unity when it emphasizes closure, neither unity nor closure depend upon the presence of return. Were the return of melodic patterning a necessary condition for unity and closure, there could be no two-part melodies such as the one shown in Example 26

Example 26

not to mention countless Bach chorales, many classical themes, and "God Save the Queen." In rounded binary structures (:A::BA:) like the folk tune in Example 21, return is a necessary condition for closure, but *not* a sufficient one. That it is not a sufficient condition can be seen by repeating phrase A, instead of A', after the B section of the tune. That return is a necessary condition for closure in such tunes is indicated by the fact that, despite their similarities, it will not do to tack the final phrase of the Mozart theme on to the B section of the folk tune—as is done in Example 27.

Example 27

The result is incongruous partly because, as noted in connection with the discussion of the Mozart, that theme has implications which should have been actualized in the B portion. Partly, however, the feeling of distortion arises because experience leads us to expect that the relative instability of the B phrase will be followed by the repose of the familiar. We are prepared for redundancy, not for novelty. It is as though we took a trip and, on returning home, discovered that a new house has been built where ours had formerly stood.

Repetition, as distinguished from return, gives rise both to formal and to processive conformant relationships. It does so because of the nature of hierarchic structures. To see how repetition works, let us begin with what

at first seems to be a rather strange irony: the more alike two successive
events are, the more separate—distinctly articulated—each appears to be.
The first two measures of Mozart's theme are related, as we have seen, by
conformance (Example 28A). Their articulation as discrete entities is clear,
but it would have been more marked had the second been an exact repetition of the first (Example 28B). The reason for this difference is that in
Mozart's theme the first two measures involve a melodic motion downward
from E to D (and from C♯ to B), and this motion creates a higher-level pattern, the first and second measures combining to form a trochaic rhythm on
level 3 (see the analysis under Example 28A). But in Example 28B no combining process creates a higher-level pattern. The first measure is initially
understood as accented. But when the second measure proves to be an exact
repetition, the first is retrospectively thought of as being weak. Both measures now seem directed toward some larger goal which will act as an organizing accent on a higher level. The difference between sequential and exact
repetition can be emphasized by eliminating the rhythms which articulate

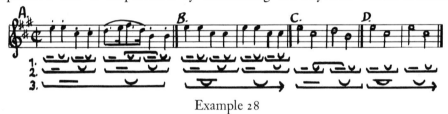

Example 28

lower-lever structure (Examples 28C and D). Now the weak beat in the
sequential version (28C, level 2) becomes a latent up-beat—as indicated by
the inverted brackets in the analysis. No such latency is present, however,
in Example 28D: each measure is a distinct, separate event.

Three points need to be made in connection with this part of our discussion of repetition. The first is that, though repetition may be exact from
a formal point of view, it is never so psychologically—for the obvious reason that *being a repetition* in itself qualifies and changes the event which is
reiterated. And it is a curious fact that immediate repetition tends to emphasize the differences between like events, while remote repetition—that is, return—tends to call attention to their similarities. The second point is that the
more exact the repetition of an event is, the more strongly we expect change
—we feel that further repetition is unlikely. Yet this statement clearly requires qualification; and this brings us to the third point. The implicative
effect of repetition depends upon context. For instance, if a reiterated pat-

tern is understood to be part of an ostinato or of a ground bass, we do not necessarily expect change. Similarly, repetition in a coda or of a cadential figure repeated as an echo, has quite a different effect from repetition which is understood to be part of some on-going process.

Any parameter—melody, rhythm, harmony, texture, timbre, or dynamics—may contribute to the articulation of musical structure. In Example 24, for instance, an abrupt change in dynamics, timbre, register, and rhythm marks the beginning of the second part of the first theme group. And closure, created by some combination of parameters, can articulate structure in the absence of repetition. The end of the consequent phrase in the Mozart theme (Example 29) is very clear, even though it is not followed by repetition.[3] Nevertheless, one of the most effective ways of emphasizing that an event is ended, is to begin it again. Repetition can articulate formal relationships not only such as that between the antecedent and consequent phrase in Example 29 but also on higher levels of structure.

Example 29

For instance, the over-all structure of a theme and variations is as a rule decisively articulated not only because the theme and each of the variations are usually closed shapes, but because the element of repetition is so pronounced. And when composers sought, as they did during the nineteenth century, to make their variation movements more processive (and less formal) in character, they tended to mask the existence of repetition.

It is perhaps partly because repetition serves as a cue that a preceding part has ended, that transitions from the first to the second theme groups in movements in sonata form often begin with a repetition of the opening melodic material. Haydn's "Clock" Symphony begins with the tune quoted in Example 30A. After some twenty-five measures, a strong cadence on the dominant is followed by a slightly varied repetition of the opening tune (Example 30B). The repetition, together with the preceding closure and the change

---

[3] This suggests that, generally speaking, the more decisive the parametric closure, the less the need for repetition in the definition of structure.

in orchestration, dynamics, and texture indicate that a major section of the exposition is completed and a new part is beginning.

Example 30

Observe that in this case Haydn does not, as he sometimes does, keep us in doubt about the function of the repetition. The new harmonization (V of II to II, rather than I to IV) with its emphasis on the minor mode and the melodic modification (C instead of D in measure 50) are understood as *signs* that this is probably the beginning of the bridge passage, not a real repetition of the opening theme.[4]

On the hierarchic level where repetition is immediate, it tends to separate events. But on the *next* level—where similar events are grouped together as part of some larger unit—repetition tends to create coherence. This is particularly the case when similar events are part of an implicative, goal-directed motion. Thus in Mozart's theme (Example 29) m and m', though formal elements with respect to one another, are processive with respect to the whole antecedent phrase, A. Similarly, A and A' are related to one another in both a formal and a processive way. In other words, relationships which are formal on one level tend to become processive on another level—usually the next higher ones.[5]

Processive conformant relationships, such as those described in connection with the first movement of Beethoven's Fifth Symphony (pp. 48–49) also play a significant role in the perception of musical structure. By "leading" the listener's ear and mind through a series of gradual modifications,

[4] Sometimes Haydn will, however, use this sort of sign in a deceptive way—he will signal that he is going to modulate, only to bring us back to the tonic and the opening theme. See, for instance, the Finale of the "Military" Symphony, in which at measure 10 a shift to the submediant (VI) suggests that the transition is beginning, but no real change of key occurs, and the first theme is repeated at measure 42.

It would, I believe, be most rewarding to analyze the procedures of the classical period as a "system of signs."

[5] This aspect of musical relationships is discussed in Chapter IV.

the successive transformation of a motive contributes to—but does not in itself create—a sense of continuity and coherence. Once again an interesting paradox is involved: the existence of motivic constancy—of varied repetition—allows the listener to attend to higher-level processes. Because low-level events are relatively regular and persistent, they can be, if not ignored, at least more or less taken for granted, so that attention can be directed to the larger patterning of the musical structure—to long-range harmonic, melodic, and rhythmic relationships. To use an analogy from visual experience: the relative constancy of size and shape of the stones in a mosaic facilitate our perception of its over-all pattern.

This perhaps explains in part why bridge passages and development sections in sonata-form movements tend to be motivically stable: motivic constancy allows the listener to focus upon and comprehend the harmonic and textural processes which are central. One can modulate without repeating motives, but then the mind has to cope with much more simultaneous information and attention tends to be diverted from the larger structures ordering musical events. The motivic constancy of classical development sections is *not*, as some have suggested, the result of the composer's desire to "exhaust" his materials—to present all the permutations and combinations he can discover. For this is seldom done. (Any third-rate composer can invent variants on the first theme of, say, Beethoven's Eighth Symphony, which Beethoven never uses.) Rather motivic constancy is used because it allows for the perception of larger processes, and because the use of *part* of a previously established whole (a motive taken from a theme) is implicative of the return of the total pattern.

These observations can be stated in more general form: the greater the amount of change—in both rate and degree—in one parameter, the smaller must be the changes in other parameters if patterning is to be perceived. If all parameters are varied simultaneously and independently of one another, the result is not necessarily a more complex and interesting pattern, but often none at all—a confused hodgepodge of sounds. The amount of simultaneous variation possible also depends upon the nature of the patterns themselves: the more patently structured and archetypal one aspect of a pattern (for instance, its melodic shape), the more other parameters (e.g., rhythm, harmony, etc.) can be varied without destroying the impression of conformance.

Because the amount of information which the human mind can comprehend at one time is limited, the more information one parameter carries the more redundant others must be if musical relationships are to be perceived. This proposition evidently applies to musical styles as well as to individual compositions. For instance, a highly complex and subtle melodic-rhythmic style, like that of the music of South India, generally minimizes (or does without) complex harmonic processes such as have characterized Western music since the Renaissance. Even more modest style differences may be distinguished, in part, in terms of which parameters tend to be varied most. Compare, for instance, the beginning phrases of two funeral marches (Example 31). In the first, from Beethoven's Third Symphony, a high degree of melodic-rhythmic variety is coupled with harmonic restraint—only one change of harmony in four measures. The second phrase, from Schumann's Piano Quintet in E♭, works the other way around: minimal melodic-rhythmic variety is accompanied by considerable harmonic change—seven changes in four measures.

Example 31

This discussion suggests one reason why thematic transformation became an important concern of nineteenth-century composers: Liszt, Schumann, Wagner, Brahms, Franck, and Strauss—to name but a few. Motivic constancy was necessary if the expressive possibilities of instrumental timbre, register, and foreground harmonic color were to be realized. On higher levels, an increase in the scope and rapidity of harmonic change could be effective only if melodic change emphasized continuity rather than contrast. But this is only part of the story.

As so often in history, a particular trend or proclivity is the result of a concatenation of causes. Another reason for the prevalence of thematic transformation was that the ideal of personal, distinctive self-expression (coupled with a tendency to write longer movements) led to the invention and use of individualized and characteristic themes and motives. Because the singularity of such materials would have been incongruous with conventional, transitional and passage-work figures such as scales and broken chords (which the eighteenth century with its less exotic themes could employ), the themes themselves were transformed so that they became part of bridge passages, subsidiary themes, and the like.

These musical tendencies were nurtured by the intellectual climate of the period.[6] A complex amalgam of interrelated, but sometimes incompatible, ideas flourished in nineteenth-century culture. A number of these became associated, formally and informally, with aesthetic notions: historical necessity was associated with the idea of inevitability (internal necessity) as a criterion for art; dialectical change, with the concept of sonata form as thematic conflict and ultimate synthesis; biological germination and evolution, with the desirability of motivic transformation and continuous musical development. The following quotations from Liszt's "Berlioz and His 'Harold' Symphony" suggest how pervasive these ideas were.[7]

> Art, like nature, is made up of *gradual transitions*, which link together the remotest classes and the most dissimilar species. (852, italics mine)

> In nature, in the human soul, and in art, the extremes, opposites, and high points are bound one to another by a continuous series of various varieties of *being*. (852)

> Art, like nature, weds related or contradictory forms. (852)

> [Art] is impelled toward an unpredicted and unpredictable *final goal* in *perpetual transformations*. (854, italics mine)

[6] The fact, noted by Gerald Abraham, that nineteenth-century composers, unlike eighteenth-century ones, were literary men and often belonged to the intelligentsia is of signal importance for the history of recent Western music. See *A Hundred Years of Music* (Chicago: Aldine Publishing, 1964), p. 20f.

[7] The excerpts are taken from Oliver Strunk, *Source Readings in Music History* (New York: W. W. Norton, 1950); page numbers are given in parentheses after each quotation.

> The poetic solution of instrumental music contained in the program
> seems to us rather one of the various steps forward which the art has
> still to take, a *necessary result of the development of our time.* (859,
> italics mine)

The particular point or argument involved in these statements is not important. What is crucial is that the general conceptual framework must at the
very least have influenced Liszt's unconscious attitude toward his art. And
it is difficult, in view of their prevalence, to doubt that these ideas affected
other composers also.

During the nineteenth century, formal conformant relationships—always vital in the articulation of musical form—became increasingly important in the minds of composers. Here Beethoven's influence was strongly
felt—particularly the example of the Ninth Symphony. Formal conformance was extended in order to relate movements to one another. Berlioz's
invention of the *idée fixe*, the cyclic principle employed by Franck, D'Indy,
Fauré, and other French composers, and the use of thematic reminiscence
in the music of Schumann, Brahms, and Bruckner are all instances of this
tendency. Wagner's case is somewhat special: his use of processive conformance is obvious, but the "return" of leitmotifs throughout the *Ring*,
though articulating structure to some extent, is also used to refer to ideas or
characters in the narrative of the operas.

The preoccupation with conformant relationships—formal as well as
processive—continued into the twentieth century. It is clear in the work
of tonal and nontonal composers alike. Bartok's Sixth String Quartet may
serve as an example. But the ultimate and "logical" consequence of the concern with conformance is found in the twelve-tone method of composition,
where the total pitch structure is derived from a single twelve-tone row.
Initially, in the music of Schönberg and Berg, the row gave rise to both
processive and formal conformant relationships. But subsequently, in the
music of Webern and his followers, processive conformance became less
and less important: emphasis was placed upon intervallic recurrence rather
than motivic resemblance. Formal conformance—the nonprocessive ordering of rows, subsets of rows, and their presentation in various permutations
and combinations—has become the chief concern of recent serialism. That
this mode of musical understanding is essentially formal, rather than processive, is indicated by the analyses made by serial composers of one anothers'
music. It tends to be in terms of row manipulation, not in terms of function,
implication, and syntactic structure that these works are discussed.

A number of reasons for the increased use of formal conformance between movements suggest themselves. From a musical-perceptual point of
view, as multimovement works (particularly symphonies) grew in size and
complexity, it became both increasingly important and increasingly difficult to remember the basic thematic ideas. The return of a pattern, between
movements as well as within them, both reduces the number of different
ideas to be remembered and reinforces the memory of those already presented.

In the area of cultural history the conceptual notions mentioned above
were influential: the prevalence of ideas of inner necessity, dialectical conflict, and resolution, and the germination of a large work from a single
motivic cell in a kind of miniature evolution. Such germination, it was
thought, would not only create audible coherence but would all but guar-
antee musical unity. This was an important concern because the diversity
of themes in a multi-movement work seemed somehow arbitrary (as opposed
to necessary), and unordered (as opposed to lawful). As intellectuals un-
prepared passively to accept tradition, these composers found it difficult to
"explain" what seemed to them a lack of coherence and elegance. The viewpoint of many of these composers is made clear in the following statements
of Webern, who was ideologically, if not compositionally, a nineteenth-
century thinker.[8]

> These lectures are intended to show the path that has led to this music,
> and to make it clear that *it had to have this natural outcome.* (33, italics
> mine)
>
> Much later I discovered that all this was a part of the *necessary develop-
> ment.* (51, italics mine)
>
> All these fugues are based on one single theme, which is *constantly trans-
> formed* (34, italics mine)
>
> To develop everything else from *one* principle idea! That's the strongest
> unity . . . (35)
>
> Composers tried to create unity in the accompaniment, to work themat-
> ically, to derive everything from one thing, and so to produce the
> tightest—maxium—unity. And now everything is derived from this
> chosen succession of twelve notes, and thematic technique works as
> before, on this basis. But—the great advantage is that I can treat the-

[8] Anton Webern, *The Path to the New Music* (Bryn Mawr, Pa.: Theodore
Presser, 1963); page numbers are given in parentheses after each quotation.

matic technique much more freely. *For unity is completely ensured by the underlying series.* (40, italics mine)

2.

Recognizing the presence of conformant relationships in music, theorists became interested in the technique and significance of thematic transformation. Notable among these was Rudolph Reti, whose book *The Thematic Process in Music*,[9] seeks to demonstrate that in the works of the "masters," all thematic ideas are derived from a single germinal motive and, further, that the succession of transformations is a process which imparts meaning and unity to whole compositions as well as to single movements. I shall discuss one of Reti's analyses not only in order to indicate some of the problems and pitfalls facing this sort of enterprise, but because this will lead to a consideration of a number of fundamental issues—methodological, theoretical, and philosophical.

There is, I think, no question that the opening phrase of Brahms's Second Symphony (Example 32, measures 1–5) presents motives which are continually varied and transformed throughout the movement—and are even used in other movements of the work. This is specially true of the neighbor-note (D-C♯-D) figure of the first measure which I shall call the

Example 32

[9] (New York: Macmillan, 1951).

"motto." And undoubtedly the composer consciously wrought the relationships. Reti, however, wants to do more than contend that Brahms used conformant relationships to create coherence; it is his conviction that *every*
important theme in the first movement is derived from the opening measures.

Reti begins by attempting to persuade us that the second tune of the
first key area (Example 32, measures 44f.) functions as a link or common
term uniting the opening phrases and the lyrical melody which begins the
second group (Example 36). That the opening measures lead to the second
tune cannot be disputed. This is an unequivocal instance of processive conformance. We *hear* the transformation of the neighbor-note figure and con-
nect its varied statement in measures 42–43 with the new theme (m. 44f.)
because of temporal proximity and pitch identity.

However, doubts begin to arise when Reti asks us to agree that measures 50 and 51 of the new tune (Example 33B, motive c′) are derived from
the end of the first phrase of the opening theme (Example 33A, motive c).
Leaving aside the fact that the first (c) phrase does not end on D as Reti's
analysis suggests, but continues to an A (see Example 32, measure 5 or its
transposed equivalent in Example 33C), the rhythmic-melodic functions of
the tones are significantly different in each phrase.

Example 33 (after Reti, p. 80)

In the opening phrase the first D (measure 3) is a weak beat, while the second (in measure 5) is accented; in the second tune just the opposite is the
case. And the rhythmic position of the E is similarly altered. Moreover, in
the opening phrase the F♯ (measure 4) is a changing-note (related to the first
measure by inversion) without marked melodic direction; but in the second
tune it is strongly directed, both because it is preceded by a gap and because
it is an appoggiatura.

The second tune of the first key area, gradually varied so that its relationship to the opening motto becomes even more apparent (Example 34), forms the basis for the transition to the lyric melody which begins the second key area. Again the processive conformant relationship is audibly clear.

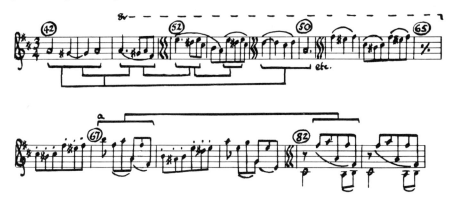

Example 34

But it does not follow from the processive character of the transition that this lyrical melody (the second theme) is related to anything which has gone before.

Reti presents an example which ostensibly shows the relationship between the second theme and the second tune of the first group (Example 35):

Example 35 (after Reti, p. 80)

and he comments: "This must strike us most forcibly . . . The composer states his first theme, which is followed by an intermediary theme that reiterates the substance of the first. But this intermediary theme is in turn, and at the same time, a foreteller of the second theme . . . *If we single out certain notes, the first theme comes to the fore; if we single out others, the second theme appears.*" [10]

[10] *Ibid.*, pp. 80–81.

Rather than striking me "most forcibly," it strikes me as being somewhat forced. To begin with, Reti did not pick the melody of the second
theme which is played by the celli (Example 36), but rather the parallel

Example 36

line played by the violas a third below the celli. The reason for this is, I
suspect, that had he used the melody itself, no half-step motion (A-G♯-A)
could have been extracted, with the result that the similarity between the
beginning of the second tune and that of the second theme would have
seemed even more tenuous. But even as it stands, the suggestion of similarity
is unconvincing because the tonal-melodic functions of the compared pitches
is so different. For instance, the A of the second tune (35B) is the fifth of a
triad, while that of the second theme is the third—and in this respect Reti
would have been better off with the cello version of the theme, for it begins
on the fifth. The G♯ which performs an important melodic function in the
second tune of the first group (leading the melodic line down through F♯ to
E and D) is an unimportant passing tone in the version of the second theme
presented by Reti. Finally, as he did with the end of the "c" motive (see
Example 33), Reti simply leaves out whatever seems incompatible with his
argument—for example, though the last A of the second tune (35B) is a
stable structural tone, the A at the end of his version of the second theme
is not: it is an unstable appoggiatura which moves to G♯ and then to G and
F♯.[11]

My reservations about Reti's analyses are both methodological and
theoretical. Methodologically, if one can pick and choose—selecting those
voices or pitches which support one's hypothesis, and disregarding those
which do not (the small notes in Reti's analyses)—then almost any melody
can be related to any other whether within or between works. In Tovey's
words: "Of all the pastimes of musical analysis, the easiest is the identifying

[11] There is, however, an explicit connection between the transition section and
the beginning of the second key area, not one of main melodic ideas, but of accompaniment figures. The chordal pattern in the first and second violins which begins in
measure 67 is the same as that which accompanies the theme in measures 82 and 83
(Example 34).

of melodic figures. An uncontrolled imagination—that is to say, an unimaginative mind—can pursue this to results as fantastic as any Baconian cipher, and composers themselves may be misled by it." [12]

The question, as Tovey suggests, is one of control—of methodological rigor. When the events being related are compared *as they are notated*—without abstracting any pitches—the question of methodological consistency does not as a rule arise. The degree of similarity between events can be ascertained by looking at the parameters defining each of the patterns, and perhaps using an *ad hoc* formula such as suggested earlier to estimate the strength of conformance. Problems arise when the demonstration of conformance depends upon analytic selection—picking some tones out of an event, while ignoring others.

I do not intend to suggest that analytic selection is wrong. Quite the contrary. Because music is hierarchic, some tones are ornamental in relation to others on a particular structural level. When higher-level structural tones are distinguished from ornamental ones, conformant relationships not at first glance apparent may be revealed. In a modest way this was done in connection with Examples 24 and 28. And without distortion, the beginnings of the second tune of the first key area and the second theme may be analyzed as ornamented prolongations of A and C♯ respectively (see Example 37).

Example 37

The prolongations are followed by a skip of a fourth, after which both melodies descend in stepwise fashion—though, as noted earlier, they have different points of closure.

What is needed is a set of rules, however informal, for distinguishing structural from ornamental tones in an objective and consistent way. Every critic who wants to illuminate the larger structure of a composition—the relationship and interaction among foreground, middleground, and back-

[12] Donald F. Tovey, *Musical Textures* (London: Oxford University Press, 1942), p. 48.

ground—must face this problem. It confronts the followers of Schenker, and will plague me later in this book. But even if a reasonable set of rules were devised, arbitrary selection would not be completely precluded. For, as argued in Chapter I, a gap necessarily exists between any general set of rules and their application to particular instances. Consequently judgment and self-criticism must remain the ultimate controls. Without them, there is a strong temptation to allow favored hypotheses to influence analytic choices.

This temptation is one to which, I think, Reti frequently succumbs. He does so because in his view thematic conformance not only creates coherence and articulates structure, but is a necessary and sufficient cause of musical unity and hence of aesthetic value.[13] ". . . in the great works of musical literature the different movements of a composition are connected in thematic unity—a unity that is brought about not merely by a vague affinity of mood but by forming the themes from one identical musical substance." [14] It is not my purpose, at this point, to dispute Reti's conception of the nature of musical unity. That must wait a bit. Rather I want to suggest that his position virtually compels him to discover the kinds of relationships he has hypothesized. For if the value of a work depends (as it does almost by definition) upon unity, and if unity in turn depends upon the "variation of one identical musical thought," [15] then, if an acknowledged masterpiece is being analyzed, the hypothesized thematic process must willy-nilly be uncovered. And Reti seems to feel that the more instances of transformation, the better (more unified) the composition.

Reti's position leads him to employ what E. H. Gombrich, criticizing the writings of cultural historians, has called the "exegetic" method: ". . . the method, that is, that bases its interpretation on the detection of that kind of 'likeness' that leads the interpreter of the scriptures to link the passage of the Jews through the Red Sea with the Baptism of Christ. . . . The assumption is always that some essential structural similarity must be detected which permits the interpreter to subsume the various aspects of culture under a single formula." [16] And just as the cultural historians who employ this method tend toward a kind of Hegelianism,[17] so Reti seems

[13] Partly he succumbs, I suspect, because, like the rest of us, he finds pleasure in discovering hidden relationships—in "solving the puzzle."

[14] *Reti, Thematic Process of Music,* p. 4.

[15] *Ibid.*

[16] *In Search of Cultural History* (London: Oxford University Press, 1969), p. 32.

[17] See *Ibid.,* Parts II through IV.

inclined toward a dialectical conception of music. Not only does a theme move *"by transformation toward a goal,"* [18] but a process of thesis, antithesis, and synthesis seems implied:

> . . . the real plan of this whole becomes apparent when the first Rhapsody [Opus 79, by Brahms] is not only complemented but almost contradicted, and so "resolved," by the structure and idea of the second.[19]
>
> Thus this Finale theme is indeed a synthesis of all the thematic impulses of the symphony.[20]

As Gombrich indicates, an important assumption underlying this method is that manifest differences mask an underlying, but more significant similarity. According to Reti, "In reality [the first and second themes of a sonata-form movement] are contrasting on the surface but identical in substance." [21] This is the crucial loophole! For there is no way of confuting this analytic method. If it is objected that a relationship is not audible or that the notes selected as significant completely change the process and organization of a theme, the answer is: Of course! it is part of the composer's plan to disguise similarities. When this occurs, cabalistic circuitry has taken the place of serious criticism.[22]

But it would be folly to let a distaste for exegetic excess blind us to the real significance of conformant relationships. For they create foreground coherence while at the same time allowing attention to be directed to higher-level syntactic processes, contribute to the formal articulation of musical structure on all hierarchic levels, and also provide the satisfaction of return, thereby enhancing the impression of closure. Whether in addition they constitute *the* basis for musical unity is another question.

Since to the best of my knowledge there has never been music without conformant relationships, it seems reasonable to assume that they are a neces-

---

[18] *Reti, Thematic Process of Music*, p. 139.

[19] *Ibid.*, p. 145.

[20] *Ibid.*, p. 164. The work referred to is Brahms' Second Symphony.

[21] *Ibid.*, p. 5.

[22] Reti believes that the similarity between the tones he has selected as "structural" and the motives from which they are presumably derived can be *heard*. In many cases this may be true, because if selection is more or less arbitrary, any motive of some complexity can be made to resemble a model motive. Moreover, as has frequently been noted, "believing is seeing" (or in this case "hearing"). For instance, a new family arrives in our community, and we remark upon the resemblance between parents and children—only to learn that the children are adopted. So, too, in analysis: our theories (beliefs) often influence how and what we hear.

sary condition for musical understanding. And in this sense at least they appear to be one basis for musical unity. They are *not* in my judgment, however, a sufficient cause for unity. Though this contention can be justified, it is difficult to prove in a rigorous way. For unity is not an objective, substantive entity like a motive, a perfect cadence, or a change in texture or dynamics. Rather it is a psychological effect—an impression of propriety, integrity, and completeness. And it is, I think, as difficult to specify the sources of this impression in music as it is to say what makes a woman attractive. When it's there, you know it. But the special combination of causes that produces the effect in any particular case defies precise definition.

Nevertheless, it seems safe to say that all the kinds of relationships present in a composition—processive, tectonic, ethetic (i.e. pertaining to ethos), as well as conformant ones—contribute to the impression of unity. The importance of a particular kind of relationship will vary not only from style to style but from one kind of work to another. For instance, ethetic relationships are a necessary condition of unity in the music of India, where mood or *rasa* is of central importance; in the music of contemporary serialism, on the other hand, conformant relationships are the prime basis for compositional integrity. In tonal music, processive and hierarchic relationships are the most important in creating a sense of unity in structures such as sonata-form movements, while conformant relationships play a vital part in unifying strophic forms such as theme and variations. An impression of unity thus depends to some extent upon the kind of relationship which dominates the ordering of a particular hierarchic level.

Despite these qualifications, conformant relationships are of secondary importance for creating unity in the repertory with which both Reti and I are concerned—that is, the repertory of Western tonal music from 1700 to 1918. To begin in a somewhat roundabout way: the great advantage of complex tectonic structures, such as those developed in Western music during the period being considered, is that patent contrasts and differences on one level can be related to one another in terms of the processes of a higher one. Were unity essentially a matter of conformance, there would be no need for such arched hierarchies. Those styles and forms which are most homogeneous—emphasizing similarity of motive, gesture, and mood—are not markedly hierarchic. One thinks, for instance, of a painting by Mark Rothko, of an imagist poem, and of the music of the Near East or of the so-called avant-garde. Let me quote from an earlier book:

. . . one of the salient ideals of Western culture and a hallmark of "greatness" in Western art, at least since the Renaissance, has been that of *monumentality*. To capture and communicate a sense of the scope and magnitude of creation—the variety and multiplicity of things, composers as well as artists and writers have found it appropriate to bring together a wealth of diverse materials, often placing these in sudden and violent juxtaposition. (One need only think of a Bach Passion, a Beethoven symphony, or a play of Shakespeare.) One way of combining and uniting contrasting ideas into a coherent whole, reconciling seemingly incompatible events, is to subsume them under some higher order—to embody them within a hierarchic structure.[23]

From this point of view, Reti chose the wrong repertory to illustrate his theory: he would have been better off analyzing recent serial music or perhaps the music of Java.

But even when conformant relationships do play a prime role in creating a sense of cohesion, similarity *per se* does not unite. For as we have seen the more two events are alike, the more they tend to be perceived as discrete, separated entities. A collection of identical buttons possesses a high degree of uniformity, but only an additive sort of unity. Conformant relationships create the strongest impression of unity when they are embodied in some sort of functional process.

From a more mundane and personal point of view, I find it difficult to believe that the kinds of correspondences, whether obvious or disguised, which Reti points to are the basis for unity or a cause of excellence in music —for this sort of motivic manipulation is so easy to do. Every third-rate composer of yesterday and today is adept at it. Having been one of them, I fully agree with Tovey that, "Nothing is easier than to derive any musical idea whatever from any other musical idea; and a long chain of such derivations is often supposed to embody the logic of music. In itself it can give us no security that it is more logical than a series of puns."[24]

Tovey's scathing reference to puns is not as negative as he perhaps took it to be. For it calls attention to an aspect of conformant relationships not previously noticed: we take pleasure in the act of perceiving transformation. Psychic parsimony—seeing a single entity or idea do double duty

[23] Leonard B. Meyer, *Music, the Arts and Ideas* (Chicago: University of Chicago Press, 1967), pp. 312–13. A true believer in the exegetic method can still have the final word, arguing that the contrasts and diversity are not *real*.

[24] *Musical Textures*, p. 50.

—is involved in the perception of conformant relationships. Just as we delight in seeing a familiar landscape in new lights—at different times of day or
in different seasons, seeing it as the same and yet different—and are en-
chanted as a magician changes a handkerchief into a rabbit, so we enjoy
discovering that something first understood as one kind of event can change
its function. For instance, that something at first understood as being a closing kind of event can be transformed into a beginning kind of event—as is
done from measure 19 to 20 in Haydn's "Surprise" Symphony (Example 24)
and from measures 42–43 to measure 44 in Brahms' Second Symphony (Example 32). For the same reasons, we are exhilarated to find that seemingly
unconnected and disparate themes really "fit together"—as in the Prelude
to Wagner's *Die Meistersinger* (Example 38).

Example 38

The basis for the unity of multimovement works is problematic. Though
composers are not always an infallible guide in critical and aesthetic matters,
their views should at least be considered seriously, the more so when there
appears to have been a cultural consensus about artistic matters. As F. E.
Kirby has pointed out, composers and theorists of the eighteenth and early
nineteenth centuries often thought of unity in terms of a characteristic
musical "style." As representative of this view, Kirby quotes Peter Lichten-
thal, who in 1826 wrote of the characteristic symphony as "one which pro-
poses a musical picture; or a moral character, as *il Distratto* by Haydn, or an
event, like *La Caduta di Fetonte;* or some phenomenon in the physical world,
as *la Tempesta, l'Incendio, la Caccia*, etc. To which belong the symphonies
pastorali, militari, etc." [25] Not only do many of the works of Haydn and
his contemporaries belong to this class of composition, but so, Kirby argues,
do quite a number of Beethoven's works: for instance, the "Pathétique"

[25] Unpublished manuscript: "Beethoven's Use of Characteristic Styles: A Contribution to the Problem of Unity in the Large Forms," p. 5.

Sonata, the "Eroica" Symphony, the "Pastoral" Symphony, the "Les Adieux" Sonata, and a number of the late works.

Though a bias favoring the obvious objectivity of a musical score has led most contemporary critics and theorists to account for music wholly in terms of pitches and durations, timbres and dynamics, an explanation of unity in terms of characteristic "styles" seems as convincing as Reti's theory. The idea of unity fostered through characterization is supported by historical evidence. And, equally important, such a view is by no means as "subjective" as might at first appear.

Evidence from many different cultures indicates that music comprehension depends to a considerable extent upon the listener's knowing a traditional tonal syntax and a set of conventional signs and schemata (even though these may be grounded in and limited by the nature and capacity of the human ear and mind). Once this is granted and the attempt to explain music solely on the basis of innate, universal responses is given up, then common traditions and conventions can be analyzed as objective aspects of a musical culture, just as images, figures of speech, poetic genres, and dramatic conventions are in literature.[26] As Kirby observes, what is meant by a characteristic style "is not necessarily a personal or subjective quality, but rather something objective and concrete: for the particular expressive character is explicit and consists of a number of distinctive elements that define it, among them particular musical forms, keys, tempi, the use of certain instruments or combinations of instruments, special melodic types, rhythmic patterns, dynamic qualities, and so on." [27]

The existence of such conventions means that there has been a continuing tradition of musical representation in which later manners of delineating a particular moral character, a kind of event, an affective state, or some phenomenon in the physical or mythical world are based upon and influenced by earlier ones. Just as there are histories of elegiac poetry and of *carpe diem* lyrics, of paintings of the Annunciation and of pastoral scenes, so there would seem to be histories of battle music, pastoral music, love music, lamentation music, and so on. In short there is, or should be, a field which

[26] Here, I believe, is the crucial mistake of studies such as Deryck Cooke's *The Language of Music* (London: Oxford University Press, 1962) and Donald N. Ferguson's *Music as Metaphor* (Minneapolis: University of Minnesota Press, 1960): neither recognizes that the expressive characterizing power they find in Western music cannot be traced to necessary "natural" sources alone, but are to a great extent a matter of learned convention.

[27] "Beethoven's Use of Characteristic Styles."

might be called *musical iconology;* and, considering that art history has to a considerable extent been a model for musicology, it is strange that (to the best of my knowledge) little work has been done in this area. It would, I think, be fascinating to study the history of the characteristics of, say, Hades (fury) music or pastoral music from the Renaissance to the twentieth century, tracing common features, describing changes of manner and means of representation, and relating these both to the history of musical style and to the history of culture generally.

3.

If the most important functions of conformant relationships are creating coherence and articulating structure, and if such similarity is not the basis for musical unity, then what is the significance of motivic correspondence *between* movements? For there is no doubt that such correspondences exist—and are specially common in the music of the nineteenth century. One explanation is that they provide the pleasure of psychic economy. In addition, the return in later movements to ideas presented in previous ones may on occasion have programmatic significance—as, for instance, in Beethoven's Ninth Symphony or Berlioz's Symphonie Fantastique. Of the other reasons for increased emphasis on conformant relationships during the nineteenth century only one need be mentioned here: namely, as the size and scope of multi-movement works increased, greater demands were placed upon the listener's memory; the use of already familiar motives made it easier for the listener to grasp new thematic ideas. Observe, however, that though this function of conformance may be important, its significance is *psychological* and generic rather than aesthetic and specific. It is a necessary condition for comprehension, not for aesthetic relationship.

Brahm's Second Symphony is, as Reti points out, an unequivocal example of the use of conformant relationships between movements. The opening theme of the Finale is audibly related to that of the first movement

Example 39

(Example 39). When he subsequently attempts to show that the second theme of the Finale is a "synthesis" of the main ideas of *all* the preceding movements, one again senses that Reti's hypothesis has driven him to remote and doubtful connections. He might, employing the same ingenuity, have related the opening theme of the third movement to that of the first by a simple inversion (Example 40).

Example 40

Why stop with correspondences between movements? An aficionado of the exegetic method might easily go further. He might, for instance, note that the changing-note motive so prominent in this Symphony occurs in other works by Brahms, notably as an important element in the Finale themes of the First Symphony (Example 41A), the Third Symphony (41B) and the Fourth Symphony (41C).

Example 41

At first, this seems an absurd thing to do. Yet nothing is forced—no tones have been ignored in order to make the themes similar. The conformance is there for all to hear. And other instances of motivic correspondence between different works by a single composer are not uncommon. In the last string quartets of Beethoven a motive moving from leading tone to tonic and from the sixth degree of the scale in minor to the fifth is used as the main theme of the first movement of Opus 131 (Example 42A), the opening of Opus 132 (42B) and, in a slightly varied form, as the introductory statement of the fugue subject in Opus 133 (42C), to cite only the most obvious cases.

Example 42

Such conformant relationships *are* significant. But their significance lies not in the area of critical analysis, but in that of style analysis. That is, they are relevant for the analysis of a particular composer's idiom—his special stylistic predilections. From this point of view, the theme of the Finale of Brahms' Second Symphony is related at least as much to the composer's general idiom—his preference for conjunct, lyrical themes for finales —as it is to other motives in the symphony. In a similar way, one could, I think, show the main ideas of Brahm's first movements tend to be disjunct and often triadic.

One can, of course, go further. For motivic similarities exist among works by different composers. For example, both the opening theme of the Finale of Tchaikowsky's Fifth Symphony (Example 43A) and the aria, "Qui sedes ad dextram patris," from Bach's B-Minor Mass (43B) use motives like the one which begins Brahms' Second Symphony. Here, too, conformant

Example 43

relationships are important for style analysis, but on a higher level—that of the style of tonal music as a whole. Their relevance for critical analysis is derivative: criticism employs concepts and generalizations developed by style analysis. Such motivic similarities are instances of archetypal schemata with which we will be concerned later in this study. They are important not because they "unify style"—whatever that might mean—but because they help listeners to comprehend and remember the particular patterns in which they are actualized. These considerations suggest that a particular composer's idiom is distinguishable from the style of which it forms a part because he tends to employ some possibilities available in a style with greater frequency than others. Thus though the motivic patterns presented in Example 42 were "stylistically available" to Beethoven throughout his career (as they were to

other composers of the time), he favored them specially in his late style
which they help to define.

The analysis of conformant relationships often leads to questions about
the composer's *intentions*. Is the resemblance between the opening themes
of the first and last movements of Brahms' Second Symphony the result of
the composer's explicit, conscious intention, or should it be ascribed to an
unconscious use of common stylistic features—or is it a chance similarity?

The relevance of the artist's intention for criticism has received considerable attention in the literature about aesthetics. And it has been argued
that even where the intention can be documented from reliable outside
sources, its relevance for criticism is questionable.[28] I do not wish to consider
the question of the relevance of the composer's intention, but rather to ask
on what grounds we base our feelings about intentionality in the absence of
extramusical information.

The excerpts in Example 44 are taken from the first movement of
Beethoven's Piano Sonata in E♭ Major, Opus 81a. The bracketed patterns
are conformant in that each involves a pitch exchange between outer voices
—or the extension of such an exchange, as in parts A and B. Although the
conformant relationships between A and B, and B and D look "intentional,"
doubts arise about the relationship of C to the others: Hasn't the correspondence been imposed, perhaps forced, in this case? Was Beethoven aware of
the similarity?

With regard to the first question, the answer is an unequivocal "no." No
exegetic ingenuity has been brought into play in order to show a correspondence. No pitches have been disregarded; nothing has been inferred or
imagined. The resemblance is there for all to see. That it is neither striking
nor obvious, is a question of the strength of the relationship, not of its
existence.

The answer to the second question is, I think, that in a borderline case
such as this, it is impossible to decide whether a relational ordering arose
from the syntax of the style being employed or was consciously contrived by
the composer. Since there is no specific point at which stylistic ordering
ends and compositional ordering begins—they form a continuum—it is impossible *in principle* to distinguish those conformant relationships attributable
to style from those we presume that the composer explicity devised. Inten-

---

[28] See W. K. Wimsatt and M. C. Beardsley, "The Intentional Fallacy," reprinted
in *Philosophy of Art and Aesthetics*, F. A. Tillman and S. M. Cahn, eds. (New York:
Harper and Row, 1969), pp. 657-699.

Example 44

tionality is a function of stylistic improbability: the more improbable it is
that a conformant relationship could have arisen for stylistic reasons alone,
the more we impute conscious intention to the composer. For this reason,
the longer comparable events are, the more certain we feel that the similarity
was intended. And we do not consider what is most normative in a style
to have been "put there" by the composer. For instance, we do not as a
rule consider the resemblances between perfect cadences as examples of intentional conformant relationships. The similarity is attributed to the syntax
of the style. But were such cadences to occur from time to time in an essentially serial work, we would probably conclude that the composer explicitly
related them to one another.

Intentional and nonintentional conformant relationships, then, differ
from one another in degree rather than in kind. The question is not essentially
one of intention, but of audible resemblance. This depends not only upon
all the factors considered earlier,[29] but also upon contextual differentiation—

[29] See p. 49.

the extent to which the event being compared is marked-off as a separable entity. The similarity between part C of Example 44 and the other motives is difficult to perceive because C is embedded in a larger and quite uniform patterning.

The question of the artist's intention intrigues us and will, no doubt, continue to do so. For our culture has, at least until recently, assigned tremendous importance to the creative act—to personal expression and individual discovery. Fortunately, however, knowledge of the composer's intention is not necessary for critical analysis. It is fortunate because such intentions are virtually impossible to ascertain, either from the music itself or from extramusical documentation. Even where documentation exists, its interpretation and reliability is problematic. Knowledge of the composer's intention is unnecessary because *a relationship is a relationship* whether it was expressly devised by the composer, resulted from the orderliness of stylistic syntax, or in rare instances was the result of chance. And a relationship is a relationship only in the light of some cognitive act, whether conscious or intuitive, learned or innate.

Though every relationship is significant, it by no means follows that all are *equally* so, or that they are so in the same respect. Some conformant relationships are relatively unimportant in creating coherence or articulating structure, while others are crucial. Some are compositionally significant—important for critical analysis—while others are most significant as aspects of the composer's idiom and of style analysis. Still others are relevant not to the analysis of particular compositions, but to an understanding of the psychology of creativity, the history of the composer, or the history of style.

The conformant relationships thus far considered were assumed to be audible; often such similarities are striking. Like those which we presume the composer intended, these tend to be ones which are less probable—given the norms of the style. Other similarities, those which are stylistically most probable, go virtually unnoticed. Once the style has been learned—through the experience of listening, not necessarily through explicit instruction—such similarities are, as it were, taken for granted. This does not mean, however, that they are not important or effective in shaping musical experience. Resemblances between similar scale and triadic patterns or between like harmonic progression are as important, and for many of the same reasons, as the conformant relationships considered throughout this chapter. The systematic study of such relationships belongs, as has been suggested, to the field of style analysis.

As a kind of "coda," I should like briefly to discuss the significance of conformant relationships which, though identifiable and unequivocal, are inaudible. Musicians, like others belonging to a professional group, enjoy the sense of exclusiveness—of clannishness—which comes not only from sharing special knowledge and using special jargon, but also from knowing "secrets" to which only initiates or members of the in-group are privy. Sometimes, as in jazz, such secret relationships are audible in performance once one has learned the repertory.[30] Then they play a significant role in aesthetic appreciation. Relating the audible tune within a florid jazz improvisation to its hidden model involves the pleasure of psychic economy. In other cases, however, covert relationships are inaudible and irrelevant for musical experience. One thinks, for instance, of cryptographic devices in which the names of friends or of admired composers are encoded through the use of the letter names of pitches, Morse Code, or some other cypher. Similarly the manipulation and ordering of pitch and time rows in serial music are often inaudible, in the sense that they are unrecognizable *as such*. They are relevant for understanding the precompositional activities of the composer, not the structure and process of the composition itself.

Such inaudible and cryptic orderings usually do more, however, than satisfy the coterie instinct. First, by limiting the number of options open to the composer at a particular point in a composition, they facilitate his choosing. That is, if the constraints present in the style are not sufficient, the composer will devise special ones of his own. As I have suggested elsewhere,[31] this need for added constraints was perhaps involved in Schönberg's invention of the twelve-tone method. In this case they were initially, at least, quite audible. But this need not be the case. Often completely arbitrary constraints which *as such* have no aesthetic significance will do. Secondly, the invention of private limitations may serve as a way to get the creative act going: cabalistic devices may suggest explicitly musical ideas to the composer. The ideas *are* aesthetically significant, but their inaudible, nonmusical, basis is not. And both reasons for the invention of special constraints are related to the composer's delight in challenge—in overcoming special, in this case self-imposed, difficulties. Such private and crytopgraphic relationships are important. But their significance lies in the areas of the psychology of creativity and the biographies of particular composers, not in that of critical analysis and musical understanding.

[30] See Frank Tirro, "The Silent Theme Tradition in Jazz," *The Musical Quarterly*, LIII, 3 (July, 1968), 313–334.
[31] *Music, the Arts and Ideas*, p. 241f.

More generally: there is a distinction between explaining the genesis
of a composition and understanding the completed work.[32] To illustrate, let
me take one final example from Reti's book. Reti wants to show that the
theme of the Trio of the Scherzo from Beethoven's "Eroica" Symphony is
a transformation of the first theme of the first movement. He writes:

> If we consider the Trio theme as it appears in the symphony itself
> [Example 45A] and the version in which this theme appears in the
> fourth, the last sketch [B], it is hardly possible to point out any actual
> affinity between these shapes and the well known theme of the first
> movement C:

Example 45

An attempt on this basis to prove that Beethoven formed the themes
of the various movements from one common thought would be refuted
as artificial. Nevertheless, the sketchbook lucidly demonstrates the true
process by which the Trio theme came into existence. Looking at the
version in which the theme appears in the *first* sketch,

Example 46

we can hardly belive our eyes. For this first original version of the
Trio theme mirrors the main theme of the symphony so distinctly in the

---

[32] This distinction, as well as that made in the first chapter between style analysis
and critical analysis, is made by William Thomson in "The Problem of Musical
Analysis and Universals," *College Music Symposium*, VI (Fall, 1966), 91–93.

rhythm and spirit of its whole shaping that the nature of the themes as
two conceptions of one identical thought cannot be doubted.[33]

But Reti's obsession with the unifying function of conformant relationships makes him miss the crucial point. True, Beethoven begins with something similar to the first movement theme. Far from being surprising or
unusual, it seems natural to start from the known—using it as a jumping-off
point, a way of getting the compositional act going. But Beethoven works
from this similarity *toward something manifestly different*. He could have
invented something related by conformance, yet subtly disguised. But that
was *not* what Beethoven was after. As Reti himself observed: "it is
hardly possible to point out any affinity" between A and C in Example 46.
As they stand, there is virtually no discernible motivic relationship between
these themes. Knowledge that one was derived from the other does not
alter this compositional fact one iota; nor does it illuminate the Trio theme.

However, the study of such motivic modifications may be vitally important in helping us understand the way Beethoven went about the act of
composing—a matter of great interest in its own right. In other words, the
sketches and notebooks of composers—not to mention ordinary biographical
information—are often crucial for the explanation of the composer's creative
process;[34] and such resources may also occasionally call attention to significant, but previously unnoticed, relationships within the composition itself.
But a compositional sketch is not a musical homunculus; it can no more be
equated with or explain the finished work than an embryo can account for
the behavior of a mature human being. Tracing the genesis of a musical
idea or a composition from the first sketch through the finished work may

[33] *The Thematic Process of Music*, p. 358.

[34] Sketches can throw light upon the compositional process *only* if they are interpreted in the light of theory about the nature of musical relationships. For example,
to explain why Beethoven removed *sforzandi* from the first version of the opening
movement of the F-Major String Quartet, Opus 18 No. 1, one must have some
hypothesis about the function of *sforzandi* in general. Otherwise all one can say is
that Beethoven didn't like their effect—which explains nothing. In the absence of a
background of theory (however informal), only description, not analytic explanation,
is possible.

One might turn this whole matter around and suggest that comparing sketches
with the finished composition would give us fairly hard data against which to test our
theories. For if theories can explain why a composer made the changes he did—or in
an ideal case, even predict from a sketch or autograph what changes seem likely,
and check these against the printed score—then our theories would have received a
kind of objective confirmation.

be illuminating psychologically and biographically, but it is not the same as, and cannot be substituted for, serious analytic criticism.[35]

[35] This does not contradict the observation in *Music, the Arts and Ideas* that we "understand an event or an object, partly at least, by understanding how it came to be what it is . . ." (p. 63; also see p. 89). Aesthetic understanding of the genesis and growth of a musical pattern is contextual; it depends upon a comprehension of the preceding patterning as it functions within the work and within its style and tradition. The psychological understanding of the act of composition depends upon our comprehension of the life of the composer, and will certainly be enhanced by the study of sketches and the like.

CHAPTER IV

Hierarchic Structures

Hierarchic Structures

This chapter will be concerned with hierarchic structures—the basis for their existence and the kind of organization possible in tonal music. These considerations will, in turn, lead to a distinction between form and process in music, and to a discussion of their interaction.

Hierarchic structures are of signal importance because they enable the composer to invent and the listener to comprehend complex interreactive musical relationships. If musical stimuli (pitches, durations, timbres, etc.) did not form brief, but partially completed events (motives, phrases, etc.), and if these did not in turn combine with one another to form more extended, higher-order patterns, all relationships would be local and transient—in the note-to-note foreground. Nonhierarchic music—that of John Cage, for instance—moves, like the ocean, in undulating or sporadic waves of activity in which we attend to, but can scarcely remember, the particular events. As Herbert A. Simon has pointed out: [1] "If there are important systems in the world that are complex without being hierarchic, they may to a considerable extent escape our observation and understanding. Analysis of their behavior would involve such detailed knowledge and calculation of the interactions of their elementary parts that it would be beyond our capacities of memory or computation." And this is specially important in the understanding of music, which, because it is abstract and successive in time, places extraordinary demands upon memory.

[1] "The Architecture of Complexity," *Proceedings of the American Philosophical Society*, CVI, 6 (1962), 477.

I.

To illustrate how hierarchic structuring works, I have chosen a theme which is both exceptionally clear and very compact. It is the first section of the second movement of Beethoven's String Quartet in B♭ Major, Opus 130. The music is given in Example 47.

Hierarchic structures such as this can arise only if the series of stimuli are articulated into more or less discrete events on the various levels of the hierarchy. In this case, the upper (1–4) analytic braces show rhythmic groupings, and the lower ones (d–a), indicate formal relationships. These groupings are the result not only of durational relationships but of melodic, harmonic, tonal, and dynamic ones as well. The first measure, for instance, is an event —a more or less discrete pattern on what is marked as level a(1). The measure is a single gesture. This first event combines with those in measures 2, 3 and 4 to form a higher-level entity: the antecedent phrase of level b(2). The consequent phrase is similar to the antecedent, and both combine to form the more complete phrase of level c(3). Though it is constructed in a somewhat different way, the second half of the theme (measures 9–16) is also hierarchically organized. And the two halves combine on a still higher level (level d, 4), creating a closed, stable shape—a rounded binary form. Finally the theme is itself a distinct event within the structure of the whole movement, which is a three-part, *da capo* form: a kind of scherzo-trio-scherzo. The section being analyzed is the "theme" or "Scherzo."

For a series of stimuli to form separable events which can act as elements within a hierarchy, there must be some degree of closure.[2] Closure—the arrival at relative stability—is a result of the action and interaction among the several parameters of music. Because melody, rhythm, harmony, texture, timbre, and dynamics are relatively independent variables, some may act to create closure at a particular point in a work, while others are mobile and on-going. To the extent that the parameters act together in the articulation of closure or, alternatively, in creating instability and mobility, they may be said to move *congruently*. Conversely, when some parameters foster closure while others remain open, the parameters are said to be *noncongruent*. A deceptive cadence is a simple instance of non-congruence: rhythm and melody act to articulate closure, but harmony remains open and mobile.

[2] The vital importance of closure in the articulation of forms and processes was made clear to me by Barbara H. Smith's book, *Poetic Closure: Or Why Poems End* (Chicago: University of Chicago Press, 1969).

Example 47

Closure, then, is an aspect of patterning. I have considered the nature and basis for patterning in music at some length in *Emotion and Meaning in Music*.[3] Here, the barest summary must suffice. The delineation of musical patterns is the result of the relationships within and among a number of factors—namely:

1) the presence of similarity and difference between successive events within a particular parameter. Both complete uniformity and total heterogeneity preclude syntactic organization, and hence establish no stability-instability relationships;

2) the separation of one event from another in time, pitch, or both; or through clear differences in dynamics, timbre, or texture;

3) immediate repetition, whether varied or exact, of part or all of a pattern;

4) the completion of previously generated implications;

5) harmonic cadence and tonal stability.

How these factors function to create patterns and articulate closure will, I hope, become clear as we proceed.

The smallest discrete event in Beethoven's theme is the motive of the first measure. Though it can be analyzed into smaller parts, these have no independent existence or stability. Rhythmically, the two eighth-notes lead to the third beat and tie it to the first, creating a closed trochaic group, as shown in Example 48. This beginning-accented patterning is supported by

Example 48

the tempo which is very fast. Melodically, the first two beats are understood as an F with a neighbor-note, E♭, followed by G♭ which functions as an *échapée*—ornamental tone. In other words, as indicated in graph b of Example 47, the main melodic line moves from the F in measure 1 to the E♭ in measure 2, with G♭ acting as an ornamental tone. But perhaps this analysis is too hasty. For on the last beat of the measure Beethoven presents the harmony—an E♭ minor triad—which would have made the G♭ a substantive, chord tone. It comes too late however. The harmonic change does not really alter our understanding of the motivic structure.

[3] (Chicago: University of Chicago Press, 1956), Chapters III–V.

The relative closure of the first measure is in part the result of rhythm
—the fact that the trochee is closed. Partly, it is due to the separation in
pitch and time between the G♭ and the following E♭. Closure is also fostered
by the varied repetition of the motive itself—in measure 2. Even had the
first two measures been connected temporally and melodically, as shown in
Example 49A, the first measure would have been perceived as a discrete event
because the second measure is a varied repetition. Or, had there been no
repetition, but a clear separation in time and pitch, as in Example 49B, two

Example 49

different, yet separable events, would have been defined. But were there
neither repetition nor separation, then, as Example 49C indicates, the two
measures would be understood as a single event—though with some internal
articulation. And the cohesiveness of the patterning would have been reinforced by the repetition presented in the example.

The first measure (Example 47) is strongly connected with the second
on the next level of the hierarchy. Melodically, the motion from F to E♭
creates a higher-level process which implies continuation down to the tonic,
B♭.[4] The first two measures are also connected harmonically. The B♭-E♭-A♭
progression in the bass begins an harmonic process through the cycle of fifths.
Note, however, that melodic and harmonic processes are coordinate only
on primary accents, not on secondary ones. Partly for this reason the G♭
in measure 1 and the F in measure 2 are understood as being ornamental.
And this is why, despite the change of harmony on the fourth beat, the
main motion is by measures. Though the motion across the barline is supported by the syncopation in the viola and the eighth-notes in the second
violin, the cello does not strongly emphasize the harmonic progression. That
is, the root motion from E♭ to A♭ would have been more emphatic had the
lower A♭ come on the first beat of measure 2. The result is that the low E♭
is almost heard as accompanimental— like a kind of "umpah" bass.

[4] The nature of and basis for implicative relationships are discussed in the second
part of this book.

The closure at the end of the second measure, like that of the first, is melodically and rhythmically unambiguous for essentially the same reasons. Because it is sequential with the first, both melodically and harmonically, the second measure strongly implies continuation to the tonic. Indeed, because the bass motion does move a fourth across the bar, the connection between measure 2 and measure 3 is a bit stronger than that between measures 1 and 2.

Measures 3 and 4 are a single event. Melodically, there is one motion—from D♮ to F. Harmonically, there is a progression from VI to IV (with a hint of II—the C on the fourth beat) to V. Rhythmically, the repeated E♭ acts as a pivot linking the weak part of measure 3 with measure 4.

The closure at the end of this phrase is the result, first and foremost, of rhythmic structure. On the first rhythmic level (1), each of the first two events ends on a mobile weak beat—even though the trochee itself is closed. And this mobility is emphasized by the final eighth-notes in the second violin part. But the final event of the phrase—measures 3 and 4—is decisively end-accented, and hence closed. This closure is emphasized by the rests in measure 4 which separate the end of the first phrase from the beginning of the second. On the second rhythmic level (2), measure 2 is an exact repetition of measure 1—in durational relationships. Because exact repetition does not create cohesive patterning, these measures do not create a clear rhythmic group. They are connected melodically and harmonically, but not rhythmically. What is needed is temporal differentiation or dynamic change. The former is provided by the two-measure group which follows. Now the first two measures cohere because they become part of the whole phrase which is an anapest group; or, from a formal point of view (analysis), a bar-form: w-w'-x. As a result, the antecedent phrase is closed, end-accented on the first two rhythmic levels.

Because rhythmic closure is forceful, the harmonic progression is understood as cadential. The progression from the subdominant to the dominant strongly implies continuation to the tonic and hence is on-going, particularly so because the bass moves linearly, without decisive root motion or disjunction. But rhythmic articulation makes us interpret measure 4 as a point of relative stability. To generalize: a semicadence might be defined as one in which a mobile, goal-directed, harmonic process is temporarily stabilized by decisive rhythmic closure. In other words, a semicadence is a case of parametric noncongruence which has become archetypal in the stylistic syntax of tonal music.

The melodic closure of the antecedent phrase, which is by no means forceful, is also primarily the result of rhythmic articulation. The F is an acceptable point of closure partly because it is the relatively stable fifth of the scale and partly because it was the first note of the tune. That is, if the implied melodic goal—the tonic, Bb—is not reached, it is preferable to return to the point at which motion began than to cadence on some other note.

Finally, the closure of the first phrase is emphasized by the fact that the second begins like a repetition. Indeed, one of the benefits of antecedent-consequent patterns is that the element of repetition makes the phrase structure crystal clear.

The cadence at the end of the antecedent phrase, though unambiguous, is only partial. Like the antecedent phrase, the consequent is rhythmically closed on the first two levels. However, the melodic implications of motion from F to Bb are realized; and so are the harmonic implications of the cycle of fifths progression. Here, in short, the parameters move congruently in creating closure.

Though the first and second rhythmic levels create clear closure at the end of the consequent phrase, the third level—the level of both phrases—is not as decisively defined as is usually the case with antecedent-consequent structures. Let me explain. Because the temporal organization of the phrases is the same, durational relationships cannot shape high-level rhythmic grouping. Melodic-harmonic syntax has to shape the high-level rhythm. Normally the melody of the antecedent phrase cadences on either the second degree of the scale or the leading tone. For instance, in the Theme from Mozart's Piano Sonata in A Major, discussed in the second chapter, the melody moves from the third of the scale to the supertonic in the antecedent phrase; in the consequent phrase the supertonic is resolved, moving to the tonic. Thus the over-all motion of both phrases is basically from the third, to the second, to the tonic. And, as in Mozart's Theme, usually the semicadence which closes the antecedent phrase is clearly articulated by a reversal of motion and a skip in the bass. But neither of these take place in Beethoven's theme. The melodic motion at the end of the antecedent phrase does not move toward the tonic, but away from it, returning to F. The harmonic motion at the beginning of each phrase is at least as strong as that at the end, and the F in the bass at measure 4 is not preceded by either a reversal or a skip, but follows from the downbeat motion begun in measure 1: that is, it is a continuation of the scale, Bb-Ab-Gb-to F. As a result, not only is the rhythm of level 3 rather weakly defined, but the high-level melodic structure, instead of being unequivocally linear, is more or less triadic—as graph b in Example 47 shows.

These considerations of closure suggest an explanation of the melodic and rhythmic structure of the second half of this Scherzo section. Melodically, the first half of the section emphasizes the fifth degree of the scale (F), with the D♭ as a point of secondary importance. The B♭ at the end of the consequent phrase is emphasized, but it is not, I think, as prominent and strong as the F. The triadic framework (F-D♭-[F-D♭]-B♭) which forms the underlying structure of the antecedent-consequent organization is, in a sense, a microcosm of the whole theme. For as graph a of Example 47 shows, the first part of the theme is a prolongation of F, the second is a prolongation of D♭, while the third is a prolongation of B♭.

Rhythmically, the highest level of the first part was not decisively defined. What is needed is a strongly end-accented grouping to create unequivocal closure. And this is what we get in the second section. The first of these phrases (measures 9–12) is a two-measure pattern exactly repeated. Both the first and second levels of the two-measure groups are trochaic. Because they end on the *un*accented part of the rhythmic group, they are mobile and on-going. Because they are alike, they are not cohesive. Together they function as weak, anacrustic groups in relation to the four final measures. That is, the whole second part is an end-accented anapest pattern (level 3); or, from a formal point of view (level b), a bar-form—m-m'-n. Measures 13–16, which are the accented goal toward which measures 9–12 lead, are also anapest or bar form (w″-w″-x″) on level 1. That is, measures 13 and 14, which are essentially alike, function as weak groups leading to the last two measures which act as an accent in relation to them. This final goal-directed patterning is intensified by the crescendo to *fortissimo*, bringing the whole section to an emphatic close.

(In a sense, the unequivocal anapest rhythm of the second A'-part of the scherzo is the realization of a potential present in the first part. That is, while the melodic-harmonic structure in the first part caused measures 2 and 6 to function as pivots on rhythmic level 2, thus weakening the sense of end-accentuation in both the antecedent and the consequent phrase, measure 14 is not processive in relation to 13, but only in relation to what follows. To put the matter more generally: in the first part of the scherzo, melodic and harmonic relationships tend to overshadow rhythmic ones; while in the second part, just the reverse is the case. In the second part rhythm is specially effective precisely because melody and harmony are quite static.)

Finally, the return in measures 13 to 16 to a varied version of the rhythmic-melodic pattern of the first part enhances the sense of closure. As noted in Chapter III, return is not the same as repetition. Repeating the first eight measures, for instance, does not enhance their closure. What is needed is the tension of "going away", of instability. Such instability, slight though it is, is provided in this case by measures 9–12.

Though the high-level closure of the second half of the theme is strong, oddly enough the low-level rhythm ends on a weak beat—is somewhat mobile. It is appropriate that closure be attenuated, because this is not the end of the movement. The Trio is about to follow. When the movement does end, not only do all rhythmic levels combine to create closure, but stability is emphasized by coming after the tension of an extension.

2.

I have considered this music in detail in order to show that closure and mobility are functions of the action and interaction among all the parameters of music. At any point in a phrase or section, some parameters will tend to create closure, while others will promote continuity. For instance, in the partial closure at the end of the first measure, pitch and time disjunctions tend to separate events, and harmonic motion and second-level melodic organization make for continuity. In other words, and this is the important point, the parameters of music do not as a rule move congruently. If they did, a passage would either be entirely on-going and without distinguishable internal organization, or it would be decisively closed—without connection with what follows. Because the parameters do not move congruently, there are degrees of closure; and these are at times quite subtle.

The degree of closure, or, alternatively, of mobility, depends upon the shaping of the particular parameters at work, the degree of articulation contributed by each, and the number of parameters promoting or preventing closure. Clearly some parameters are more important shaping forces than others. In tonal music, for instance, melody, rhythm, and harmony are on the whole more important than timbre, dynamics, and register. Thus, though the crescendo at the end of the passage we have been analyzing contributes to the feeling of finality, closure would have been clear without it. But closure would not have been strong had the final harmony been a G♭ major chord.

A given parameter may articulate various degrees of closure. For instance, at the end of measure 4, the rhythmic closure of the second level is quite strong; but there is virtually no rhythmic closure on the same level at the end of measure 12. Or, if the end of the antecedent phrase is contrasted with that of the consequent, the latter is more markedly closed because, although the degree of rhythmic closure is essentially the same, melodic and harmonic closure are much more forceful.

Every composition, then, exhibits a hierarchy of closures. The more decisive the closure at a particular point, the more important the structural articulation. Or, *the structure of a composition is something which we infer from the hierarchy of closures which it presents.* A composition continues—is mobile and on-going—partly because of the tendency of parameters to act independently of one another, to be noncongruent. The end of a movement is not merely a cessation of sound. It is the point at which all parameters move congruently to create the stability of closure.

Musical structures are hierarchic not only in this combinational sense, but also because the individual parameters—particularly those that are most important in the formation of patterns—are themselves structured hierarchically. Considering the melodic structure of the Beethoven theme, we perceive not only the note-to-note motion within measure 1, but the motion of the motives themselves. On the next level, we perceive the relationship between antecedent and consequent melodic structures. And so on. The same is true of rhythm and of harmony—and to a smaller extent, of texture.

The way in which a particular parameter acts in articulating structure may be different on different hierarchic levels. For example, on lower levels dynamics and orchestration tend to contribute to the articulation of rhythmic patterns, but on higher levels they generally serve in the structuring of large-scale formal relationships. Similarly durational relationships are crucial in the shaping of low-level events such as motives and phrases; while tonality and texture are especially important for the organization of high-level structures. Moreover, the role played by a particular parameter depends not only upon hierarchic level, but also upon style. Harmonic relationships play a central role in the structuring of tonal music, but none in the ordering of most serial compositions. Timbre plays a very significant role in defining relationships in Webern's music, but only a minor role in the music of Bach.

Also the syntax of particular parameters tends to change as one moves from one level of the hierarchy to another. For instance, the syntax of chord-to-chord progression in the foreground harmony is different from that which governs long-range harmonic structures—tonal relationships. Thus the probability of the tonic chord (I) being followed by the mediant

(III) is low in foreground harmony, but it is quite high in the succession of tonal areas—particularly in the minor mode—witness measures 9–12 in the music we have been discussing. In like manner, it is more likely, in the music of the second half of the eighteenth century, that a low-level melodic event, a motive or phrase, will begin with a triadic pattern than that the higher-level connection between phrases will be triadic—though, as this Scherzo or the Minuetto of Mozart's Symphony No. 40 shows, this is not impossible. In other words, hierarchic structures are nonuniform and discontinuous. Just as the ways in which chemicals unite to form molecules are different from those involved in the organization of molecules into cells, so the ways in which tones combine to form motives are different from the ways in which motives cohere to create larger, more complex musical events.[5]

A motive, a phrase, or a period is defined by some degree of closure. On the level of its closure—the level on which it is understood as a separable event—it is a relatively stable, formal entity. Though it contains and is defined by internal processes, once closed, it is not a process but a palpable "thing." When in turn it combines with other events on the same level and thereby becomes part of a higher-level event, it again functions in a processive way. Measure 1 of Beethoven's theme, for instance, is a formal entity—defined, as we have seen, by internal rhythmic, melodic, and harmonic relationships. It combines in a processive, syntactic way with subsequent events to form a higher-level entity which is completed—partially closed—at measure 4. On the level of its closure, the antecedent phrase is also a formal entity; and it, in turn, combines with the consequent phrase forming the first part of a rounded binary structure. From this it appears that the same event may be characterized as either form or process depending upon the hierarchic context being considered.

A general principle of hierarchically structured music is that, as one moves from one level to another, there is always an alternation of functional significance. What is processive on one level (for instance, the note-to-note relationships within the first measure of the theme) becomes formal (a motive) on the next; what is formal on one level tends to become processive on the next. And such alternation continues until the highest level—that of the composition or movement—is reached.[6]

----

[5] This matter is considered in more detail in, *Music, the Arts and Ideas* (Chicago: University of Chicago Press, 1967), pp. 96–97, 257–259, 306–308, and passim.

[6] Events may follow one another without creating hierarchic structure, as, for instance, in the successive statement of an ostinato figure. An ostinato pattern will

In complex compositions the highest structural level—that which is the basis for naming the form—is usually mixed. It is formal in that relatively stable themes are presented; and it is processive in that such stable events are functionally related to less stable parts. The clearest example of this sort of organization is the rounded binary form. And the most complex rounded binary structures are sonata-form movements. Though one might argue that the highest level of a sonata-form movement is essentially processive—a single entity in which two similar subevents, the exposition and recapitulation, are functionally bound together by the development—it is, I think, closer to actual experience to say that the recapitulation is an aspect of formal organization, not just of syntactic structure. Indeed, this is the case even with small rounded binary forms such as the Beethoven theme we have been concerned with. The final four measures are part both of a syntactic process, the resolution of a tension, and of a formal entity, recognizable because of conformant relationships with the first part of the section.

The distinction is difficult to make because the word "form" has at least two meanings: these might be characterized as the difference between a composition "having form" and "being a form." We say that something has form if its parts are related to one another in a functional, syntactic way. A cadential chord progression, a sequence, a development section are processes which *have* form. In the same sense, a play and a novel have form. But they are not forms. When we say that something *is* a particular form— usually giving it a name like sonata-form, rondo, theme and variations, etc. —we are referring both to its hierarchic structure and to its conformant organization on the highest level. When both types of relationship are articulated by clear differentiation, then relationships will be formal. That is, the complex event will be said to be a form.

Sometimes themes—particularly fugue themes—are essentially processive entities. They have form in the sense of having a beginning or generative event, a middle or process which moves toward some goal, and an end—the arrival at some sort of closure. The subject of the F Minor Fugue from Book I of the Well-Tempered Clavier, as Example 50 shows, is essentially a single process—a chromatic decent from the fifth of the scale to the tonic. The changing-note figure, C-D♭-C, is the beginning or generative event; the con-

---

itself be hierarchic, but the series of identical patterns can create no higher-level organization. The series of statements is additive, not processive. Thus ostinatos give rise to what Herbert Simon has called "flat hierarchies." See "The Architecture of Complexity," p. 469.

junct motion toward F is the medial process; and the arrival at the tonic
in measure 4 is the conclusion, and in this case the beginning of a new event.
Though the conjunct process is interrupted by the motion from E to F, this
is understood as being separate from the "real" melodic motion. (The inter-
jection creates what will be called a potential structural tone. Because its
melodic prominence is not matched by its functional importance, structural
emphasis is called for. This emphais takes place—the potential is actualized
—when the answer begins on the F.) [7] The basic melodic process cannot
be divided or labeled "A" and "B," etc. Compare this with the consequent
phrase of the Beethoven example, which also descends from the fifth to the
tonic in the minor mode. The Bach is pure process. In the Beethoven, the
same process is embodied in a set of formal relationships which can be
labeled—w-w'-x—and classified as a bar-form.[8]

Example 50

There are even complete pieces which are basically syntactic processes.
In the first two preludes of Book I of Bach's Well-Tempered Clavier, for instance, there are no closed stable events—motives or themes—which are repeated on the highest level. Neither prelude *is* a form which can be labeled
as A-BA or the like. But both *have* form. Syntactic coherence is a result of
the functional relationships between the beginning, which has a relatively
closed harmonic shape; the middle, in which a less stable, sequential melodic-
harmonic process moves toward the goal of stabilizing tension on the dominant; and the conclusion, which consists of a prolonged cadential progression.
The only repetition—that of the keyboard figure within the measure, which
serves to sustain the harmony—is not syntactically structured. Its constant

[7] Potential tones are discussed in Part II, pp. 196–201.

[8] Patterns which are not strongly structured from a formal point of view—which
are primarily processive—are specially suitable for contrapuntal treatment. They become formal entities on higher levels, usually through imitation.

Example 51

repetition precludes process. Consequently it is understood as an active ground rather than as an implicative patterning.

Purely formal structures are additive. Though successive events may be related by conformance (as in a strophic form: A-A'-A″ . . . Aⁿ), no syntactic processes create higher levels of organization. And because they do not readily give rise to higher levels of organization, such formal structures seldom occur on lower levels. The single exception is the ostinato; and such unvaried patterns generally function as grounds over which processive patterns appear. For instance, the motive F-E-D-C♯ in Ravel's *Rhapsodie Espagnole* (Example 51) is repeated over and over, and, after one or two repetitions, is understood as a patterned ground against which the "real" tunes are heard. The peculiar circumstance in this case is that the ground is almost as well shaped as some of the figures. The result is a subtle ambiguity which Ravel enhances by modifying the orchestration and dynamics of the ostinato so that at times it becomes the focus of attention and seems to change its function.

At times *axial melodies* have something of the character of additive form.[9] The first measures of the Second Movement of Brahms' Fourth Symphony consist, as Example 52 shows, of an axial E embellished with upper and lower neighbor-notes. Though the embellishments suggest directions of motion, and though the addition of octave doublings in the oboes, bassoons and flutes provide variety and a sense of motion, a true syntactic process is not generated until measure 5, where the repetition of the axial pattern a third higher makes it probable that the theme will be triadic on the phrase level. And this indeed proves to be the case: the axial pattern moves to B in measure 15.

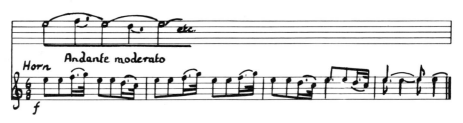

Example 52

But the clearest instance of purely formal structure occurs on higher architectonic levels—namely, the theme and variations. The first movement of Mozart's A-Major Piano Sonata, of which the Theme was discussed in the second chapter, may serve as an example. The Theme, and consequently

[9] Axial melodies are discussed in Part II, pp. 183–191.

each of the variations based upon it, is both syntactically and formally structured (Example 17). The first part, an antecedent-consequent phrase, though internally syntactic, is a formal entity on the level of its closure. The next four measures (9–12) are primarily syntactic in function, creating sufficient tension and change to call for a return to the consequent phrase, whose closure is enhanced by a brief extension.

Though the theme itself is a mixture of form and process, the movement as a whole is essentially formal. Parts—the theme and its variations—are related to one another not in terms of any over-all process, but in terms of conformance, in terms of harmonic structural parallelism and motivic similarity. There may, however, be implicative connections between parts. We saw, for instance, that the potential fourth, E to B across the first barline implies and is related to its actualization in the first variation. But such foreground connections, however interesting and important they may be, do not create or depend upon the existence of high-level processive relationships.

Observe that because the highest level is additive, rather than processive, the series lacks an internally structured point of probable termination. The number of parts is variable—many or few—depending upon the ingenuity of the composer, the taste of the time, and the patience of the audience. Of course additive structures can be ordered in some non-processive way. For instance, variation movements often have a tendency to move in the direction of greater complexity, faster tempi, and louder dynamics. But these are "trended" changes, not processive ones. That is, a number of variations of increasing complexity and so on may be followed by a variation that is simple, slow, and soft. Formal, additive structures may be ordered in still other ways: for instance, in terms of some set of key relationships—as in the Well-Tempered Clavier, the suite, or the symphony; or in terms of a text—as in a strophic song. In this last case, the text may provide syntactic connections which the music itself lacks. In all these kinds, however, the structure will be formal, not processive, unless there is some sort of functional differentiation among parts.

A theme and variations, a strophic song, a set of preludes or etudes is similar to what Herbert A. Simon has called a flat hierarchy. He observes that "a diamond is hierarchic, for it is a crystal structure of carbon atoms that can be further decomposed into protons, neutrons, and electrons. However, it is a 'flat' hierarchy, in which the number of first order subsystems can be indefinitely large." [10] From this point of view, the history of the theme

[10] Simon, "The Architecture of Complexity," p. 469.

and variations in the eighteenth and nineteenth centuries might be understood as the search for a way of transforming a "naturally" flat, additive
hierarchy (as in most Baroque and early classical variations) into an arched,
processive one—one with functionally differentiated parts (as in variations
of Schumann, Franck, and some of Beethoven).

Though the form of a composition is generally classified in terms of
the organization of the highest level, formal structures are found on all
levels of any work of reasonable complexity. And with some qualification,
the same formal types may arise on different hierarchic levels. The Beethoven
theme given in Example 47 is a clear case in point. On the first level (a), both
the antecedent and consequent phrases are bar-forms. Unless, like some
theorists, one considers a sonata-form movement that repeats the exposition
to be a bar-form:

Exposition	-	Exposition	-	Development and Recapitulation
A		A′		B

or one follows Alfred Lorenz in discovering large-scale bar-forms in
Wagner's operas, such formal structures are usually low-level: confined to
melodies or parts of melodies.

On the second level (b), the first part of Beethoven's theme is an antecedent-consequent phrase. Such formal types do at times form the highest
level of a composition—usually rather short ones. Chopin's Prelude in E
Minor, Opus 28 No. 4, would be an example. In this case, incidentally, the
two phrases are themselves essentially processive—without significant internal formal structure as in Beethoven's theme. On the highest level (c), the
scherzando section of Beethoven's movement is a rounded binary form:
A-BA. This is perhaps the most common form in tonal music. It is the
basis of countless melodies and themes within sonata-form movements,
rondos, minuettos, themes and variations, and so on. On higher levels,
elaborated by subsidiary formal events, rounded-binary organization is the
basis for most dance forms of the eighteenth century and of sonta-form
itself.

The Beethoven theme is, of course, part of a movement which is ternary,
A-B-A, in form. Though first and last parts are related to one another by
repetition (that is, by conformance), *da capo* structures such as this, like
strophic structures such as the theme and variations, are essentially formal,
not processive, on the highest level. This is the case, not only because clear
closure and satisfactory stability are established at the end of each part, but

because the parts themselves are not processively related: neither implies the other in a functional way, as is the case, for instance, with the development section of a sonata-form movement. For these reasons, even though conformant relationships may furnish the comfort of familiarity, may act as an aid to memory, or may provide the pleasure of recognition and psychic economy, the parts of most multimovement works—symphonies and sonatas, dance suites and song cycles, or collections of pieces in the same genre like preludes, etudes and so on—are related to one another in a formal way.

Many forms fall between the purely processive and the exclusively formal. Ritornello movements, rondos, fugues, and characteristic pieces such as rhapsodies, nocturnes, and so on are not, as a rule, highly arched. For unlike sonata-form movements, they contain no centrally processive part. Nor, on the other hand, are they strictly additive and formal. For though basically on the same hierarchic level, the several stable parts are processively connected to each other by less stable modulatory episodes. Such structures might be called conjunctive flat hierarchies. Because they contain processive parts, such conjunctive hierarchies can easily become more highly arched—as in many of Bach's fugues or in the so-called sonata-rondo. Finally, falling between the formal and the processive, are contrapuntal forms which are mixed. For instance, in a ground bass aria, such as the final lament in Purcell's *Dido and Aeneas,* the bass is strophic and additive, while the voice and upper instrumental parts are significantly processive. In canons, the imitative relationships between the voices tend to preclude marked functional differentiation between parts. Yet canons are continuous, not additive. An interlacing of complementary, but like, strands of music creates what I have called a *braided* hierarchy, which is processive and continuous, yet at the same time quite flat—in the foreground.[11]

3.

The distinction between form and process is important for the analysis and classification of hierarchic structures and because they at times function independently of one another. As a rule, formal organization—the part-whole relationships of a composition—and syntactic processes support and comple-

[11] With important exceptions, most formal types of organization can themselves become parts of larger wholes. For instance, a canon may be part of an essentially additive whole, such as Bach's Art of the Fugue; or it may be part of a processive structure, like the opening theme of the last movement of Franck's Sonata for Violin and Piano.

ment one another in the articulation of musical structure. For instance, at the end of the consequent phrase of the Beethoven theme in Example 47, rhythmic, melodic, and harmonic processes reach closure and at the same time a clearly shaped formal event comes to an end. In the second half of the theme, however, measures 9–12 are processive and unstable both rhythmically and harmonically. Their process carries over into the next four measures. But there is a clear formal division between these parts. That is, the last four measures constitute a formal entity, but are at the same time the continuation of a process generated earlier. Because this example might be analyzed in terms of the alternation of formal and processive functions within a hierarchy, rather than in terms of their bifurcation or division, it may seem somewhat equivocal. Let us, therefore, consider other examples.

Example 53 is the beginning, through the first beat of measure 12, of Bach's Fugue in F Minor from the second Book of the Well-Tempered Clavier. From a formal point of view the subject is a bar-form—not a one-part form like the subject of the F-Minor Fugue of Book I (Example 50). As the analysis indicates, the first event, ♪ ♫ ♪ is an amphibrach group

lasting for four eighth-notes. And so is the second event. These together imply that the next group will be twice as long—a gesture of eight eighth-notes. And this is basically what follows, except that the group has no clearly defined closure. The momentum of the sixteenth-notes continues on into measures 5 and 6, despite the entrance of the answer on the last eighth of measure 4.

Melodically, the subject contains three distinguishable strands, as the analysis over the example shows. The first of these, graph a, involves a motion from F in measure 1 to the E in measure 2 which is left unresolved until the answer enters in measure 4. (Notice that in like manner, the C to B of the answer implies the second entrance of the subject in measure 11.) Strand b consists of the upbeats to measures 1 and 2. Because they are functionally parallel and conjunct in pitch, they are perceived as a latent, subsidiary pattern whose linear continuation, probably to E♭, is implied. Like the F in Example 50, the C and D♭ are potential structural tones. That is, their melodic prominence suggests that they should be important structurally; but because they are rhythmically weak, that function is denied them. Consequently, they are implicative of a structural tone within the

Example 53

linear pattern already generated. That implication is realized—their potential is actualized—by the E♭ in measure 5. Bach reinforces the D♭ in measure
3 and moves through D♮ in measure 4 to the E♭.

The main melodic line, strand c, consists of the first beats of the measures,
each of which is prolonged—essentially for the whole measure. This line
moves from F to E, then, through a skip of a diminished fifth, to B♭ and A♭.
And here "theoretically" the fugue subject ends. Except that it doesn't. The
melodic process generated in the first four measures continues on as the A♭
is followed by a skip of a fifth to E♭ which moves by conjunct motion to

the D. The E♮ is important not merely because it is the highest note and accompanies the first accented beat of the answer, but because the main line of substantive tones and the line of potential tones *converge* on that pitch.

Though the melodic process of the subject continues through measure 6, and possibly beyond, the entrance of the answer creates a clear and unambiguous formal articulation. This is the beginning of a new shape, and of a new process. For two measures—measures 5 and 6—the continuation of subject and the answer move in parallel motion. Then the processes generated in the answer become the guiding force as both voices move sequentially toward the cadence in measure 12.[12]

This is a clear instance of the bifurcation of form and process: a second formal-processive event begins before a previously generated one has been completed. What are called elisions involve this kind of division of form and process. But not all bifurcations are, strictly speaking, elisions.

The articulation of a new formal division may be the result not of the generation of a second process, as in the Bach fugue, but may occur simply because a single processive event receives decisive, internal articulation. Consider the beginning of Beethoven's String Quartet in E♭ Major, Opus 127. As Example 54 shows, the movement opens with a six-measure Maestoso. For the first five measures, tonic harmony, complemented by dominant-seventh chords, prevails. At the end of measure 5, a progression through the submediant (C minor) leads to the subdominant. The main motion—from E♭ to A♭—leaves the harmonic situation open and mobile. The harmonic implications of the Maestoso are ambiguous. Rhythmically, the first level—that of two-measure groups—is trochaic, as the *sforzandi* of measures 1, 3 and 5 suggest.[13] On the next level, the pairs of measures form a dactyl grouping, but one which, because of the trill and the harmony in measure 6, is open and mobile. As a result, the sixth measure also functions as an anacrusis.

Whatever the ambiguities of rhythm and harmony may be, the melodic structure is clear and palpable. As the analysis over Example 54 indicates, it consists essentially of a triadic motion, E♭-G-B♭, which moves to C in the sixth measure. Though the theoretical-psychological basis for the contention

[12] Here, too, there is a division between form and process—albeit a slight one. Though the harmony and the process of the lower melodic line end with the first beat of the subject in measure 12, the fourth species counterpoint implicit in the upper line continues to the second eighth-note, the F, in measure 12—and perhaps beyond.

[13] I suspect that the *sforzandi* on the syncopated quarter-notes in measures 2 and 4 are there in order to prevent the final eighth-notes in these measures from functioning as upbeats.

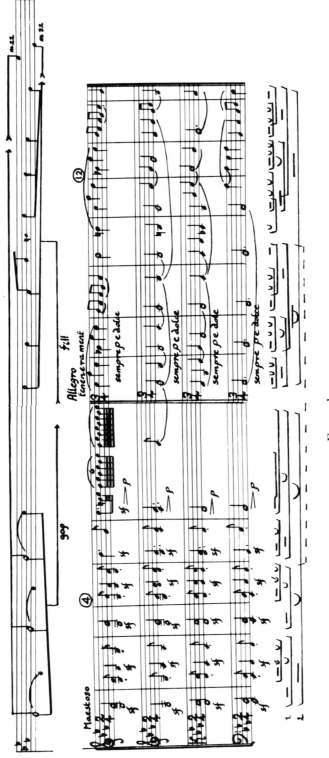

Example 54

cannot be explained here,[14] triadic patterns can function in two ways. They can imply their own continuation to a point of relative stability, usually the octave above the first note of the pattern—in this case, the high E♭. And triadic patterns can also function as disjunctions (gaps to be filled) implying conjunct motion back to the note from which they began—in this case, the lower E♭. Both implications can be actualized, as they are in this quartet.

The implications generated by the triadic process of the Maestoso are realized in the Allegro which follows. The lovely lyrical melody which begins the Allegro, descends conjunctly to the A♭ in measure 9. It is temporarily deflected up to the B♭ in a kind of spurious semicadence (the harmony, E♭, is the dominant of A♭ and the melodic pitch, B♭, is the fifth of the tonic, E♭), so that the first four measures of the Allegro function as a kind of antecedent phrase. The consequent follows reaching a tonic chord with G in the soprano. This "antecedent-consequent" structure is repeated, this time reaching the E♭ in the upper octave in measure 22 and realizing the implication of triadic continuation. But the decisive closure—the end of the first-theme group—comes only in measure 32, with the lower E♭ as the cadential pitch. And there, the second violin leads linearly through F to the tonic.

In short, the melodic, harmonic, and rhythmic processes generated in the Maestoso are continued and actualized in the Allegro. No alternative events are generated. But the beginning of the Allegro, clearly articulated by the changes in meter, tempo, dynamics, texture, expression, and character, is nevertheless established as a new formal entity. There is a bifurcation of form and process.

That Beethoven considers the melody which begins the Allergo as an entity in its own right is shown in the fact that its returns in the recapitulation are not preceded by the Maestoso. This independence is made possible by the special nature of the conjunct part of the gap-fill structure. Let me explain.

In most gap-fill themes—and they are legion in tonal music—the conjunct "fill" is not divided into paralell structures such as antecedent-consequent phrases or what Joseph Kerman has called "doublets." [15] The subject of the D♯-Minor Fugue from Book I of the Well-Tempered Clavier is, as Example 55 shows, a gap-fill melody. However, though it contains internal

---

[14] See the discussion of "Disjunct patterns" in Part II, and the analysis of the melody of the fourth movement of Beethoven's Fourth Symphony, p. 218.

[15] *The Beethoven Quartets* (New York: Alfred A. Knopf, 1967), pp. 201–204.

Example 55

articulation—the gap is renewed by the skip from D♯ to G♯—the parts have no rhythmic-structural independence. The subject is essentially a single gesture. On the other hand, if a melody is divided into parallel structural parts, then the generating disjunction is usually repeated at the beginning of the second part. For instance, in the Minuetto from Mozart's Flute Quartet (K.298) both the antecedent and the consequent phrases are preceded by a triadic gap (Example 56).[16]

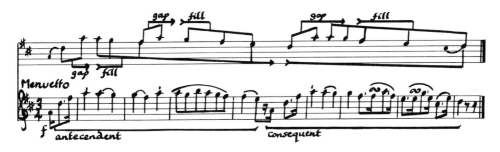

Example 56

In neither of these cases does the conjunct "fill" itself form a quasi antecedent-consequent doublet structure, as in the descending motion in the Allegro melody of Opus 127. It is because the "fill" is itself clearly structured that the Allegro theme of this movement can become independent of the Maestoso which first generated it. The reason why it does in fact become separated from the Maestoso—why the Maestoso does not return in the recapitulation—is convincingly stated by Joseph Kerman: ". . . the *Maestoso* never appears again, neither to introduce its consequent in the recapitulation, nor anywhere in the coda. It falls victim to the single-minded lyric ambition

---

[16] The skip from the first (lower) A to the D above it does not function as a gap to be filled but as an harmonic interval and a basis for octave definition.

of the movement as a whole . . . The movement lives not on contrast but on the inherent beauty of the consequent doublet phrase." [17]

In these examples of bifurcation, a previously generated process continues beyond and transcends formal articulation. The reverse is also possible. That is, process may reach closure before the formal structure has been completed. Echoes and extensions, for instance, often serve to normalize the morphological length of a phrase or period after cadential closure.[18] Since this sort of adjustment is well understood, a single example will serve as an illustration.

The "Dumka" from Dvořák's Piano Quintet, Opus 81, begins with the four-bar melody given in Example 57. The harmony moves from the tonic to an altered subdominant which is followed by the dominant—all over a tonic pedal—and then back to the tonic, and is completed in measure 3. So are

Example 57

both melodic and rhythmic processes. Because the melodic accent is suppressed at the beginning of measure 2, as well as for harmonic reasons, the second measure functions as a weak group linking measures 1 and 3. Melodically, the second measure leads back to, and emphasizes, the C♯ and F♯ previously presented. What process there is, is clearly closed by the end of measure 3. But the morphological length established by the opening two-measure group—and which in addition is normative in this style—calls for another measure. To normalize the length, a fourth measure—an echo—is added. The echo is not part of the process; it is an aspect only of form. In other words, in this case form transcends process, while in the Beethoven and Bach examples, process transcends form. But both types involve bifurcation.

[17] *The Beethoven Quartets*, pp. 204–205. By "antecedent" Kerman means the Maestoso "gap" structure; by "consequent," he means the descending conjunct "fill."
[18] Prolongations are discussed in Part II, pp. 226–241.

I should like to close on a more general note. The basis and nature of hierarchic structures is of more than purely musical interest. In a climate of disciplinary diversity and specialization such as the one we live in, the need for common unifying concepts—cross-disciplinary fields—is pressing. The young in particular, I think, feel that knowledge is fragmented and disjointed. One feature which almost all disciplines have in common is that they are concerned with the analysis and understanding of hierarchic structures. In the physical world, scientists study relationships ranging from the level of micro-particles to that of the cosmos; biologists are concerned with levels of organization running from microbiology to the ecology of the planet; in the social sciences, the hierarchy includes a span ranging from the psychology of the individual to the behavior of nations and cultures. Within the humanities, naming only the most obvious fields, literature and history as well as music are necessarily concerned with hierarchic structures. Much work needs to be done. For even in the physical and biological sciences, the precise ways in which hierarchies arise and levels interact are not fully known. In the social sciences and the humanities only the barest beginning has been made.

But there is no real alternative. For most of us at least, the patent diversity of the world will not be made comprehensible by the transcendental visions of mysticism. Nor will it be united by trying to make the humanities more scientific, in the sense of striving for exhaustive systematization or exact quantification. Particularly, if one is concerned with the explanation of particular instances, then, as I argued in my first chapter, the exhaustive is impossible and the definitive unattainable. Different disciplines and diverse conceptual frameworks will be brought together through careful inquiry into problems and modes of organization which are really common and shared. The nature of hierarchic structures is certainly an area of such commonality.

Part *Two*
EXPLORATIONS–
Implication in Tonal
Melody

CHAPTER V

Introduction

I.

Understanding music is simply a matter of attending to and comprehending tonal-temporal relationships, however subtle and complex they may prove to be. Two kinds of relationships—conformant and hierarchic ones—have already been considered. This part of the book will be primarily concerned with another kind of relationship which I shall call *implicative*. And, as the title of Part Two indicates, the main focus of attention will be upon implication as it occurs in tonal melody.

There is at present virtually no viable conceptual framework for the analytic criticism of melody. Most analyses consist of an unilluminating amalgam of blatant description (the melody rises to a climactic F♯ and descends to a cadence on B), of routine formal classification (the first phrase is an antecedent, the second a consequent), and of a naïve account of motivic similarity (the motive of the first measure is repeated in the third and is inverted in the seventh measure). One reason for this sorry state of affairs is that, at least of late, too many writers have attempted to discuss melody in general. But it is difficult, if not impossible, to construct a theory which will encompass the melodic styles of Machaut, Mozart, and Webern—not to mention Javanese and Japanese music, and so on. We have a pretty good theory of tonal harmony precisely because we have not asked "what is harmony?" but have built a theory of tonal harmonic practice.

We also have an illuminating theory of the larger tonal structure of music—that developed by Heinrich Schenker and his disciples. What follows in this part owes much to Schenker's way of thinking. But there are significant differences. For Schenker's theories are primarily concerned to explain the middleground and background organization of tonal music—the large-scale structure. My concern will be to explain the foreground and its adjacent levels. This being the case, it is worth recalling that, as I argued in Chapter IV, the concepts and principles pertinent and illuminating for the analysis of one hierarchic level may not be useful for the analysis of other levels.

Though I believe, perhaps fondly, that the concepts and principles developed in this part of the book are genuinely illuminating, there is no pretense of completeness. I do not claim that the concepts developed in this study will be useful in the analysis of all melodies—even all tonal ones. Fortunately, one does not have to be able to explain everything in order to account for some things. Though some aspects of the physical world and the realm of biology remain to be explained, we nevertheless are confident that we do have valid explanations of many aspects of physical and biological events.

The melodies analyzed here, are those which I think I can explain. Beyond this, they have been chosen because they illustrate the concepts and ideas being developed as simply and unambiguously as possible. In other words, no attempt has been made to "cover" the repertory of tonal music. If there are more examples from the music of Beethoven than from that of Wagner, this does not mean that Wagner's melodies cannot be analyzed using the same concepts as for those of Beethoven. Nor is any value judgment implied. It is simply that, because their proportions are more manageable, the music of Bach and Beethoven illustrates the points to be made more concisely and, at times, more clearly.

2.

An implicative relationship is one in which an event—be it a motive, a phrase, and so on—is patterned in such a way that reasonable inferences can be made both about its connections with preceding events and about how the event itself might be continued and perhaps reach closure and stability. By "reasonable inferences" I mean those which a competent, experienced listener —one familiar with and sensitive to the particular style—might make. Though patterns are properly implicative only for such listeners, the listener need not be explicitly referred to in an analysis. One can simply say that "this pattern implies such and such," taking the listener's competency for granted.

Making such inferences—understanding implicative relationships—is something which all of us do much of the time, in reading novels or histories, in observing changes in nature or in human behavior. The rumble of distant thunder and the piling-up of dark clouds suggests that it will rain. Denied a sweet, a child pouts and his eyes water—and we surmise that tears will soon follow. The end of a consequent phrase moves toward the cadence and a competent listener feels that the tonic will probably follow. None of these implications may be realized. The clouds may blow away; the child hold back his tears; and the cadence may prove to be deceptive. But this does not mean that the presumed consequents were not implied. Only that the implication was not in fact realized—did not happen. As these examples suggest, patternings are implicative *signs* which experienced observers know how to interpret.

These examples also call attention to the fact that our understanding of temporal events—our conception and characterization of them—is both prospective and retrospective. It includes both an awareness of what might have happened and our knowledge, after the fact, of what actually did occur. The fact of implication, in other words, affects our understanding of both the antecedent and the consequent event, whether the consequent was the one thought to be implied or not. If the stormy conditions do not actually lead to rain, then that fact is included in our retrospective understanding of those conditions: they implied, but were not followed by, rain. And our understanding of the consequent is similarly modified: the pleasant day is one which had been threatened by rain and is in that respect different from fair days not so threatened. And the same kind of change occurs if the implied event does take place. In retrospect, the stormy conditions are understood not only to have implied, but actually to have led to rain; and the consequent rain is not something which came out of the blue, an unexpected squall, but a possibility implied by antecedent conditions.

We tend to be aware of the contingency of temporal events. This is specially true when the antecedent situation is ambiguous, when a number of alternative consequents seem more or less equally probable. But even when the implications of some situation seem unequivocal, the possibility of alternatives is somehow present—if only unconsciously so. Moreover, even if the probable consequent actually occurs, we are frequently aware that things might have been otherwise—that it might not have rained, that the child might not have cried, that the cadence might have been deceptive. For our proclivity to consider alternatives, though significantly related to the patterning of the particular event being considered, also stems from a fundamental fact of human existence: namely, the necessity of choosing. Because human behavior is not for the most part genetically determined, man must choose.

To do so successfully, he must envisage the consequences—understand the implications—of alternative courses of action. Perhaps for this reason considering alternatives is a deep human habit.

The importance that we attach to alternatives is shown in the fact that our understanding of a past event often includes not only our knowledge of what actually occurred but also our awareness of what might have happened. Particularly when temporal events are being analyzed, we are prone to make contrary-to-fact statements—to say, for instance, that if it had not rained, we would have gone to the zoo; or, if the phrase had not been extended, it would have reached a cadence in the eighth measure. From this point of view, what is of interest about counterfactuals is not their logical, but their psychological significance. They are rhetorical devices which, by calling attention to the contingency of alternatives, modify our understanding of events.

Clearly, however, we do not always consider all alternatives. If we did, surprise would be impossible. Unanticipated events certainly occur. For instance, a child who seems quietly contented all at once begins to weep. Searching for an explanation of this behavior, we recall his earlier disappointment at not receiving a sweet. At the time perhaps there was no implicative behavior, or it was not noticed or has been forgotten in the meantime. But now, in retrospect, we recognize the relationship between antecedent and consequent events. Many detective stories depend upon our not noticing or not grasping the implications of events earlier recounted. Only in retrospect do we understand their significance. This sort of retrospective understanding is the basis for what has been called "The Aha!" or recognition experience.

Retrospective understanding is an aspect of musical experience as well. Because patterns are seldom simple and "single-minded," alternative consequents or continuations are as a rule implied by musical events. Sometimes, however, one alternative may be so strongly implied that others are obscured and tend to go unnoticed. At other times, we may sense the possibility of alternative continuations, but the realization of one of these—particularly if it is the most probable one—may cause us to lose sight of others. We are specially liable to overlook or forget if the alternative consequent is separated from the implicative antecedent by time and the demands of contrasting, intervening events. In cases like these, implicative relationships may be understood largely, perhaps entirely, in retrospect. Such retrospective understanding of implications at first missed or but dimly divined is in part responsible for our feelings about propriety, unity, and even necessity in a composition.

Most of the time a pattern can be fully comprehended and its internal relationships analyzed only by seeing what follows from it. Criticism based upon this sort of method may seem a kind of "post hoc, propter hoc" way of reasoning. Doubtless there is some danger on this score; and we must, therefore, work to refine theoretical formulations, stylistic concepts, and critical methods. But I see no alternative to retrospective analytic criticism. We understand temporal events, whether in the arts or the sciences, not only in terms of where they have come from and what they are, but also in terms of their consequences—both proximate and remote. As a number of philosophers of history have pointed out, this is a common mode of understanding and explanation in this discipline too.

Though we do it with amazing facility and considerable accuracy, understanding implicative relationships is a complex and subtle cognitive activity. And it is an activity of our whole being, not just that artificial abstraction, the mind. The many facets of the human nervous system, physiological changes and adjustments, motor behavior and the like, are all involved. For this reason, implicative relationships may be experienced as kinetic tension and resolution—that is, as feeling and affect. However, though they can be experienced without explicit conceptualization, implicative relationships cannot be explained without conceptualization—without theories and hypotheses, classes and norms.

Implicative inferences, then, are like hypotheses which experienced listeners entertain (perhaps unconsciously) about the connections between musical events—past and present, present and future ones—on the several levels of hierarchic organization in a particular movement or work. Like hypotheses in other realms, reasonable inferences can be made about relationships only if individual sounds and groups of sounds combine in relatively orderly and regular ways: that is, if they form patterns.

CHAPTER VI

Definitions and Methodology

Melodies are implicative because they are orderly patternings. Paradoxically, however, the more regular and orderly a pattern is, the less conscious we are that it is implicative. The implicative relationships are grasped with a kind of intuitive immediacy. Only when a pattern proves to be problematic do we tend to become consciously aware that it is implicative.[1] For instance, just before the end of the Minuetto of Haydn's "London" Symphony (No. 104), a compellingly goal-directed process is abruptly broken off (Example 58).

Example 58

There is, I think, no doubt whatsoever that we are explicitly conscious of the fact of implication.

---

[1] Partly for this reason I have chosen to describe this sort of relationship in terms of "implication" rather than in terms of "expectation"—the word used in *Emotion and Meaning in Music* to denote essentially the same sort of cognitive behavior. Another difficulty with the latter term is that expectations tend to be thought of as mental acts in which a single, exclusive consequent event is envisaged. Because a particular antecedent event may be related to a number of alternative consequents, and because the parameters of music may not act congruently in the articulation of processes and structures, the term expectation is often awkward and at times tends to misrepresent the act of musical understanding. For instance, to suggest that a passage

One is not, however, really aware that the events within the simple folk tune which occurs toward the end of the Finale of Bartók's Fifth String Quartet are implicative (Example 59). The melody is smoothly linear in the

Example 59

foreground (graph 1), and regularly triadic on the next level of organization (graph 3). Nevertheless the tune contains specific and strong implicative relationships, as can be easily tested by stopping the melodic motion after, say, the C♯ in measure 6. The tonic, A, is clearly implied (graphs 2a and 4). We "hear" that the melody should descend through B to the tonic. Moreover, while the lower A is implied both by the tendency of tunes to return to starting points, particularly if they are the tonic, and by the change of melodic direction which begins in measure 5, the high A reached in measure 13 is implied not only by linear and triadic motions of the first two hierarchic levels (graphs 1 and 3), but by the motion from tonic to fifth (E) on the third level (graph 5).

---

gives rise to simultaneous expectations seems strange, but to say that a pattern implies alternative modes of continuation is quite natural. Similarly, it is anomalous to assert that harmony leads the listener to expect closure while rhythm does not, but it seems reasonable to say that harmony implies closure, while rhythm implies continuation. Finally, the term implication seems preferable because it does not entail continuing reference to the listener. Assuming a competent listener, it describes the cognitive-musical process in "objective" terms. However, what is changed is *not* the basic way of viewing and explaining music—though these essays present a more accurate and refined understanding of the nature of musical experience—but the terminology used to describe musical structures and processes.

This example calls attention to a number of important matters of methodology:

1) Earlier it was suggested that implicative relationships are like hypotheses which competent listeners entertain about the connections among musical events. To explain a melody which such listeners comprehend without conscious effort, the critic must make these implicative hypotheses explicit. He must discover the patternings present in the melody, and he must speculate—formulate explicit hypotheses—about how each of the patternings might be continued to reach the stability of relative closure, or perhaps silence: the end of the patterning. To do so, the critic will often perform a kind of mental "experiment." He will "stop" the melodic flow at particular points and try to imagine what continuations seem probable. This was done in connection with the Bartók example when we asked what was implied by the patterning up to the C♯ in measure 6, and by the motion of the opening measures.

From the critic's point of view, there is a problem to be solved: given some theoretical premises, what do these incomplete patterns, these partial events, imply? What—given the style and musical context, as well as the structure of the event itself—will probably follow? The critic will study the composer's score to see whether any of the envisaged (alternative) continuations actually occur. If they do, his understanding of the implicative relationships discovered in the patterning is probably correct. Very often this is the case, even though the realization of an implication may at times be much delayed. If the envisaged continuations do not occur, then the critic's understanding of the melodic pattern may have been incomplete or simply mistaken. In such a case, he will restudy the melody and attempt, *without modifying his theoretical premises*, to formulate an alternative hypothesis. Often new insights can be gained by analyzing events in retrospect—in terms of their known consequences. For later events can call attention to aspects of earlier ones which may have gone unnoticed or not been fully appreciated.

Here methodological considerations begin to arise. For if the realization of an implication can be significantly delayed, then in a work of even moderate duration and complexity envisaged consequent events would be virtually bound to occur—as a matter of statistical probability. Suppose, for instance, that in a movement in B♭, the opening melody is hypothetized as implying motion from the fifth (F) to the upper tonic (B♭). But this motion does not occur within the melody itself. As the movement unfolds, the implied B♭ is almost certain to occur in some context—as part of a scale or arpeggio figure, a harmony or another melody: simply because it will be an important tone in the syntax of all closely related keys. To a considerable extent, however, this danger can be avoided by stipulating as *precisely as possible* what the antecedent events are understood to imply. For the more precisely the organization of each parameter in the consequent event is specified, the less likely that an event matching those specifications is the result of statistical distribution. Therefore, the implications of an antecedent pattern should be made as exact as possible with respect to rhythmic position, harmonic context, registral placement, and timbre—as well as pitch relationships. The possibility of theoretical concepts determining analytic choices will be further diminished if the analysis exhibits a coherent and consistent order in which one part fits with and thereby "confirms" others.

More difficult methodological problems are posed when apparently patent implications are not realized at all. At times, a complex pattern may imply a number of alternative implications only some of which—though usually the most important ones—the composer has chosen to realize. In other cases, such nonrealization may rest on historical-stylistic grounds: for instance, composers of the Romantic Period may sometimes have left implications unrealized so that the work would remain "open"—so that its implications would, so to speak, transcend the limiting frame of cadential closure and continue to reverberate in the silence of subsequent time. In still other cases, however, unrealized implications might constitute a compositional weakness or defect. Frankly, I do not know how to resolve this dilemma in any systematic and rigorous way. Until theories of musical structure and style are considerably more refined, I suspect that such problems will have to be dealt with on an informal, individual basis. At this point, all that can be expected is plausibility.

Implications must, of course, be realized with considerable regularity and frequency—often enough that the listener's confidence in his own understanding of the style of the work is sustained and reinforced. Often this is accomplished by what will be called *provisional realization* of implication: for instance, when the particular pitch implied is realized, but in the "wrong" register or in a tonal-harmonic context which is not the one called for by the generating pattern.

2) More common than the nonrealization of previously generated implication is its converse: the occurrence of an event not implied by or connected with preceding patternings. As a rule, such unanticipated events, taken together with preceding ones and with those which follow, are understand-

able in retrospect as part of a higher-level ordering of events. However, this is not always the case. Sometimes, as was argued in Chapter I, an event cannot be accounted for in terms of relationships with preceding or following events. It seems convincing and effective, yet remains in a sense anomalous.

This is, I think, the case with Example 59. The use of this simple folk tune with its regular and unassuming accompaniment just before the close of a movement characterized by considerable intensity and complexity must be regarded as an arbitrary decision by the composer. One can suggest psychological reasons—*ad hoc* ones, in this case—why the passage makes musical-aesthetic sense: a release from the tension of syntactic complexity, it (at the same time) checks the forward motion of the music for a brief moment, making the subsequent resumption of tension and the drive toward final closure particularly forceful and decisive. And because this "composed *firmata*" is not unlike places in other movements, it is stylistically understandable as well. But to attempt to explain this passage by relating it to earlier events by conformance, implication, or formal ordering is, in my judgment, to misrepresent its significance and to miss the point; namely, that it is genuinely aberrant and anomalous.

3) Implications arise because patterns are incomplete or unstable in some respect. That aspect of a pattern which is the basis for implicative inferences will be called a *generative event*. As events follow one another in time, some of the implications of a pattern may be realized immediately; others may be realized only after other events, which may be implicitive of alternative goals, have intervened. For instance, the linear motion of the first two measures of Example 59 is a generative event, implying continuation to the E (graph 2), which follows without delay. Once E is reached, a higher-level generative event—a triadic pattern which implies the high A—is formed (graph 3). But the realization of this implication is temporarily delayed not only by the prolongation of the E, but by the motion from F♯ to E to D, which changes the direction of the melody and in so doing implies descending motion to A. Events which generate such alternative goals will be called *deflections*. Because return to the pitch of an initial accented tone—particularly when it is the tonic—is quite probable, this deflection in a sense only actualizes what was already potential in the melodic-tonal structure. Notice, too, that the implication of motion down to A is itself briefly delayed by a subsidiary deflection—when the C♯ moves back to E instead of descending directly to A. The opening pattern is repeated, beginning in measure 9. Thus reinforced by repetition, the second-level generative event is realized as the scalar-

triadic motion reaches temporary closure on the high A (graphs 1, 1a, 3 and 3a).

Deflections seldom change the implications generated by the initial, primary patternings. They create alternative goals which are as a rule subsidiary. A special case of deflection is what I called *reversal*.[2] Particularly when they tend toward uniformity, so that no decisive points of structural stability are established, patterns develop a strong internal momentum. In such cases, a marked, unequivocal break in process is needed if closure is to be effective and convincing. Since as a rule such uniform patterns take the form of linear sequences, reversals generally involve a skip followed by a change in the direction of the motion—from descending to ascending, or vice versa.

4) Because the patterns which generate implications are usually complex, a number of alternative consequent events will be implied. Indeed, even a single motive may imply alternative continuations. For instance, the skip of a third may function both as a gap, implying motion to the pitch skipped-over, and as part of a triad, implying continuation to the fifth or the tonic depending upon the harmonic context. Because melodic events are necessarily successive, implications will be realized one after another. This being so, some realizations will almost always be delayed. Those realizations which occur before the main melodic cadence or before the end of the section containing the melody, will be called *proximate realizations;* and those which happen only after the events generating them have reached significant closure, will be called *remote realizations.* At times, such delayed realizations may be very remote indeed; for instance, in cases where the implications generated by the opening theme of a sonata-form movement are not realized until the final coda.

5) Not all patterns, however, are implicative. For instance, realizations which complete and close a preceding process may not be so. And this is also true of many prolongations and extensions. Even beginning events such as opening themes may be complete, stable shapes which, though internally implicative, do not imply particular, specific continuations. Because of their position at the beginning of a movement, such *declarative* prolongations will, of course, imply continuation in the general sense that more music is expected. Similarly, some medial events—such as *parentheses* and *internal extensions*—generate no new goals. With some reservations, it might be said that the folk melody in Example 59 (together with its varied repetition in the following

[2] See *Emotion and Meaning in Music* (Chicago: University of Chicago Press, 1956), p. 93 and passim.

measures) is an interpolation which, while intensifying the sense of goal-directed motion by interrupting it, generates no alternative, novel implications. There are also *terminal* events which are not implicative—for instance, the echo which closes the Dvorak melody (Example 57) discussed at the end of Chapter IV. However implicative its internal processes may be, to the extent that a pattern is understood to be complete and stable on some hierarchic level, it is not implicative on *that* level. In terms of the viewpoint developed in Chapter IV, on that level it is a formal entity, not a processive one.

6) Just as patterns are structured hierarchically, so are the implications they generate. In Example 59, for instance, rhythmic-metric accents on the relatively stable tones of the tonic triad give rise, as we have seen, to a second level of organization. Because the E follows directly from the preceding linear-triadic patterning, continuation to the high A is implied. More concretely: had the relative uniformity of the preceding patterning been broken, as shown in Example 59A, the implications of the second structural level would have been different. The reversal of motion created by the

Example 59A

skip of a third (D to F♯) which the following E fills not only makes the E a more stable goal, but prevents the F♯ from acting as part of the rising line as it was able to do in Example 59. As a result, the triadic structure of the first three measures [3] no longer implies continuation to the high A, but only descent to the tonic. An on-going folklike melody has been transformed into a cadential figure. In other words, because it is not a clearly articulated, stable goal, the E in Example 59 implies continuation to the upper A. The prolongation of the E does not diminish its mobility; rather the emphasis it provides suggests a third level of organization—a pentachordal-tetrachordal division of the octave (A'-E'-)—which also implies A''. (graphs 5 and 5a). Notice that the foreground scalar motion, which implies E, is supported and reinforced by the second-level triadic pattern, and that the triadic pattern,

[3] The E is still a structural tone. See below.

implying the upper tonic (A''), is in turn supported by the even more fundamental division of the octave.

This discussion calls attention to a point of importance: a single melody may exhibit different kinds of patternings on each of its hierarchic levels. Differences in the organization of the several levels of a hierarchy are the rule rather than the exception; the reinforcement of lower-level implications by higher-level patterns is by no means necessary. At times different levels will imply alternative modes of continuation. Such melodies will, almost by definition, be relatively complex. Or, put the other way around: the simplicity of Bartok's folk tune is in part the result of the coordination of implications among its several levels of organization.

The analysis of hierarchic patterns and, consequently, of the implicative relationships they generate, involves a methodological problem of considerable difficulty: how to establish reasonably objective grounds for distinguishing structural from ornamental tones on a particular hierarchic level. Without some relatively rigorous and explicit criteria, there is a real danger that theoretical preconceptions will influence, if not determine, the analysis of structural versus ornamental tones. And when this occurs, analysis becomes circular and self-confirming.

The problem is difficult because the structural importance of a tone on a particular hierarchic level depends not only upon its place and function within the specific sequence of melodic events, but also upon the particular disposition and interaction of the other parameters which may be involved —rhythm and harmony, dynamics and timbre. Because these may not move congruently and because their relative importance may vary even within a single composition, the matter is a delicate one about which competent critics may differ. More fundamentally, to revert to a point made in Chapter I: since each pattern is a particular instance, it is doubtful whether hard and fast criteria can be devised for distinguishing ornamental from structural tones. The best one can do at present is to suggest reasonable rules of thumb. The most important ones used in this study are as follows:

a. Meter is regarded as the prime, though by no means the only, guide to structural importance. This is not unreasonable considering the basic regularity of metric organization and harmonic rhythm in the style of tonal music. Tones which occur on a main metric accent are analyzed as being on a higher structural level than those which occur on secondary metric accents, with exceptions that are explained on an individual basis. Thus a tone coming on the first beat in ¼ meter is in general considered to be on a higher level than one which comes on the third beat. Tones occurring on weak beats are structurally less important than either of these. As measures group together, larger metric entities are formed, and these serve as guides for distinguishing structural from ornamental tones on still higher levels.

b. A general exception to this rule is that goal tones—tones of resolution, like the G in measure 4 of Example 62—are considered to be structural on the hierarchic level on which they are goals, regardless of their metric position. It follows from this that appoggiaturas, though metrically emphasized, are *not* construed as structural tones. In an appoggiatura figure, the structural tone is the note of resolution—for instance, in Example 59A it is the E, not the F♯ that comes on the accent, which is structural.

c. Relatively regular patterning is the basis for implicative inferences. Consequently, sometimes a note that comes on a secondary metric accent will be assigned the same structural importance as one coming on a primary accent. Thus in Example 60, the opening measures of Haydn's String Quartet, Opus 50 No. 3, the G on the fourth eighth-note of measure 2 is considered to be on the same structural level as the F which comes on the primary accent. And the same is true of the B♭ in measure 3. For the motivic parallelism makes it clear that the pattern is linear, moving through the scale from E♭ to B♭. This analysis is supported by

Example 60

the harmonic changes and by the dynamic emphasis provided by the other instruments of the quartet. But even when the patterning of other parameters provides no confirmation, parallelism of patterning makes it reasonable to assign equal structural importance to like melodic events, even though their metric placement is different. Thus though the metric position of the perfect fourth (C—F) which begins the subphrases of Till's tune (Example 85) changes, the fourths are analyzed as being structurally equivalent.

7) Using the term in the special, analytic sense suggested earlier, two basic kinds of implicative "problems" can be distinguished: incompleteness and potentiality. Potentiality refers to some discrepancy that calls for resolution. The discrepancy may be a consequence of the syntactic structure of the event itself: for instance, when melodic prominence is not complemented by functional importance—as was the case with the two upbeats, C and Db, in the Bach Fugue subject analyzed in Chapter IV (Example 53). Or discrepancy may arise because the event as a whole implies a function not realized when it is first presented; for instance, when a movement begins with what is unquestionably a closing, cadential gesture (see Example 115).

Incompleteness may be the result either of the specific patterning of a particular melody, or of the syntax of tonality characteristic of the style as a whole. The former, which will be our main concern in what follows, might be called processive incompleteness; the latter, tonal incompleteness. Though these kinds of implicative incompleteness often complement one another, this is not always the case. At least some of the implications of a melody will as a rule be realized before tonal closure takes place. Conversely, tonal goals may be reached, though some of the implications generated by the melodic pattern remain unrealized. Indeed, were this not the case, the "reverberation of unrealized implications," mentioned above (p. 117), would not be possible.

Two examples will not only help to clarify this point, but will, in addition, serve to illustrate some of the concepts considered earlier in this section.

A. In the folk tune from Stravinsky's *Petrouchka*, given in Example 61, melodic process and tonal syntax have a common goal: the tonic, Bb. From a tonal point of view, the most mobile note of the tonic triad is the third, which sooner or later almost always moves by conjunct motion to the tonic.[4] As the first important structural tone of this melody, the D, accordingly, implies the Bb below it. This implication is strengthened and specified by the melodic process.

On the lowest level, the conjunct motion from F to D implies continuation to C, as graph 1 indicates. But this is a subsidiary pattern, as the preceding quarter-note motion of the triangle, which indicates the main metric

[4] See, for instance, Examples 129 and 130.

levels, has made clear. The more important melodic motion is from F to D. Because it is harmonized by the tonic, this third strongly implies triadic continuation to B♭ as an important structural tone (graph 2). However, this possibility is not realized directly. Instead, the D is prolonged, and this serves to establish a higher-level metric structure in which the half-note becomes the chief measure of motion and a two-measure unit is the main morphological

Example 61

length. As a result, the B♭ in measure 2 does not have the same structural-morphological importance—is not on the same hierarchic level—as the D. For this reason (and because of the lack of harmonic motion), the B♭ is only a *provisional*, not a definitive, realization of the implications generated by the preceding triadic pattern.

The skip from D to B♭ has a number of consequences. It creates a gap (reinforced in inversion at the end of measure 3), which implies filling-in motion to the missing tone, C—already implied by the first generative event. Second, it deflects the descending pattern which might, had it been regular, have continued sequentially as shown in Part A of Example 61. And as the *deflection* itself becomes a pattern, the complementary motions shown in graphs 5 and 6 are generated. To explain: just as the beginning linear motion, F-E♭-D, implied C, so the reverse pattern, B♭-C-D (m.2), implies continuation to E♭ and perhaps beyond. This implication, together with the fact that the E♭ fills the gap from F to D (see graph 3), helps to make the E♭ a convincing beginning for the second phrase. In like manner, just as the falling third, F-D (graph 2), implied B♭, so the rising third, B♭-D (graph 6) implies continuation to F—a note which, as we shall see, plays an important role in the reversal and closure of the tune.

The tonal tendency of the D in this context, the opening conjunct motion, and the D-B♭ gap in measure 2 all imply the C reached in measure 4, making it a strong point of arrival. Here, a higher-level linear pattern is generated (see graph 4), and it, too, implies the tonic. This implication is reinforced not only by the linear patterning (E♭-D-C → B♭) which begins the second phrase (graph 1), but by the parallelism between the opening of the second phrase and that of the first. But the sequential conformance is broken in measure 6. Instead of skipping down to A, paralleling the skip from D to B♭ in measure 2, the C is repeated and then skips across the barline to F, after which descending conjunct motion leads towards the tonic.

Notice that, as indicated in Part B of Example 61, had the second phrase paralleled the first exactly, the tonic would have been reached at the same point in measure 8. But had this been the case, the momentum created by considerable melodic uniformity and parallelism would have tended to carry the motion beyond the B♭—perhaps down to the low F. In other words, the complementary motion which follows the deflection in measure 2 establishes F as an alternative, subsidiary goal and thereby makes the *reversal* of the ongoing motion possible. Although the second phrase is not exactly parallel to the first, a kind of higher similarity prevails: the break in phrase similarity (the repetition of the C) which begins the reversal occurs at the same place in the phrase as did the deflection which presaged the reversal. Finally, in this context the gap from C to F not only strongly implies linear return to B♭, but in some sense "summarizes" the melodic motion of the tune as a whole.

B. The first and last eight measures of the "Soldier's March" from Schumann's *Album for the Young* are given in Example 62. As was the case with the tune from *Petrouchka*, the first accented, structural tone is the third of the scale. Consequently, from a tonal point of view, descending motion to the tonic, G, is implied. This tonal tendency does not go unrealized, but the melodic patterning implies alternative goals—as the patterning in the tune from *Petrouchka* did not.

The main generative event is the third, B to D, in the first measure. Two possible continuations are implied: thirds, particularly ascending ones such as this, may function as gaps making a conjunct fill probable; or thirds may be understood as part of a triadic pattern, and continuation to the third note of the triad may be implied. Whether both of these alternatives are probable depends, as we shall see, upon rhythmic relationships as well as melodic ones.

In Schumann's melody the gap-fill patterning is realized first. In retrospect the D is understood to have been "prolonged" by the neighbor-note, E, after which the melody descends by conjunct motion, filling the gap and moving on to the tonic (graph 1). At the end of this motion, as B continues down to G, the tonal tendency of the third to reach the tonic is realized

Example 62

(graph 2). The second alternative—that the triadic pattern will be completed by reaching the high G (graph 3)—is regenerated by the repetition of the first two measures of the tune at the beginning of the second phrase (graph 3a). The high G is presented. But because it forms part of a mobile, secondary dominant, rather than a stable tonic harmony, the realization is only provisional. The resolution of this secondary dominant, in turn, generates a descending conjunct motion which fills the gap that preceded the G (graph 1b).

Like the G in measure 4, the D in measure 8 is a point of arrival and of relative stability—a structural tone. Looking at the melody in this way—in terms of beginning and ending structural tones—calls attention to the fact that the melody is triadic on a still higher level. That is, the first phrase moves from B to G, and this patterning implies the low D (not shown in the example; measures 16–24) around which the middle part of the piece centers (graph 4). The second phrase, moving from the B in measure 5 to the D in measure 8 (graph 5), reinforces the rising triadic motion generated in the first and fifth measures (graph 3 and 3a). Though implied from the first measure, the realization of a satisfactory high G—one which is part of tonic harmony and which comes on an accent—is remote. It occurs only at the very end of the piece (graph 3), after being once again implied by the repetition of the opening measures (graph 3b), as the final cadential note. As Schumann himself wrote: "The beginning is the main thing; once one has begun, then the end comes of its own accord." [5]

Just how important beginnings may be, can be seen by comparing the melody of Schumann's "Soldier's March" with that of the Scherzo from Beethoven's Sonata for Violin and Piano, Opus 24 (Example 63). The first eight measures of the two melodies are almost identical in pitch contour. But the differences, though seemingly slight, are by no means inconsequential. Consider the first rhythmic groups. In Schumann's "March," the third of the scale, B, is an accented, structural tone, while the fifth, D, which follows, is weak and mobile. Because the trochaic group is open and on-going, the fifth of the tonic triad implies continuation to G. In Beethoven's Scherzo, on the other hand, the first note—the third, A—is an upbeat to the fifth, C, which is the first structural tone. Because the C occurs as the relatively stable goal of

---

[5] Robert Schumann, *Briefe, Neue folge* (Leipzig: Breitkopf und Härtel, 1886), p. 338. "Der Anfang ist die Hauptsache; hat man angefangen, dann kommt Einem das Ende wie von selbst engegen." I am grateful to my daughter, Carlin, for calling this quotation to my attention and for helping me find the title for this book.

an end-accented iamb, the third (A—C) scarcely implies triadic continuation. The opening third functions only as a gap, and the high F in measure 6 is understood as defining the area of melodic activity and not as triadic continuation. In short, as is the case with countless melodies whose first structural tone is the fifth of the scale—particularly those where the fifth is preceded by a gap—what is implied is conjunct descending motion to the tonic.[6]

Because the structural tone which begins each phrase in Example 63 is the fifth, the implications of the high-level structure are different. Because of the high-level motion from third (m.5) to fifth (m.8), the second phrase of the Schumann melody implied triadic continuation to the high G. In the Beethoven, however, the second phrase begins and ends on the fifth (C). Consequently, no triadic pattern is suggested; instead the implications generated in the first phrase are reinforced. In contrast, then, with Schumann's "March," it is not unexpected that, articulated by the clear closure of an end-accented rhythmic group (measure 32–35), the final cadence of Beethoven's Scherzo is on the low F.

One tangential point having to do with the relationships among syntax, tempo and dynamics, and character. In a sense, Schumann has written the meter "against" the natural melodic-harmonic patterning: the first quarter-note "should" have been an upbeat, as in Beethoven's Scherzo. Though the organization of the Scherzo is similar to that of the "March" in the following measures, it involves no ambiguity; for, despite a kind of off-beating effect, the triple meter permits no alternative metric-rhythmic patterning. But, except for the final measures, the barline in Schumann's "March" might have been placed one quarter-note to the left.

I suspect that Schumann writes the "March" in this way—making the rhythmic groups trochaic—because to play the piece properly (as notated), considerable stress must be placed upon downbeats. Otherwise the "natural" mode of organization—an iambic grouping—will result. This is specially the case because the tempo ($\downarrow$ =120) is not really fast. To put the matter the other way around: had the tempo been quick, then metric accents would have been strong, and no particular stress would have been needed to make the groups trochaic.[7] As it is, however, the "Soldier's March" must be played with somewhat exaggerated emphasis upon downbeats. And this has an important effect upon character. For the music becomes almost too assertive

---

[6] See, for instance, Example 47.

[7] See the discussion of tempo and grouping at the end of Chapter II.

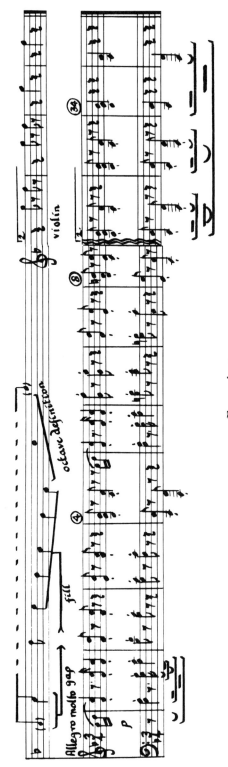

Example 63

(*deciso*)—like a small child's self-consciously imperious and ostentatious way of exhibiting "marching behavior."

To summarize. Implicative inferences are possible because the regularity and orderliness of a pattern suggest probable continuations which the competent listener understands and which the conscientious critic attempts to explain. This matter can also be stated objectively—as though stylistically coherent and syntactically structured melodies themselves actually obeyed, or "behaved" according to, certain basic principles. In terms of proximate realizations, the general rule would then be: *Once established, a patterning tends to be continued until a point of relative tonal-rhythmic stability is reached.* Prolongations and extension may, as we shall see, delay closure; and deflections may give rise to subsidiary or alternative goals as points for closure. In terms of remote realizations, the general rule would be: *Continuations not realized—or realized only provisionally—before significant pattern closure has taken place will probably be so subsequently.* Often such delayed realization will take place after a repetition of the intial pattern has reinforced the implications generated when it was first presented.

These "laws" may, in turn, be subsumed under a still more general principle: *Patterns tend to be continued until they become as complete and stable as possible.* Completeness and stability are determined not only by the particular attributes of the pattern itself, but by norms of the particular style being employed—its syntax, traditional forms, and conventional schemata.

CHAPTER VII

Melodic Structures

There are but two kinds of pitch relationships: conjunct intervals and disjunct ones. Though this distinction may seem somewhat simpleminded, it is fundamental because disjunct patterns may imply not only continuation but gap-closure and return. Our concern, then, will be with the ways conjunct and disjunct patternings, and their interactions, generate implicative relationships on different hierarchic levels. Though some melodies are primarily conjunct, and others—usually those which are triadic—are primarily disjunct, most melodies involve both kinds of motion. Furthermore a melody may be conjunct on one hierarchic level, but disjunct on another. For both these reasons, a rigorous, systematic classification of melodies is out of the question. In what follows, the melodies analyzed have been grouped, generally speaking, according to what seems to be the main hierarchic level generating implicative relationships. Though some sort of classification is necessary as a way of ordering the discussion, what is important is the analysis of the individual melody.

CONJUNCT PATTERNS

Linear patterns are scales—diatonic, chromatic, or some mixture of these. The basic implicative principle, to repeat the point made at the end of the last chapter, is that, once begun, a linear, conjunct motion implies continuation to a point of relative stability. To turn to our first example.

The opening melody of Mozart's Divertimento in B♭ Major (K.287; New 271b) for strings and two horns consists of two similar phrases (Example 64). As graph 2 shows, both phrases begin on the fifth (F), and descend by conjunct motion toward the tonic (B♭). Though it comes on a weak beat, the D in measure 3 (and the one in measure 7) is analyzed as a structural tone both because it is the resolution of a cadential harmonic progression (II $\frac{6}{5}$ —V/V—V⁷—I) and because, particularly in retrospect, the simplest way of understanding the over-all motion is as a conjunct pattern. The II⁶—I $\frac{6}{4}$ —V⁷ progression in measure 4 is resolved to tonic harmony in measure 5. But instead of moving to the implied B♭, the melody moves back to the fifth, as the second phrase begins. This time the authentic cadence is complemented by a clearly end-accented rhythm and by melodic closure, when the B♭ is reached in measure 9.

Example 64

Though the implications of the main melodic motion are clear, the phrase structure is complex and equivocal. When the movement begins, we assume that the *forte* chords are part of the first phrase. The cadential progression in measures 2 and 3, however, seems to articulate a half-phrase which will be answered by a second two-measure group reaching closure in measure 5. Though harmony cadences on the tonic in measure 5, the repetition of the opening chords makes it clear that this is also the beginning of a new phrase: the motion from tonic to subdominant makes the harmony on-going, the trochaic grouping creates rhythmic mobility, the melodic F is implicative—and all this is emphasized by the abrupt change in dynamics and texture. Because measure 5 functions both as the end of the first phrase and the beginning of the second, it has the effect of an interruption. The result is that even though there is a cadence on the tonic, the first phrase sounds like an antecedent.

When the second phrase reaches closure in measure 9, our feeling that the basic phrase structure is 2 + 2 is confirmed. But even in retrospect, the function of the chords in measures 1 and 5 is equivocal. Though measure 1 begins the main melodic pattern, it is at the same time separate from the basic morphological structure—both because of the organization of the following phrase and because of the marked contrast in dynamics and texture between measures 1 and 2. Consequently, it is also understood as introductory. The witty play on function is even more complex in measure 5: it is not only a beginning and an introduction, but also an end.

Because these measures are set off in dynamics and texture, separated from what follows syntactically, and equivocal functionally, they are particularly prominent. We are aware not only of the descending conjunct motion from F to B♭ which begins here, but of an alternative possibility. As shown in graph 1, the low-level conjunct motion from F to G suggests linear continuation to the high B♭. Both the mobility of the trochaic rhythm and the on-going harmonic motion support the implication of a melodic A, harmonized by a dominant, followed by a melodic B♭ complemented by tonic harmony.

However, the high B♭ never occurs as a stable goal harmonized by a tonic chord in the exposition section. When it occurs toward the end of the recapitulation—after measure 238—it follows descending motion from C. For the recapitulation begins not with the melody we have been discussing, but with the motives which follow that cadence in measure 9. The opening melody does not recur until the coda, where, as Example 65 shows, it leads through a melodic A harmonized as part of a dominant seventh chord to an accented high B♭—the note on which the movement ends. Not only is the continuation the one implied by the opening theme, but the relationship be-

Example 65

tween the chords of measures 1 and 5 and this remote realization is emphasized by the fact that in both places the violins play triple-stops.

Though Mozart's movement ends on the high B♭, the main linear motion —the one understood as being *the* melody—is undoubtedly the descending one. And if the examples analyzed in this book represent a fair sample, it seems that descending melodies are considerably more common in the repertory of tonal music than ones whose main motion rises. One important reason for this is that ascending melodic motions involve a sense of effort and concomitant tension (probably because of our own kinesthetic motor behavior); falling melodic lines represent relaxation and are motions toward the repose required for closure. Partly for this reason melodies which begin on the third and the fifth of the scale tend to descend; [1] and, further, gap-fill melodies usually begin with a rising skip which is followed by descending conjunct motion.

Needless to say, there are exceptions. The Scherzo from Schubert's String Quartet in Eb Major, Opus 125 (Example 66) is a very striking one.

The movement begins with a clearly defined motive (m)—an amphibrach rhythmic group in which the first Eb, acting as an upbeat and creating an octave gap, is followed by rising conjunct motion, Eb-F, that suggests that the gap is going to be filled. The linear part of the motive is continued when the F in measure 3 moves to G in measure 4. The conjunct rising motion, both within and between motives, generates the implications shown in graph 3.

The Eb upbeats are implicative not only because the gaps they create suggest linear fill, but also because they are *potential structural tones* (see graph 1). Though aurally conspicuous, the Eb's are weak beats lacking structural importance. The incongruity between function and prominence is emphasized by the reiteration of the Eb's, which seem unaffected by and, consequently, separate from, the rising motion of the melodic line. What is implied —more strongly with each repetition—is that Eb will become an actualized structural tone, as it does when it comes as the downbeat in measure 8.

The arrival of the Eb in measure 8 actualizes the preceding potential tones and is a realization of the implications of the preceding scale (see graph 2). But it does *not* constitute a satisfactory realization of the implications generated by the linear motion of the first four measures. For the satisfactory realization of an implication is governed by what might be called the *law of hierarchic equivalence:* an event is an adequate realization of an implication only if it is on a hierarchic level which is the same as, or more extended than, the level of the pattern which generated the implications in question.

What is required, if the implications generated by the opening measures of Schubert's Scherzo are to be satisfactorily realized, is the arrival at a goal— probably one of the notes of the tonic triad—which follows from and is on the same hierarchic level as the linear pattern of measures 1–4 (graph 3). Though it continues the motion implied by the opening measures, the scale

---

[1] This tendency is also related to their proximity to the lower tonic. This is obvious in the case of the third. In the case of the fifth, the third, acting as a point of intermediate stability, is proximate and influences the probable direction of motion.

Example 66

in measures 5–8 is not on the same hierarchic level as the earlier pattern.[2] For in the first four measures, the fundamental level of motion is a two-measure unit, while in measures 5–8 the motion is at least twice as fast. For this reason, the scale is only a *provisional* realization of the implications generated by the earlier linear pattern.

Closure at the end of the first part of the Scherzo is definite and unmistakable: the whole movement concludes with almost exactly the same eight-measure phrase. Harmonically, there is a full cadence. Rhythm is end-accented on the lowest level and on the highest one, which is a clear anapest group of 2 + 2 + 4 measures. Melodically, the scale creates foreground closure. However (and this point will concern us later), though it ends on the tonic, the linear motion is quite uniform—without reversal or significant articulation—and, for this reason, further motion seems probable.

There must be more music. This for two reasons. First, because no digression from the stability of tonic harmony and cohesive patterning has taken place. What is needed is the tension of tonal contrast and motivic change, so that the return to stability can create a sense of arrival and conclusive finality. Second, and our primary concern here: the implications of the main melodic motion generated in the first measures have been realized only provisionally. Adequate realization is still to come. Both these requirements are met in the second part of the movement.

The linear processes of the first part of the Scherzo are continued in the second. As graph 3 indicates, the melody moves sequentially from the G—the point reached in measure 4—up to the D in measure 16. In both the first four measures and in these eight, the linearity of the violin melody is supported by parallel motion in the cello. Both lines—and the harmonic motion as well—could have gone directly from measure 4 to measure 9. Observe, too, that the mobility of the pattern is partly a result of the instability of the sequence of first-inversion harmonies.

There is a cadence in measure 16. But it is by no means decisive. Though the rhythm is end-accented on the highest level—measures 9–16 are a pyramided anapest: 2 + 2 + (1 + 1 + 2)—the low-level group is a mobile amphibrach. Harmony, too, is on-going: both the lack of root motion and the $II_5^{6\sharp}$—V progression in G strongly imply continuation. The low-level, fore-

---

[2] It might be argued that the whole scale-phrase is a prolongation of E♭ and therefore on the same level as the previous patterning. But in that case, the low E♭ in measure 55 is the tone prolonged. The result would be a high-level neighbor-note motion, E♭(m.1)—F(m.3)—E♭(m.5), which is scarcely a satisfactory continuation for the strongly linear pattern of the first four measures.

ground melody creates a degree of closure, for the skip of a diminished fifth from G to C♯ resolving to D is a cadential gesture. (As shown in graph 1, this cadential pattern makes the G, a potential structural tone like the earlier E♭, part of the melodic-rhythmic structure.) On the higher level of melodic motion, however, the uniformity of the chromatic line from B on implies continuation. Thus, while the cadence in measure 16 has somewhat checked the goal-directed momentum, arriving at a kind of tension within equilibrium, the implication of continued motion is still strong.

But the implied continuation of melodic motion from the leading tone, D (measure 16) to the tonic, E♭, does not follow directly. The D is prolonged (and thus emphasized) from measure 17 to measure 30 (see graph 3), but in a context that is unstable and hence implicative. Harmonically, the D functions as part of an alien tonality (G minor rather than E♭). The harmonic rhythm is open and mobile because the temporary tonic (G) comes as the weak part of the rhythmic pattern, rather than as a goal. In addition tension and mobility are a result of the weakening of the melodic-rhythmic shape. That is, the reiterated D's and the repeated low-level iambs of the melody do not give rise to higher level patterns.[3] And this lack of palpable patterning also implies change.

An octave transfer at the end of measure 22 brings the melody back to the original register. Because the same motive is repeated an octave lower, it is, I think, a legitimate instance of registral transfer. That is, it is legitimate to analyze the melodic line as continuing in the lower octave. Often, however, the situation is more problematic. In general, analysis has posited such transfers with unwarranted casualness. This is, in my judgment, a mistake. For the implications of melodic patterns are in principle specific not only with respect to pitch-class (C's, F♯'s, B♭'s, etc.), but with respect to register as well.

At measure 25, D is harmonized as the third of the dominant-seventh of E♭. The foreground pattern rises through that harmony to the B♭ which is, so to speak, left hanging in mid-air—without explicit connection with the following pattern. The progression through the dominant to the tonic constitutes a reversal of the harmonic process and creates high-level closure.

Melodically, the arrival of the E♭ in measure 31 represents not only the arrival of the stability of the tonic, but the realization of the implication generated in the opening measures of the Scherzo. The processes begun

[3] See Meyer, *Emotion and Meaning in Music* (Chicago: University of Chicago Press, 1956), pp. 160–196.

there have moved (with an octave transfer) in linear fashion from the E♭ in measure 1 to the one in measure 31. Since the first part of the movement ended with a full cadence, the realization in measure 31 is remote. Melodic and harmonic closure, as well as the return to strongly structured rhythmic organization, are complemented by formal closure. For the repetition of the first part of the Scherzo, following the harmonic, melodic, and rhythmic tension of the middle part, enhances the feeling of closure by providing the satisfaction of return.

But the first part is not repeated exactly. The E♭ major scale (m. 35–36), whose linear continuation (m. 7) in the first part weakened the sense of closure, is broken off and replaced in measures 38 and 39 by a disjunct cadential gesture. This change accomplishes three things. First, it establishes a conformant relationship between the cadence of the middle part (m. 14–16) and the final closure. Second, it provides a continuation for the A♭ and B♭ which were left "hanging in mid air" at the end of the second part and leads them to the cadence. And most important of all, by reversing the linear motion of the preceding measure it creates decisive closure.

Rounded binary forms, such as this, raise an important analytic-critical question. If a particular patterning of events—for instance, the linear motion of measures 1–4 in the first part of Schubert's Scherzo—implies continuation when first presented, why isn't the restatement of the patterning in measures 29–33 implicative even after the second half has been repeated? How can the piece end satisfactorily? From an aesthetic-theoretical point of view, once an implication has been adequately realized, the resolution of the tensions of the middle part, together with the satisfaction provided by return, seem to create a psychological situation in which closure takes precedence over implication. On the practical side, to emphasize the closure of the second part of the form, the composer may extend the final cadence, as Mozart does in the Theme of his A-Major Piano Sonata (see Example 17). At times a final coda, following the repetition of the whole first part of a da capo form, serves to create a sense of finality. This is the case in the Menuetto movement of Beethoven's String Quartet in C Major, Opus 59 No. 3. The performer, too, often helps to make closure clear by slowing the tempo or perhaps changing dynamics. And, finally, the competent listener knows, as a result of his stylistic experience, how such forms generally "behave"—that the second part of a rounded binary structure is repeated, but only once.

Because it is the stable goal toward which all other tones tend to move, the tonic (in contrast to the third and fifth) implies no particular direction of motion. Consequently, if the main melodic patterning begins on the tonic, ascending and descending motions are equally probable—at least in terms of tonal theory. But a sense of direction may be provided by other means. For instance, a prefatory gap may indicate the probable direction of motion, as the upbeat in Schubert's Scherzo does. Or, the probable direction of motion may be suggested by other means. One of these is register.

The melody of the "Notturno" from Borodin's String Quartet in D Major, for instance, begins with the tonic, A, played softly by the cello (Example 67). The tonic harmony provides no clue as to the probable direction of melodic motion. Because the cello enters on the second beat of the measure, over a gently syncopated accompaniment, there is a suggestion of instability. But the particular feeling of poignant tension, which the slow tempo enables us to savor from the very first note, arises in large part because, though it is the tonic, the A is nonetheless implicative.

Example 67

It is so, because timbre and register serve as substitutes for tonal tension. Relative to the over-all range of the cello, the A is quite high. Consequently, simply from a statistical point of view, descending motion is probable. Had the "same" A been played on a violin—say, on the D-string—no clear direction of motion would have been implied. But the sense of implied direction has an even more important kinesthetic basis. We understand and respond to the effort involved in playing the "high" A with our whole being—with our bodies as well as our minds. This feeling of tension is heightened by the fact that the note is played softly. Let me explain. "High" and "loud" are associated with one another: not only is there a tendency to play louder as pitch rises, but even when intensity remains constant, perceived loudness increases as pitch rises. Because they require special effort and control, we are particularly sensitive to the covert tension of high, cantabile tones. Through sympathetic identification with the sound itself, the listener experiences tension—as though he were performing or singing the music himself—and, consequently, he not only knows, but feels, that descending motion is probable.

The implications of the "high" A, though persuasive, are general. Reg-

ister, dynamics, and timbre are, so to speak, protogenerative. There is a
sense of directionality, but no specific goals are defined. When the patterning does generate particular implications, these prove to be both complex
and ambiguous. The motion from A, through G♯ and E, to D implies continuation of the descending line; the ascending pattern in measure 3 suggests a return to the tonic. And neither of these is clearly dominant. Moreover, because melodic relationships suggest modality as much as tonality,
neither of the implications is particularly forceful. Though the stress created
by the grace-notes to the first beat of measure 2 helps to clarify the meter,
they also have the effect of making the G♯ seem ornamental rather than
structural—as though it functioned first as an appoggiatura to the F♯ and
then as an *échappée*. This weakening of the leading-tone, the durational
emphasis of the E and F♯, and the absence of a strong C♯ defining a triadic
tonal motion—all complement one another in giving the melody its modal,
quasi-pentatonic flavor. And the combination of alternative goals with the
somewhat attenuated and ambiguous implications of modality is to a considerable extent responsible for the subtly static and contemplative lyricism
of the melody.

In Borodin's melody, as well as in Schumann's "March" (Example 62)
and Mozart's Divertimento (Example 64), different aspects of the melodic
patterning implied alternative goals. But this need not be the case. Different
melodic processes may imply a single common goal. This is true of the subject of the fugue that is the second movement of Handel's Concerto Grosso
in G Minor, Opus 6 No. 6 (Example 68).

Example 68

Because it is in a more or less normal register for violins, the tonic on
which the subject begins is implicatively neutral. The uniformity of the

initial chromatic pattern is strongly implicative of continuation, as graph 1 indicates.[4] After the first measure, this motion is abruptly broken off, and a second pattern begins on B♭. The foreground motion of this pattern is patently linear, moving up to E♭. However, though the second level of motion (graph 2)—that of half-note groups—begins as conjunct motion, implying continuation to D, it skips from C to E♭. The gap thus created not only closes, but reverses the preceding rising pattern. Thus both lines converge to a common goal, D. Such *convergence*, articulating structural points of importance, is common in bilinear melodies.[5]

As is often the case with linear, descending fugue subjects, the last note of the subject becomes the first note of the answer.[6] The answer, played by the second violins beginning on D (measure 3), not only continues but renews the implications generated by the patterning of the subject. The alternative lines converge on A, which, harmonically as well as melodically, implies motion to G—at which point the violas and a solo cello continue the linear motion as they restate the subject.

Not only can bilinear melodies that converge be distinguished from those that do not, but bilinear patterning should be differentiated from what might be called "bilevel" ones. The subject of Bach's Fugue in C♯ Major from Book I of the Well-Tempered Clavier is a clear example of a bilevel melody (Example 69).

Example 69

As the analysis shows, the two melodic strands are parallel, with the upper one related to the lower one by latent fourth-species counterpoint. The "suspensions" are resolved when both voices move to a C♯. The tonal tendency of the fifth to descend to the tonic is the framework within which patterning takes place. The first generative event, the skip of a sixth to E♯, both establishes a second strand of melodic activity and, at the same time,

---

[4] In these respects and others, Handel's fugue subject is in marked contrast to Borodin's melody.

[5] See Examples 70, 92, and 105.

[6] See Bach's Prelude and Fugue in G Minor (BWV 542) for Organ.

implies the descending motion of a fill. The main generative event, which moves the harmony away from the tonic and sets the contrapuntal pattern, is the motion from G♯ to F♯ in the lower line. Because the upper strand (graph 2) is contrapuntally dependent upon the lower one (graph 1), there is no contrary or oblique motion. Therefore, though both lines move to the same pitch-class (C♯), there is no melodic convergence. Incidentally, like the Handel fugue, this one is linearly continuous: the answer begins on the lower C♯ (where the subject ended), and moves down the scale to G♯, at which pitch the subject is repeated.

Convergence may not take place as directly and immediately as it does in Handel's fugue subject (Example 68). The theme which begins the exposition section of Beethoven's Seventh Symphony illustrates this point. The melody, given in Example 70, consists of an antecedent and a consequent phrase. Though it is adequate, closure at measure 74 is scarcely decisive. Mostly it depends upon rhythmic relationships. As the rhythmic analysis under the example indicates, each part is end-accented on the phrase level, and the consequent phrase is so on the lowest level as well. The antecedent phrase ends on a weak beat (B), but, because the weak beat is longer than the accent, closure is enhanced. Though the theme is also closed harmonically, it is not forcefully so. For the cadential progression lacks emphasis on the subdominant. Generally speaking, then, rhythmic and harmonic closure are low-level, and this is the case with melody as well.

Example 70

Melodically, the foreground structure is coherent and complete. But the high level is not. Like the Handel theme, this is a bilinear melody. As the graph above Example 70 shows, both the descending line, E-D, and the rising line, G♯-A-B, imply continuation to a common C♯. Because it is an appoggiatura, not a structural tone, the C♯ in measure 70 cannot count as a realization of the implications generated by these linear events. The consequent phrase reaffirms the implication, but the C♯ in measure 73 is even weaker.

The implication generated by the first theme proper is powerfully reinforced in the following measures. After a six-measure prolongation of the tonic (measures 75–81), emphasizing A and E but *not* C♯, there is a passage on the dominant (Example 71). This moves through the triad to the seventh, D, and in the same register as the D of the theme. This dominant-seventh chord, emphasized by *fortissimo* dynamics and a fermata, unequivocally implies a resolution to tonic harmony with C♯ in the upper line.

Example 71

But C♯ does not follow. In fact, no satisfactory, structural C♯ occurs until the recapitulation. One can look through the transition passage, the second key area, the closing section, and the whole of the development and not find a single C♯ which can function as a stable, goal tone in the appropriate harmonic context and in the right register. There are, of course, some important C♯'s. One occurs in the transition passage of the exposition section at measure 111 (Example 72). However, though it comes at the end of a sequence, this is not a satisfactory realization of the implications generated in the first theme group. As the harmony sketched under Example 72 shows, the tonal context is not the proper one. Instead of functioning as part of tonic harmony, this C♯ is the fifth of an F♯-minor triad which itself functions as the subdominant of C♯ minor. Moreover, this C♯ is in the wrong register —an octave lower than that specified by the generating event.

Example 72

Only in the recapulation, two hundred and thirty measures after it was first implied, is C♯ realized as a satisfactory structural tone. And perhaps because it has been so long delayed, it is emphasized again and again. The

implication is regenerated by the return of the first theme group at the beginning of the recapitulation. This time, however, the dominant-seventh
fermata, D, is resolved to C♯ (Example 73A). And the resolution is specially
striking—marked by the preceding rest, the sixteenth-note upbeat, and the
change in instrumentation and dynamics. Though the melodic C♯ is clearly
structural—in the right register and part of tonic harmony—the chord itself
is a mobile secondary dominant, V of IV.

Example 73

When it occurs at the beginning of the second tune in the recapitulation,
however, the C♯ is structural and the harmony stable (Example 73B). The
phrase also ends on the third of the scale, but as part of a six-four chord. In
a sense, this is a function it *should* have had in the opening theme—as is the
case, for instance, at the end of the antecedent phrase of the Theme of
Mozart's A-Major Piano Sonata (Chapter 2, Example 17). This six-four
chord receives its main resolution when the C♯ moves through B to A in
measure 346. Subsequently, a strongly implicative, sequential passage, reaf-
firming C♯ as a goal (Example 74) is followed by a cadential progression,
N⁶—V—I (measures 368–370), which also arrives at a forceful structural
C♯. And the movement ends with the third of the scale as the melodic note.

Example 74

DISJUNCT PATTERNS

Disjunct patterns may be implicative in two ways. A disjunct interval
may be understood as a kind of incompleteness—a gap—which implies that
the note or notes skipped over will be presented in what follows. Or, when
understood as part of a triad, a disjunct interval—such as a third, a fourth,

or a fifth—may imply continuation of the triadic pattern until a point of relative stability is reached. A single disjunct interval may imply both these possibilities—as was the case in Schumann's "Soldier's March" (Example 62).

Gap-fill melodies

Gap-fill melodies consist of two elements: a disjunct-interval—the gap—and conjunct intervals which fill the gap. As a rule, gaps are not larger than an octave. Given this qualification, it is generally the case that the larger the skip, the more strongly conjunct fill is implied. A skip of a sixth, for instance, is more forcefully implicative than a skip of a third. For the larger the disjunct interval, the more noticeable the incompleteness it creates, and a triadic continuation of a large disjunct interval is not probable because the melody would be carried beyond the octave,[7] which would be unusual—particularly in the early period of this style. Rising gaps are much more common than falling ones [8]—probably because it is natural for the tension of effort, associated with both rising and disjunct intervals, to precede the relaxation associated with descending conjunct motion and with the approach toward closure. In such melodies, it is not only the disjunct gap which generates implications. As with other linear patterns, the conjunct motion functions as a generative event in its own right and, once begun, tends to be continued until relative stability is reached. Finally, an important exception must be mentioned: an upbeat interval of a perfect fourth, moving to the tonic, does not necessarily function as a gap, but may be understood as a rhythmic-harmonic event emphasizing the tonic on which the melody proper begins. Let us now consider some examples.

The subject of the fugue from Geminiani's Concerto Grosso in E Minor, Opus 3 No. 3, is an almost archetypal instance of a gap-fill melody. As Example 75A shows, the main gap consists of an octave skip. Because it is an upbeat to the lower E, the B emphasizes this disjunction and at the same time acts as a subsidiary gap to the upper E. These gaps are followed by uninterrupted descending conjunct motion to the tonic.[9]

---

[7] For instance, the triadic continuation of a sixth, E to C, would take the pattern to the G outside the octave above the initial E.

[8] Though there are notable exceptions: for instance, the melody of Schubert's Scherzo (Example 66).

[9] I have discussed the shortcomings of such unimpeded conjunct motion in *Music, the Arts and Ideas* (Chicago: University of Chicago Press, 1967), Chapter 2.

Example 75

The only analytic problem that arises in connection with this example is that of hierarchic equivalence: is the motion following the B in measure 3 linear or triadic? In my judgment, it should be analyzed as both. The tones on the primary and secondary accents—the B, G, and E—are structurally more important than the A and F♯ which come on weak beats. On the other hand, the initial octave gap is so strongly implicative of completion that the fill notes acquire an importance which they would not otherwise have. More important still, the preceding linear motion (D♯–C♯) tends to shape our understanding of later events; it leads us to hear the conjunct motion as a continuing pattern. Consequently, the conjunct part of the pattern seems a satisfactory realization of the implications generated by the antecedent gap.

Because it is a single event without marked internal articulation, this gap (E-E) is ancillary: though it generates and gives direction to the following conjunct motion, the "real" melody is understood to be the consequent descending pattern. Gaps can be even more clearly ancillary than this— emphasizing the probable direction of motion, but not really becoming part of the essential patterning. This is the case, for instance, with the octave upbeat to the melody of Chopin's Prelude in E Minor, Opus 28 No. 4, the first measures of which are given in Example 75B. As the abstraction given above the example shows, the essential melodic motion consists of a conjunct descent, delayed by repetition and diversion, from B to E. In addition to emphasizing the direction of motion, the gap serves to define the basic area of melodic activity. Partly for this reason and partly because of the restrained motion of the melody itself, the *stretto* marked by Chopin in measures 16 and 17 is felt to be a "bursting out"—a gesture releasing previously pent-up tension. That the gap is ancillary is shown in the fact that the accompaniment does not begin until the downbeat.

Whether a gap is ancillary or is part of the main melodic motion depends, then, upon whether its tones are structural. This distinction can be made clear by comparing two menuetto melodies by Mozart—both of which begin with triadic gaps. The first, given in Chapter 4, Example 56, is from the Flute Quartet in A Major. In this case, the gap is an upbeat which precedes the first structural tone of the melody—the high A. The gap is ancillary, for our understanding of the structure of the conjunct fill, which consists of an antecedent and a consequent phrase, is not dependent upon the presence of the gap. Though the melody would undoubtedly have been poorer without the gap—for instance, had it begun with a changing-note upbeat, A-B-A—the antecedent-consequent structure would nevertheless have made musical "sense."

But in the melody of the Menuetto from the String Quartet in D Minor (K. 421), as Example 76 shows, the gap—a D-minor triad—is made up of structural tones. Because the descending fill is on the same hierarchic level as the generating gap, and because the repeated A's in measure 3 act both as the end of the gap pattern and as the beginning of the conjunct motion, the gap is part of the fundamental melodic structure. The conjunct fill does not form an independent pattern, understandable in its own right—as was the case with the Menuetto from the Flute Quartet (also see Example 54).

Once begun, the triadic motion is implicative both of its own continuation to the high A and of descending conjunct fill. The lower A in measure 1 performs two important functions. It establishes the lower limit of melodic activity, and thereby makes it probable that its octave in measure 3 is the upper limit and, therefore, a relatively stable goal for the triadic motion. Also, it emphasizes the disjunct character of the higher-level triadic pattern (graph 1). Indeed, gaps implying further motion occur throughout the melody: the A to F in measure 1, the low-level triad, D—F—A, from measure 2 to 3, and the falling fourths and rising thirds in measures 4 and 6.

Because the descending conjunct motion (graph 1a) is both strongly goal-directed and quite regular—and the sense of uniformity is heightened by the chromatic bass line—the melody generates considerable momentum. For this reason direct motion to the tonic would not create satisfactory closure. The on-going motion must be slowed down. This, the reversal in measure 8 does. When the foreground gap (E to C♯) is filled (by D), the direction of motion changes from descending to ascending. This change of direction is strengthened by the primary patterning (graph 1) and the secondary line (graph 2) converging in this motion. At this point, too, rhythm becomes relatively closed: previously the weak beats had been highly mobile;

Example 76

but here the eighth-note motion at the beginning of the measure creates a *closed* dactylic group (♪ ♪ ♪ ♪ ♩), and, as a result, rhythm is considerably less on-going and implicative. The closure of the whole part is assured by the arrival of the implied tonic, by the gap-fill structure (E—[A]—C♯ to D) in the middle-ground melody, by the motion of the tertiary voice (graph 3) to the tonic, and, finally, by the disjunct cadential motion of the bass.

In the preceding examples, disjunction was explicit and obvious, and the implications generated by each patterning were basically simple. However, a gap consisting of structural tones may be embedded in conjunct fore-ground motion, and disjunct patterns may be complex—implying a number of continuations. The subject of the D-Minor Fugue from Book II of the Well-Tempered Clavier is a case in point (Example 77). The sixteenth-note triplets at the beginning create foreground continuity. But they are essentially ornamental rather than structural. As shown in graph 1, there is a higher-level pattern: the eighth-notes on beats 1, 2, and 3 are structural tones outlining the tonic triad, D—F—A, and these are connected by foreground passing-tones. The importance of these structural tones is due not only to their metric position, but to their function in the patterning: the D is emphasized because it is the first note of the melody; the F, because it begins to repeat the motive just presented; and the A, because it ends the triplet motive and is followed by the first disjunct motion in the foreground.

The triadic pattern might seem to lead to the octave, D, on the second half of beat 3. However, though the D marks the extent of the over-all motion—the probable area of melodic activity—it does not follow from or form part of the preceding triadic pattern. Because the D, F, and A occur on main beats, not on weak eighth-notes, the D enters at the wrong point (too early) to fit the triadic patterning on the hierarchic level on which it was generated. The A represents the end of the triadic pattern. Its motion is continued in the next measure when A moves to G and then to F.[10] The completion of this conjunct fill does not occur until the penultimate cadence of the fugue —four measures before the end.

The high D is implied not by the triadic motion, but by the less patent gap-fill pattern shown in graph 2. This pattern consists of the series of eighth-notes which skip up a fourth, creating a gap, and then descend a second—implying further linear motion. There are three statements of the pattern, each beginning on the last note of the previous one: that is, D—G— F, implying continuation down to E and D; F—B♭—A, implying descending motion to G, etc.; and, finally, A—D—C♯ implying a still more extensive linear fill. As the conjunct motion descends from D, and the gaps are filled, the several lines converge and merge into a single motion.

Example 77

If the richness and complexity of these intertwining implicative structures is to be perceived, the fugue should be performed as "neutrally" as possible. For instance, it would be a mistake to think of the second triplet

[10] The last eighth-note, A, in measure 2 is not part of this line, but an upbeat leading to the statement of the answer.

as an upbeat to the F, but it would also be wrong to think of it as grouped with the preceding triplet thereby emphasizing the triadic structure. Because none of the subpatterns should be thought of as being dominant, no special articulation or phrasing is called for. Either of the two basic kinds of patterning embedded in this subject might form the basis of a separate melody, and it is instructive to see what happens when this is the case.

The first part of the aria "Se vuol ballare" from Mozart's *Le Nozze di Figaro*, like the patterning of Bach's fugue subject shown in graph 1 of Example 77, is a triadic gap-fill melody. The first eight measures are made up of two four-measure phrases related to each other by conformance (Example 78). Though each contains linear motion, the main patterning is unequivocally triadic (see graph 1) because of the phrase relationships: the first begins on F and moves to A, the second begins on A and moves to C, and the third—that of the conjunct-fill—begins on C. This high-level triadic structure is emphasized by the foreground patterning; because the first phrase returns to F and the second to A, the major-third relationships between phrases is aurally explicit. And because the triadic patterning is so strong, the G in measure 3 and the B♭ in measure 7 are understood as high-level passing tones rather than as structural tones. The triadic, gap structure of these first phrases implies linear fill.

The second part of the melody realizes this implication. It begins by descending conjunctly, filling the preceding gap as far as the G (graph 1).[11] Though the descent to G takes only four measures—the gap-creating pattern was twice as long—the filling-in is a satisfactory completion from a melodic point of view. For not only is each of the conjunct steps explicitly emphasized by rhythm and the articulation of the sequential pattern, but the first two-beat group in each of these measures (the falling third) is related by conformance to the important points of structural arrival in measures 4 and 8.

From a temporal point of view, however, the descent is too short. To balance the morphological length of the first half, four more measures are needed. But we are given twice that number. This is not because the text needs more music—the words of measures 15 and 16, "le suonerò, sì" are simply repeated in the last four measures. Rather these "extra" measures are

---

[11] The third phrase begins with the same two notes, C and A, which ended the second. However, though the interval is the same, the rhythmic placement and function of the notes is different. An end has become a beginning. When, as is the case here, a single "idea" is made to do double duty, there is the pleasure of psychic economy mentioned in Chapter 3 (pp. 67f.).

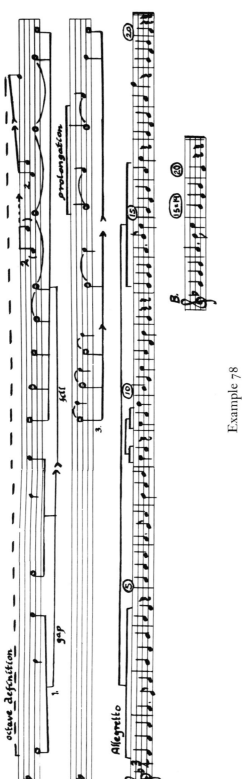

Example 78

appropriate because the descending motion of measures 9–12 is so patent and direct that a cadence after only four measures—such as is given in Part B of Example 78—would have seemed flat and uninteresting, and closure would have been weak and ineffective.

The last eight measures, which from one point of view are little more than a prolongation of the G in measure 12, subtly combine an intensification of implication with an equally effective feeling of closure. The sense of implication arises not only because the preceding descent stopped short of its goal, F, but because the lower-level *échappée* figure, shown in graph 3, would, if continued, have moved from G—A to F. And this possible continuation of the sequence in measures 9–12 is repeatedly suggested in the last eight measures. Secondly, the skip to C in measure 16 and to F in measure 18 tends to make these notes seem implicative and mobile. As the analysis in graph 2 shows, the motion from A to C implies F.

Though aurally prominent, the high F is understood not as a potential structural tone, but as part of the cadential process. Here context is crucial. Because it comes toward the end of a pattern, the F not only provides stability through octave definition (see Example 78), but is understood as part of the cadential pattern—one common in the style of Viennese classical music. For instance, the cadence at the end of the Minuetto from Haydn's "London" Symphony (No. 104) (Example 58) employs almost the same set of pitch-time relationships: the tonic, D, in measure 44, on a weak beat, moving to the second degree of the scale, E, in measure 47, on an accent— and then to the lower tonic. Closure is also enhanced by the fact that, despite vital differences in function, these measures are a kind of return. As indicated by the brackets over the example, they are rhythmically the same as, and melodically similar to, the first four measures of the melody.

A nontriadic gap-fill patterning—the skip of a fourth followed by descending conjunct motion, as in graph 2 of Example 77—is the basis for the opening melodic pattern of the song "Das Wandern" from Schubert's *Die schöne Müllerin*. Since the same melody is used for a number of different verses, so that prosodic patterns vary from one stanza to another, the text can be disregarded for purposes of analysis. And since our concern will be with melodic implication rather than with high-level rhythm and form, the repetition of the first four measures will not be considered. The melody is given in Example 79.

The first melodically generative event is the skip of a fourth, from F to Bb. When A follows, continued conjunct descent, filling in the missing

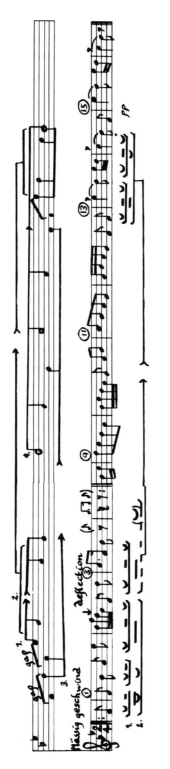

Example 79

tone G and returning to F, is implied (graph 3). This patterning is analogous to the first eighth-note motion, D—G—F, in Bach's fugue subject. As in the Bach, this implication is not realized directly. Instead, the gap pattern is repeated: the A skips to E♭ which moves down to D. Continuation through C to B♭ is implied (graph 1). The second gap-fill pattern is more forcefully implicative than the first, both because the diminished fifth (A—E♭) is harmonically goal-directed and because the over-all motion from F to E♭ makes a progression to the tonic, B♭, very probable. This motion does follow, as graph 1 indicates. But it does so only after a delay of three eighth-notes: the B♭ comes on the second beat of measure 3, rather than on the second beat of measure 2.

This delay creates a break in process which has important consequences later in the melody, but it need not have occurred. The implied B♭ might have followed directly, as shown in Example 80. Had this direct descent to

Example 80

B♭ taken place, continuation of the linear patterning would have been probable. And such continuation would have led to the realization of the first implication generated: the B♭—A of measure 1 would have moved through G to F.

What is crucial here is the relationship between rhythmic structure and melodic patterning. As the analyses under both these examples show, the grouping of the second rhythmic level is an anapest, 1 + 1 + 2, which is completed on the third eighth-note of measure 2. In the spurious version (Example 80), the rhythmic closure created by the end-accented anapest is complemented by partial melodic closure on the B♭—the implied goal of the second generative event. But in Schubert's melody this is *not* the case. The tune is deflected away from closure by the prolongation of the D, which moves through the B♭ major triad to the lower F. In other words, though the rhythmic group in Schubert's song is closed in measure 2, the melodic pattern remains to be completed. The result is that the motive (D—C—B♭), which realizes the implications noted in graph 1, sounds both like an ending "tacked on" to the first phrase and like a beginning of a new event. It sounds like an ending because from a melodic point of view it is related to and closes the previous phrase. It seems like a beginning both because the rhythmic closure in measure 2 is quite strong and because the two-measure morphological lengths established by the piano introduction and the first phrase suggest that a new unit should begin here.[12] And for reasons of morphology, this "beginning" seems abortive: a second measure of melody is wanted. Indeed, this need is such that, as indicated by the parenthesis in Example 79, one can easily imagine the piano echoing the motive in the following measure.

This noncongruence of rhythm and melody is itself implicative, as graph 2 indicates. What is implied is a patterning in which the motion from E♭ down to B♭ occurs without a deflection or break. In the last two events of the melody, this implication is realized: melodic motion and rhythmic grouping form a single coherent pattern. The rhythmic grouping potential in measures 3 and 4—an amphibrach on the first level and a trochee on the second—is actualized in measures 13 and 14 (and measures 15 and 16), and the echo potential in the earlier measures is made manifest in the higher-level organization. As Schubert's marking of *pianissimo* shows, measures 15 and 16 are an echo of measures 13 and 14.

On the highest level, the second part of Schubert's melody (measures 9–16) moves in two-measure units. As graph 4 of Example 79 shows, both the primary line, D—C, and the secondary line, B♭—A, imply B♭ as a point of closure. On a lower level, the G in measure 10 and the F in measure 12 are realizations of the implications generated by the first melodic event of the song—the gapfill pattern, F—B♭—A (graph 3). Because they are goal-notes harmonized as temporary tonics and because they occur on a hierarchic level equivalent to that of the generating event, the G and F are satisfactory realizations.

But this is not true of the main linear motion of the second part of the song. The B♭'s in measures 14 and 16 are *not* on the same hierarchic level as the conjunct motion from D to C. Nevertheless the melody does achieve satisfactory closure. This is so for five main reasons. First, the echo repetition at the end of the song acts as a sign of relaxation and hence of closure. Second, the restatement of the B♭ emphasizes its function as a goal—though it does not change its hierarchic level. Furthermore, the skip of a seventh, F to E♭, represents a condensation of the melodic motion of the first measure, and measures 13 and 14 (and their repetition) are, in like manner, condensations of measures 2 and 3. The sense of return thus created enhances the

---

[12] And such lengths are normative in this style.

feeling of closure.[13] Fourth, the harmonic process—the cycle of fifths progression begun in measure 9—reaches a full cadence in measures 14 and 16. And, finally, the high-level rhythmic structure, including the repetition of the first four measures, is closed, as Example 81 shows:

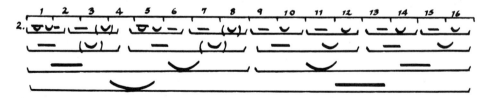

Example 81

The analyses presented in Examples 79 and 81 indicate that rhythmic and melodic closure complement one another. The low-level melodic structure is closed, but the highest level—the D to C motion generated in the second part of the song—is not. Conversely, the rhythmic pattern is closed —end-accented—on the highest level, but on lower levels the last groups are mobile, ending on weak parts of the rhythmic group. When one considers the text, which emphasizes the continuation of "wandering," the strophic nature of the song, which must remain somewhat open to allow for repetition, and the fact that this is the first song in a cycle—then the lack of absolute and unequivocal closure seems entirely appropriate.

Other points merit consideration in connection with this song. At the outset, two different gap-fill implications are generated. The second of these —the conjunct motion from E♭ to B♭—is realized, after a brief delay, before the first cadence. It is proximate. The first generative event is realized remotely—in the second half of the melody. Thus the realization of gap-generated implications may, as was the case with linear patternings, be significantly delayed. Also, though large skips, like octaves and sixths, tend to be more forcefully implicative than smaller ones, even modest disjunctions may function as gaps implying fill. This is true not only of the fourths which begin the melodic patterning of "Das Wandern"; it is also the case with some of the thirds in the melody (Example 82). For instance, the closure

---

[13] Despite the gap of a seventh, motion beyond the B♭ is not implied. Partly this is because the F can be understood as moving "harmonically" to the B♭—as dominant to tonic—and more importantly because the implications generated by a comparable earlier event (in measure 1) have already been realized satisfactorily, and, as noted above (p. 138), once a set of implications have been adequately realized, closure takes precedence over implication.

Example 82

on the B♮ in measure 3 is enhanced by the preceding skip of a third from C to A. As graph 1 indicates, this is a gap—albeit an unobtrusive one—which the B♮ fills. Had the C merely been repeated as a sixteenth-note, closure would have been slightly weaker. More important: in the second half of the melody, the descending motion of measure 9 is given impetus by the skip from the preceding B♮ (graph 3a). Similarly, the following third from A to C implies motion down to F (graph 3b). Thirdly, the implications generated by the opening fourth and those generated in the second half of the melody converge on the G and the F (graph 2 and 3a and b). This convergence facilitates the penultimate closure. Finally, despite the dominant sense of linearity (shown in graphs 2 and 3), the middleground structure is triadic (graph 4).

Triadic melodies

Some disjunct intervals—such as thirds, fourths, and fifths—are implicative because, within the style of tonal music, they are understood as possible parts of larger, syntactically normative patternings—namely, triads. Though they are uncommon, other regular, disjunct patterns do occur. For instance, in measures 5–8 of Schubert's Scherzo (Example 66), foreground linearity includes a higher-level disjunct motion: the two adjacent tetrachords, E♭—A♭ and B♭—E♭ (see graph 2). The symmetry of the relationship, reinforcing the tendency of the E♭ scale to continue its linear motion, evidently implies the high E♭. However, because triadic patternings are by far the most important in generating implications in the repertory of tonal music, nontriadic disjunctions will not be considered here.

The extent implied triadic motion—whether a pattern will move to the octave above and, if so, whether the octave will be a structural tone—depends upon the particular structure of the generating event. A pattern that begins on the root of a triad may continue only to the fifth, touching the upper octave as a way of defining the area of melodic activity, but not as a structural tone. This, as we have seen, is the case in Mozart's aria, "Se vuol ballare" (Example 78). However, some triadic melodies begin on the root and imply continuation beyond the fifth to the upper octave as a structural tone—the melody of the second movement of Telemann's Suite for Flute and Strings in A Minor is an example. To consider why the upper octave is implied as a structural tone in Telemann's melody, but not in Mozart's is not only instructive, but a clear instance of the need for *ad hoc* explanation.

Mozart's melody begins with two similar phrases: the first on the root of the triad, F; the second on the third, A. As a result, the third of the triad receives the same emphasis, is on the same structural level, as the root. The fifth of the triad, C, is structurally important not only for the melodic reasons considered earlier, but for rhythmic ones as well. Because of their similiarity, the first two phrases are understood as elements in a high-level anapest rhythm: $4 + 4 + 8$ —plus a four measure internal extension. Consequently the C, which begins the "accented" phrase, functions as the goal of the preceding motion. Because each element in the triadic motion is stable, with C (in measure 8) as a point of closure, continuation to the octave as a structural tone is not strongly implied.

In Telemann's melody, on the other hand, the tones of the triad are not structurally equal (Example 83). The root (A) and the fifth (E), which come on primary accents, are on a higher level than the third (C). As the proximate goal of both linear and triadic patterns, and as the accented fifth of the scale, the E is potentially stable. But this potential is diminished by three circumstances. First, because it is rhythmically weak and is not articulated as a separable patterning, the C is mobile—much more so than the third in Mozart's melody. Since some of this mobility is, so to speak, carried over to the E, there is a tendency for the triad to be continued. Second, instead of closing an end-accented rhythmic group or beginning a new event, the E moves on to a weak beat on the low A. The stability of the E is so reduced that there is a strong possibility of continuation. And third, the structural importance of the root and fifth emphasize the pentachordal relationships implicit in the root-position triad, making it probable that the upper tetra-

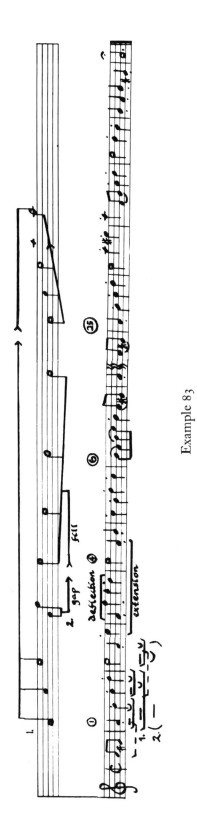

Example 83

chord will be completed. For all these reasons, continuation to the high A is strongly implied.

The high A is not, however, realized in the first part of the movement. Instead, the motion to the lower tonic, initiating a series of gaps—of which the sixth, A—F, is the most important—deflects the motion downward (graph 2). This, together with the tension created by the internal extension, leads to conjunct motion and closure on the low A. The high A is realized only remotely—when the melody is restated at the end of the movement. As in Mozart's melody, the arrival of the octave contributes to the sense of closure. The realization of the previously implied A is marked melodically by the disjunct motion which surrounds it. Rhythmically it is emphasized because it is both the beginning and end of an unequivocal end-accented group.[14]

Both Mozart's melody and Telemann's reach the octave above the first structural tone. But this is not always the case with triadic patterns—even those that begin with the root. The main melody of Smetana's *Vltava* (The Moldau) (Example 84), for instance, is similar in a number of ways to the one from Telemann's Suite. The first structural note, the tonic, is followed by conjunct foreground motion to the fifth. And on the second level, the pattern is triadic. But continuation to the upper tonic is not implied.[15]

Example 84

[14] Telemann's melody is similar, at least in general motion, to the folk tune from Bartók's Fifth String Quartet (Example 59). In the Quartet, the melody is repeated beginning on the high A of measure 13—and again beginning on Bb. In this final statement, Bartók takes care to articulate the leading-tone to tonic progression so that clear closure is assured.

[15] In all these cases the matter is one of relative probability. It is more probable that Telemann's melody will move to the upper tonic than that Smetana's will. But Smetana's melody might have done so anyway. Had this been the case, our understanding of the earlier events would be changed in retrospect. Our understanding of the beginning of the Telemann tune is also changed in retrospect when the implied high A is realized. For the "hypothesis" generated by the opening pattern has now been "confirmed."

Because of the phrasing and the structure of the accompaniment figure, the third of the triad (G) receives some articulation as a separate event. Though the articulation is not nearly as forceful as in Mozart's melody, it is somewhat stronger than in Telemann's. The fifth (B) is a clear stable goal which, instead of being weakened by a feminine ending as in Telemann's melody, is reinforced by prolongation. Moreover, the neighbor-note pattern —from fifth to sixth to fifth in the minor mode—makes descending conjunct motion probable. Finally, and perhaps most important, the fifth of this triadic motion is an octave above the initial upbeat. Consequently, when the upper B is reached, the main area of melodic activity is understood as defined, and continuation to the high E is not felt to be probable.[16]

The first melody from Richard Strauss' *Till Eulenspiegel* is also triadic (Example 85). Like Smetana's melody, it begins with a skip of a fourth and moves through the third of the scale to the fifth, which is the goal of the preceding motion. However, despite these surface similarities, the tunes are obviously very different. In the "Moldau" melody, the triad functions as a gap implying linear fill. The motion to the fifth is smoothly regular and is accomplished without significant delay. What delay there is occurs in the "main" part of the melody—the descending conjunct motion. In the Strauss melody, on the other hand, a triad is the basis for the patterning of the *whole* event. It is a note of the triad—the fifth, C—which is delayed. And what the disjunct pattern implies is not complementary conjunct fill, but continuation *within* the triad.

Till's tune begins with a skip of a fourth, C to F.[17] The probability of triadic continuation is supported by the accompanying tonic harmony, which is sustained throughout the melody and which helps to emphasize the structural importance of all the tones of the triad. The implied continuation to A is at once delayed and strengthened by the "interposition" of the G. It is delayed because the A might have followed the F directly; it is strengthened because the linear motion, F—G, is itself implicative of A. In a similar way, the following G♯ performs a dual role. But here, because of its greater duration and its function as an appoggiatura, the delay is so emphasized that we become explicitly aware of the fact of implication.

[16] This is an example showing that a upbeat fourth need not function as a gap.

[17] As in Smetana's melody, the fourth is adjunctive: it is understood as part of the triad, but not as a gap. Compare these adjunctive fourths with the one which begins the first melody of the second movement of Beethoven's Second Symphony. In that melody, the fourth is not an upbeat and is not adjunctive. It functions as part of the melody proper and, consequently, as a gap implying linear fill—an implication realized at the end of the phrase.

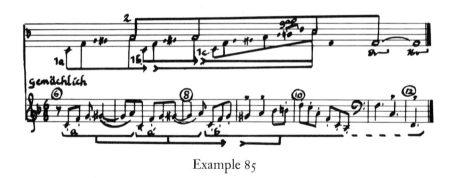

Example 85

Once the A is heard, further continuation is forcefully implied for three main reasons: the uniformity of the chromatic motion creates no clear point for closure; the A comes on a weak beat and is rhythmically mobile; and ascending triads which begin on the fifth tend to reach closure on the upper octave. Nevertheless there is partial closure—because the A is part of the harmony, which G and G♯ are not; and because the A is followed by a marked pitch disjunction. When the pattern is repeated, the triadic impression is stronger. For the F now comes on a secondary accent. Not only are melodic implications reinforced by the repetition, but a clear sense of higher-level rhythmic structure emerges, and this, too, is implicative. The similarity of the two phrases, a and a′, makes it likely that the following phrase will be twice as long—an anapest group, 1 + 1 + 2. And though the momentum of melodic motion carries the b phrase beyond the "predicted" limits, this is the basic patterning (see the analysis under Example 85).

The third statement of the motive not only takes the linear motion beyond A, but it does so chromatically. Because the uniformity of the patterning creates no inherent syntactic stopping place, a break and reversal of process is necessary if the C is to constitute a relatively stable goal. Such articulation is created by the disjunction—the gap from B to D—which the C fills. And harmony contributes to the relative stability of the C, whose structural force is also the result of the fact that it is the first goal tone which comes on a primary accent. The accumulated tension of the ascending triadic motion with its conjunct delay is, so to speak, released when the C is reached—is realized as the goal of the preceding process—and its momentum carries the pattern through the descending triad and beyond the confines of what would have been its normal morphological length.

In the analysis over Example 85, two levels of triadic motion are distinguishable, though they are not really as distinct as the graphs make them appear. The first level (graph 1a, b and c) consists of the patternings which imply the C in measure 10. The second (graph 2) is a higher-level, yet some-how less forceful, motion from A to C to F. The foreground patterning has already been discussed. The higher-level motion arises because the A and C are considerably more important structurally than the F's in measures 6, 7, and 8. The importance of the C has already been considered. While the eighth-note F's are parts of the low-level triadic motion, they are clearly subsidiary points on the way to the A's. The latter are more important not only because they are goals and ends of phrases but because they are em-phasized by appoggiaturas. The F's in measures 11 and 12 are structurally important for both tonal and rhythmic reasons.[18]

Despite considerable foreground complexity—rhythmically, because each phrase begins on a different part of the beat; melodically, because of the chromaticism and the long appoggiaturas—the structure of Strauss' melody is essentially simple. There is a single, basic patterning, a single primary goal. Although even more patently triadic, the first part of the theme of the slow movement of Haydn's Symphony No. 97 is much more complex. For under deceptively simple foreground relationships, analysis reveals an intri-cate network of alternative patterns and goals (Example 86).

The first motive (m) is conjunct on the lowest level, and perhaps im-plies linear descent. On the next level, the A—F is part of a triadic pattern implying continuation to the low C. These implications are not realized until measure 3, where a return to F is followed by conjunct foreground motion and second-level triadic motion to the C in measure 4 (graph 1a). The motive is repeated a third higher (m'), and again, after a modest delay, the implied patternings are continued—the conjunct motion on the G at the end of measure 2, and the triadic motion on the F of measure 3 (graph 1b). A third version of the motive, beginning on the high F, moves triadically from the F and linearly from the D down to the C at the end of the phrase (graph 1c). All three linear and triadic patternings converge as they ap-proach the C.

The first two statements of the motive (m and m') create an alterna-tive, higher-level patterning which is also triadic (graph 2a and 2b). The structural tones of this patterning move from F—A to C. Because it is the chief accent of an anapest rhythmic group, the C functions as the immediate goal of the high-level triadic pattern (shown as unfilled notes in the analysis). Both this high-level triad and its auxiliary pattern (graph 2a) imply con-tinuation to, and completion at, the upper octave. But arrival at this goal is

[18] Because they follow from the prolonged tonic triad of measure 10, the F's seem to be octave transfers, as shown in the analysis.

delayed until the lower-level implications are realized (graphs 1a, 1b, and c).

The convergence of the descending conjunct and triadic patternings in measures 3 and 4 is accompanied by the first harmonic changes thus far. The subsequent melodic motion to the goal, C, is complemented by a strong cadential progression (V/V—V). As a result, the C becomes a structural tone of such major importance that it not only functions as the end of the first phrase, but, as graph 3 shows, it also participates in the triadic patterning of the second phrase. And, once that triadic motion has taken shape, a structural C an octave higher is implied. But just as the realization of the high F was delayed in order that the alternative descending patternings might be continued, so now the realization of the triadic motion from the low C to the higher one is put off so that another, previously generated, implication can be realized—namely, that generated by the high-level triadic motion of the first phrase (graph 2a and b).

Example 86

When the high A and F are reached in the second phrase, there is no doubt that the opening motive, here displaced an octave (m‴), implies and is followed by conjunct descending motion to C. The implication of conjunct descending motion is reinforced by the high-level gap from the A in measure 5 to the F in measure 6. The descending conjunct motion not only makes patent and direct what was latent and delayed in the first part of the melody, but it also constitutes the realization of a foreground implication generated earlier. For, given the conjunct motion within the first two motives, the skip from F to D at the end of measure 1 is understood as a foreground gap. The highly conjunct motion from F to D in measures 6 and 7 fills this gap and thereby contributes to the sense of closure created by the cadence in measure 8.

The closure of this first part of Haydn's theme is assured not only by the strong harmonic progression to the dominant, but by the convergence on C of the high-level patternings—that is, by the fact of realization itself. Of course this is not the end of the theme. Return to the tonic is implied—both melodically and harmonically. And in contrast with the intricate and predominantly triadic motion of the first part of the melody, the second consists of relatively simple conjunct motion, somewhat delayed, from the C reached in measure 8 down to the tonic, F, in measure 24.

In the above examples of triadic motion, disjunct motion took place within a single triad. But this need not be the case. Because triads a third apart share a common interval of a third—for instance, the third F—A belongs to both the F major and the D minor triads—*different* triads may follow one another yet create a single disjunct patterning. Two kinds of triadic overlapping may be distinguished: linked triads and continuous triads.

1.) *Linked triads* occur where the patterning contains both thirds and fourths in alternation. The well-known melody "and He shall reign for ever and ever" from the Hallelujah Chorus of Handel's *Messiah* illustrates this kind of overlapping triadic patterning (Example 87). The foreground motion consists of three rising fourths separated from one another by falling sixths. The pattern's convincing coherence comes from this patent intervallic regularity (which is significantly due to rhythmic structure) and from the orderliness underlying the succession of disjunct intervals. For when the pitches of the melody are written as a single "line"—with the sixths inverted to thirds, as in the first staff of the analysis—it is even more evident that the pattern is one of overlapping triads: the D and F♯ of measure 1 are not only part of D major, but of B minor; and the B and D of measure 2

Example 87

are not only part of B minor, but of G major. The forceful patterning of the melody comes not only from this triadic linking, but from the higher-level motion which, as indicated in graph 2, is also triadic. On this level continuation to the lower D is implied.

Though not directly relevant to the problem at hand, two aspects of this melody merit consideration. Though rising fourths, which begin on weak beats need not function as gaps, implying conjunct fill, they do so here. For, instead of being adjunctive, like the upbeat in Smetana's melody (Example 84), the fourths in this case are part of the main melodic pattern. The first two are "filled," as it were, by proxy when the fourth from D to G is followed by descending conjunct motion. Perhaps to compensate for the lack of fill for the preceding fourths, an extension emphasizes the conjunct motion. For the two similar iambic groups of the beginning imply that the higher-level rhythm will be an anapest group of four-beats duration. Had this been the patterning, the D would have come on the first beat of measure 3. The two-beat extension not only serves to emphasize the conjunct fill, but to symbolize the meaning of the text. It is clearly appropriate that the word "ever" is coupled with the stretching of the phrase created by an extension.

The forthright, spirited character of Handel's jubilant affirmation derives both from its manifest regularity and from the emphasis created by disjunct motion—as well as by tempo and dynamics. How much the former contribute to the ethos of the melody may be seen by comparing it with one in which the same fundamental structure is embellished by foreground connection and in which the impression of regularity is weakened by rhythmic displacement. Though it is hard to believe, the first melody of Mahler's Fourth Symphony (Example 88), meets these specifications.

Example 88

As the abstraction over the example shows (graph 1), the basic triadic structure is exactly that of Handel's melody! Indeed, even the rising-fourth—falling-sixth pattern is the same. But this simple organization is veiled in foreground embellishment. There is but one explicit disjunct motion—the falling-sixth in measure 1. All the other intervals are connected by conjunct motion, emphasized by a phrasing which calls for smooth continuousness. As a result, the fundamentally end-accented organization, so emphatic in Handel's melody, is much attentuated. Moreover, the rhythmic-formal organization is complicated by the fact that the G in measure 3 is an accent, not an upbeat conforming with the preceding patterning—as was the case with the equivalent D in Handel's melody. As a result, the C is so much less emphatic than is the G in Handel's version of this schema that the analysis may seem "forced" in order to emphasize the similarity between the two themes.

But this is not, I think, really the case. Mahler makes it clear that he thinks the C is important by emphasizing it with an accent and calling attention to it with the grace-notes. Moreover, though it comes on the downbeat, the G is unstable because it is harmonized by a six-four chord which moves to and is "resolved" on the dominant that harmonizes the C. Finally the C is brought out because it is the turning point in a traditional and familiar cadential gesture—as a comparison between the last measure of Mahler's melody and the closing motive of the slow movement of Mozart's "Haffner" Symphony makes clear (Example 89).

Example 89

2) *Continuous Triads* consist only of thirds (or, by inversion, of sixths), rather than of an alternation of thirds with fourths or fifths. The melody which begins the second key area of the first movement of Mozart's Sonata for Violin and Piano in A Major (K.305) is a conspicuous, but by no means uncomplicated, instance of this sort of organization (Example 90). The C♯ in measure 24, which begins the patterning, is followed by a succession of

thirds: C♯—A—F♯—D♯—B—and so on. As staff A of the example shows, this creates a series of overlapping triads: f♯—d♯°—B—g♯—etc. (The super-script "o" means diminished; lower-case letters designate minor triads; upper-case letters, major triads).

This disjunct, foreground patterning is the basis for a higher-level con-junct motion. The groups of four eighth-notes create an implied bilinear organization, shown in staff B of the example. As the "tie" in the analysis indicates, the falling seventh (C♯ down to D♯) creates an implied dissonance such that the following B acts as the resolution of an imagined suspension. In other words, the pattern is one of latent fourth-species counterpoint—as, for instance in Example 69. Both the foreground and higher-level pattern-ings are continued to the F♯ in measure 27, after which the momentum created by uniformity is slowed down and brought to stability by a reversal.

The noncongruence of melodic motion and metric structure makes the passage complex and equivocal, creating subtle, yet effective, tension. As the brackets above and below the music make clear, the melodic pattern con-sists of groups of four eighth-notes, while the meter is in threes. For this reason, the relationship between melody and meter is continually changing. The first melodic pattern begins on the fourth eighth-note of measure 24 (C♯), the second begins on the second eighth-note (B) of the next measure, and the third begins on the last eighth-note (A) of measure 25. Even when the original relationship between meter and melody is reestablished at the G♯

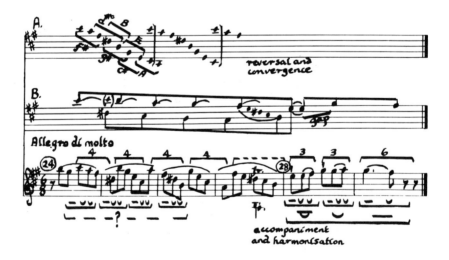

Example 90

in measure 26, there is little sense of stability and return because the G♯ is not a beginning, preceded by an upbeat figure (as the C♯ in measure 24 was), but is part of an on-going process. This noncongruence of melody and meter should, I think, be brought out by the performer: the low-level triple meter must be made evident by slightly stressing the primary and secondary metric accents—beats 1 and 4—within each measure.

That the passage is without accompaniment until the second half of measure 27 is important, for this allows the metric-melodic conflict to be fully effective. Moreover, because no accompaniment emphasizes one of the triads latent in the uniform succession rather than another thus creating a sense of progression, the harmonic structure of the passage is ambiguous. Because melody suggests one patterning and meter another, where harmonic events begin and end is not certain. From a melodic point of view, for instance, the D♯ at the beginning of measure 25 is part of the preceding patterning, largely because it is separated from what follows by a larger disjunction—the skip of a sixth. Metrically, however, the D♯ is the beginning of a triad and should be grouped with the weak beats that follow it. Similarly, the following B and G♯ are part of one harmony from a metric point of view, but melodically they begin new harmonic events. In other words, the triads are truly continuous, following one another without clearly defined boundaries.

Though the low-level dactyl grouping indicated in the analysis will be clear if the passage is played as I have suggested, the lack of lucidly articulated harmonic progression and the shifting relationships between melodic and metric patterns prevent higher-level rhythmic groups from arising. Above the primary level, rhythm is ambiguous—or at least inchoate. And from this point of view, arrival at a more clearly articulated higher-level patterning is implied.

Melodically, the passage is equivocal in the sense that neither the foreground thirds nor the higher-level linear pattern imply an unambiguous syntactic goal. Like any succession of thirds within a tonal framework, the series of triads in this melody is potentially endless. It is repeated (in a new metric context) beginning with the C♯ in measure 25, and might have continued in this established way after the C♯—A—F♯ in measures 26 and 27. On the higher-level, the implied fourth-species counterpoint is also ambiguous. Not only is the connection between substantive tone, dissonance, and resolution veiled by the intervening thirds,[19] but the metric placement of

---

[19] Compare with Example 69 where this is *not* the case.

dissonance and resolution keeps shifting. Moreover, here, too, continuation is implied—at least for another one and a half measures at which point a cadence to the tonic would be quite strongly implied.[20]

Because both the foreground and higher-level melodic patternings, as well as the rhythmic-metric organization, imply continuation, a decisive and unequivocal reversal of the on-going motion is required if the phrase is to reach stability and closure. The reversal is made clear by a number of changes in the musical organization. The most important of these is the end of the triadic motion. When the foreground becomes conjunct in measure 27, the two strands of the melody are connected by a scale and converge to the E in measure 28. Second, the ambiguity of the rhythmic structure is resolved in measures 28 and 29, where the foreground dactyls become part of a higher-level anapest group. Finally, the entrance of the violin and piano accompaniment in measure 27 not only defines the harmony, but clarifies the rhythmic relationship between the preceding measures and the cadential ones. The dominant-seventh chord functions as an upbeat to the next two-measure group, and partly through this the anacrustic function of the earlier measures is made explicit.

The reversal is emphasized—or signaled—by the trill on the D♯ as well as by the change in texture and the beginning of the accompaniment in the violin and piano. The ultimate closure of the phrase is assured both by the end-accented rhythmic group and by the strong and explicit harmonic progression to the dominant. Melodically, the F♯ is a satisfactory goal because it has been implied by the preceding gap of a third, E—G♯, and is delayed and emphasized by an appoggiatura.

A continuous triadic structure need not, however, be patently uniform and ambiguous in process. When harmonic functions are clearly defined and rhythmic-melodic organization is decisively patterned, a succession of foreground thirds may be the basis for a strong and unequivocal melodic structure. This is true of the melody which begins the first movement of Brahms' Fourth Symphony (Example 91). Not only does the rhythmic structure distinguish between structural and ornamental tones on several levels, but this differentiation is supported by a clear and normative harmonic progression (see chord analysis under part B of the example). As in Mozart's melody, the foreground succession of thirds is the basis for higher-levels of melodic patterning. The highest level (the "half-notes" in graph 1) is linear—a scale moving from G in measure 1 down to B in measure 18, with a lower-level

─────────

[20] Had the pattern been continued, the tonic, E, would have occurred on a downbeat at the beginning of measure 28—as it does in Mozart's music.

continuation to E. The middle-level motion begins as a series of falling fifths (or rising fourths), G—C—F♯—B; but the process is altered in measure 4 after which the pattern consists of rising fifths and falling sixths, E—B—D—A—C.

This alteration is the result of a change in both the direction and the timing of the underlying triadic organization. As line A of Example 91 shows, the first four measures are based upon a *descending* series of thirds (x), and the second part of the melody (beginning in measure 5) is based upon an *ascending* series of thirds (y). When the second part of a melody has the same basic patterning as the first but changes the direction of motion, the first part will be called the model, the second the complement. The whole pattern will be referred to as a complementary melody. Such melodies will be considered in the next section.

The manifest melodic organization, however, is not essentially complementary. For, despite the change in the direction of triadic succession from falling to rising (see line A), the main aural patterning—the high-level conjunct motion—continues in the second part of the melody. For the conjunct pattern to continue, the rate at which triads succeed one another must be modified, and this entails a concomitant change in the middle-level pattern. Instead of a rate of four different pitches in eight quarter-notes as in the first part, the octave repetition of the E, D, and C across the barlines slows down the rate of change so that there are only three different pitch-classes in eight quarter-notes. On the high level the consequence is greater emphasis

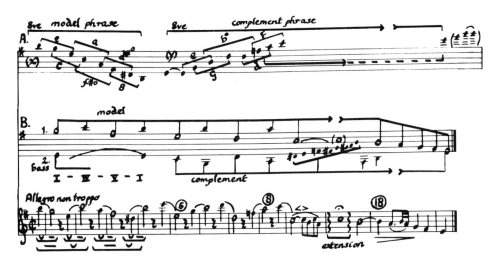

Example 91

on conjunct motion. On the middle level, though the alternation of rising and falling iambs continues, the intervals are changed from fourths and fifths (as in the first part) to fifths and sixths in the second.

Though the change from falling to rising triadic motion is significantly masked by the dominant conjunct motion, explicit complementary relationship is not entirely absent. The bass line, which was static (a sustained E, over which the harmony changed) in the first part of the melody, begins to move in measure 5. It ascends through the cycle of fifths (C—G—D—A), complementing the middle-level cycle of falling fifths of the first four measures in the melody. Had the series of fifths in the bass continued, the next bass note would have been an E, but this possibility does not follow directly. Instead, the sequential disjunct fifths are followed first by a chromatic rising line moving from D♯ to A (measures 9–14 which are only sketched in the analysis) and then by an authentic cadence, IV^6—V^7/V—I_4^6—V^7—I, at the end of which the implied E is realized.

An analogous delay occurs in the triadic motion which underlies the melody. Just as the first four measures of the melody move through a series of thirds from B to B (see line A), so once the complementary motion starting on E is begun, continuation to the structural stability of the octave-tonic is strongly suggested. But the melodic E, like the harmonic one, is put off: first by the extension-repetition of the C (measures 10–12, indicated by the fermata in the example), and then by bilevel conjunct motion followed by straight descending scales (measures 13–16, not given in the example). The E, implied by the underlying triadic pattern, is reached in measure 19, following a melodic reversal emphasizing the B of the main melodic line.

The second part of the melody raises an interesting question: is the succession of low-level conjunct motions following the prolonged C hierarchically equivalent to the high-level linear pattern of the preceding nine measures. In other words, can the whole theme be analyzed as a linear melody moving down from the G in measure 1 to the E in measure 19? Although none of the individual conjunct patternings in measures 13–19 are on the same hierarchic level as the preceding pattern, which moved in two-measure units, several aspects of the passage suggest that these measures are a structurally equivalent continuation of the first part of the melody (Example 92).

a) The prolongation of the C, delaying the previously generated process, lends psychological importance to the linear motion in these measures.
b) The cadential motion in measures 17–19 begins with a marked gap

which strongly implies and thereby calls attention to the descending conjunct pattern.

c) The iambic rhythm and bilevel melodic organization of measures 13 and 14 relate this part of the melody to the opening measures, as a kind of varied diminution. The patterning is linear and, as indicated in line A of the analysis, both the primary and secondary strands suggest conjunct motion converging to the E in measure 19.

d) Both strands—particularly the subsidiary one—seem to be continued in measures 15 and 16,—though to nonsubstantive E's. The succession of descending linear motions toward E, has a cumulative, summational effect—as though a single descending line were spread over these five measures (analysis line B).

e) This suggestion is not as fanciful as it might at first appear. For had the conjunct motion in two-measure units (the rate of motion in the first nine measures) been continued in the second half, then, as line D shows, the pattern would have reached the E precisely as it does in the actual theme. Accompanying the underlying triadic patterning is a fundamental and consistent rate of pattern change.

Though Brahms' melody creates a strong and persistent sense of linearity, the two-measure units of the second part do not, in fact, move con-

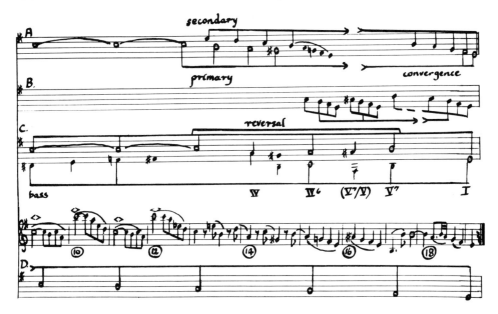

Example 92

junctly. Rather, as graph C (Example 92) shows, the momentum of the conjunct motion which led to the prolonged C is checked by a reversal. On both the middle and the high level, a skip from C to A not only breaks the preceding linear pattern, but creates a gap implying conjunct fill. The fill follows when the A moves chromatically (through A♯ in measure 16) to B—the first high-level ascending motion in the melody. On the high level, the B then moves in disjunct motion down to the tonic. This articulation of the melodic process is accompanied by a reversal in the motion of the bass. The chromatic line begun in measure 9 ends in measure 14, and a clarification of the harmonic syntax is followed by an authentic cadence.[21]

That this melody is based upon a pattern of continuous triads is shown in the recapitulation. In the restatement of the first part of the melody, Brahms eliminates the bilevel patterning, as well as the iambic rhythm with which it was associated in the exposition. As a result, the underlying triadic structure is made manifest in the audible foreground (Example 93).

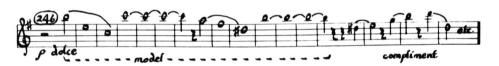

Example 93

SYMMETRICAL PATTERNS

In most of the melodies considered thus far, successive events were related to one another by: repetition—as in the linear melody from Mozart's Divertimento (Example 64), or the triadic tune from Strauss' *Till Eulenspiegel* (Example 85); continuation—whether conjunct, as in the Scherzo from Schubert's String Quartet (Example 66), or disjunct, as in the melody from Handel's *Messiah* (Example 87); and contrast of function, as in gap-fill melodies like the subject of Bach's Fugue in D Minor (Example 77). In symmetrical melodies, the relationship between successive events is such that one event *mirrors* the patterning of another. In other words, there is a balance of motion and countermotion. When such countermotions are primarily

[21] Again, the dual character of critical explanations is clear. For, though rule reasons were frequently employed in the analysis of this melody, common-sense, *ad hoc* reasons were indispensable.

melodic, successive events are similar in intervallic relationships, and often in rhythm as well, but opposite in direction of motion. This is true of complementary and axial melodies. Or, the mirroring may be primarily harmonic. Then the events involved may move in the same melodic direction, but they have an harmonic pattern of, as a rule, I—V, V—I and a high-level melodic structure which moves by conjunct motion away from and back to one of the notes of the tonic triad. Most changing-note melodies are of this type.

Complementary melodies

.The first theme of Brahms' Fourth Symphony is based, as we have seen, upon a symmetrical pattern of two continuous triads moving in opposite directions over a two-octave range (Example 91). However clearly sensed this complementary relationship may be, it is not explicitly presented. The manifest motion is predominantly linear. But complementary patterns can be explicit and manifest. The clearest instances are those in which one melodic event is an exact inversion of another, and in which durational relationships are the same for both. Another melody by Brahms—that which begins the third movement of his First Symphony—is such an unequivocal instance (Example 94).

The analysis shows the main patterning of the first phrase as being linear—a conjunct motion from E♭ down to B♭ (graph 1). Because the C is the most important tone in measures 2 and 3—as the A♭ pedal in the second clarinet and the bassoon, and the counterpoint in the horn and celli, make clear—there is also a hint of triadic motion. But the metric position and repetition of the D♭, as well as the emphatically conjunct motion of the foreground and of the bass line, suggest that the pattern is essentially linear. Both this linearity and the prototriadic structure (E♭—C, with tonic harmony) strongly imply continuation down to A♭.

The second phrase, an exact inversion of the first employing the same durational relationships, rises conjunctly from C to F (graph 2). This patterning, too, implies continuation—to the upper tonic. However, because the interval from the first note of the phrase, C, to the potential goal, A♭, is a sixth (rather than a fifth as in the first phrase), immediate continuation is necessary if the ends of the two phrases are to correspond; that is, if the second is to reach the leading tone below A♭, as the first reached the supertonic above it. This continuation, which takes place when the next phrase begins on G, reinforces the implication of motion to the high A♭.

Example 94

Though the stability of tonic harmony is reached at the end of the whole theme (measure 19) and at the beginning of its repetition in measure 109, the melodic Ab's, implied by the opening phrases and by their subsequent repetitions, are delayed until the beginning of the coda (measure 154). There, as the example shows, both lines move linearly through octave transfers to their respective goals. Yet even here, the rhythmic placement of the upper Ab keeps it from functioning as a structural tone. Only in the final cadence, as a sustained G moves up to the tonic, is there satisfactory closure and congruent arrival at implied goals.

The melody which begins the exposition section of the first movement of Mozart's "Linz" Symphony (K.425) consists of complementary phrases which are linear on the lowest level and triadic on the next (Example 95). Despite its seeming simplicity, it is so complex that to do it justice would require a discussion of the whole movement of which it forms a part. What follows must, therefore, be regarded as illustrating a type of organization, rather than as an adequate analysis.

The melody begins with a foreground pattern of conjunct whole-notes (motive *x*). Because tonic harmony persists throughout the first four measures, however, the E and G are understood as structural, while the F functions as a passing-tone. The main patterning is therefore triadic (graph 1)—implying continuation to C—rather than linear. But the C which follows in measure 22 is not a satisfactory realization of the implied triadic motion, for it is not on a hierarchic level equivalent to that of the two-measure lengths which generated the patterning. Because the melodic prominence of the C is not matched by its structural importance, it is a potential structural tone (graph 3) which strengthens the implication of a structural C.

The C in measure 24, which occurs in the right register and at the right point in time, is a satisfactory realization of the implied triadic patterning.

Nevertheless, it is only a temporary goal. For, though the triadic patterning is confirmed and thereby reinforced, the C is not stable, either harmonically or rhythmically. Consequently, triadic continuation to, and completion on, the E an octave above the first note of the tune is a strong possibility. At the same time, the C functions as the beginning of the second phrase.

The descending, conjunct, and whole-note motion (x′) with which the new phrase begins is a conformant inversion of the opening pattern (x), and, as a result, the complementary relationship between the phrases is clearly audible. The bass, moving in parallel tenths with the melody, strengthens the impression of foreground linearity. The harmonic progression

$$\text{IV}^6\text{—V}^{6\flat}_{\substack{4\\3}}/\text{IV—IV}$$

establishes the C and A as stable, structural tones and creates the complementary triadic patterning (graph 1a) which implies continuation to F, and perhaps beyond. This possible patterning is not, however, realized immediately.

Deflected—or perhaps "attracted" by alternative possibilities—the melody changes direction, rising conjunctly from the A in measure 26. The E, implied by the triadic patterning of the model, is reached in measure 27. It functions as a relatively stable goal, not only because of the satisfaction of octave completion, but because it is preceded by a gap-fill pattern (graph 4) which articulates closure.

Example 95

A descending triadic pattern follows the E. Its motion is both more explicit (the linear connections of the foreground are unequivocally ornamental) and more rapid (the structural tones occur every half-measure,
rather than every other measure) than that of the model and the beginning of
the complement. These two measures (27 and 28) join model and complement in a single pattern—moving from E which belongs to the model, to C
which is common to model and complement, and then to A which belongs
only to the complement. The F which follows is the continuation of the triadic motion of the complement begun in measure 24 (graph 1a).

The probable continuation of the triadic pattern begun in measure 24
is to C in the lower octave. But this C is not reached in the antecedent period.
Instead, the motion continues to D, where the appoggiatura progression
($^{6-5}_{4-3}$) to the semicadence creates temporary closure.

The consequent period (of which only the first measure is given in
Example 95) begins with an octave transfer to the upper E. This transfer, as
well as the octave motion of the model phrase, is made explicit and, as it
were, comprehended by the octave leaps in the first measures of the period.

In the consequent period the structural C which begins the complement is delayed by a varied repetition of the pattern in measures 22 and 23.
This is important because the reiteration of the potential structural tone and
the extension of the phrase length make the C a more emphatic and stable
goal. As a result, continuation to the high E is not strongly implied—and
does not in fact follow. Instead of being deflected, as in the antecedent period, the triadic pattern begun on the C continues down to the D in measure
40, and perhaps even to the B in measure 41. A reversal of the melodic motion in measure 41 leads to the stability and closure of a cadence on the
tonic, C—a goal implied not only by the triadic motion of the complementary phrase, but by the highest level of motion (graph 5), a linear progression from the third of the scale, through the second (measures 29 and
40), to the tonic (measure 42).

In the melodies from Mozart's "Linz" Symphony and from Brahms'
First Symphony, the complementary relationships are evident not only because durational relationships are essentially the same in model and complement, but because the intervallic structure of the several hierarchic levels is
basically preserved in the inversion of the pattern. But this need not always
be the case. For the sake of comparison, let us consider another melody by
Mozart—the one which begins the Menuetto of the String Quartet in A
Major (K.464). It, too, is complementary (Example 96).

On the highest level—that of two-measure units—the rising conjunct motion (A—B) of the first part of the phrase is apparently mirrored by the descending conjunct motion (E—D) of the second part. Even on a lower level, the beginnings and endings óf the two-measure events (*x* and *x'*) complement one another. Each of the first two events ends on a weak beat a perfect fourth above its first note, and in the second part each event closes on a weak beat (but the third beat rather than the second), a perfect fourth below its first note. There is another sort of symmetry as well. For, if the pattern is considered to consist of structurally equivalent tones, then the second part of the phrase is a retrograde of the first, and the whole phrase is symmetrical around the E: A—D—B—E / E—B—D—A.[22]

These relational similarities tend to be masked, however, by differences in foreground patterning. Melodically, the motives (x) of the model create an impression of triadic motion, while those of the complement seem predominantly linear. Rhythmically, the differences are even more striking. On the lowest level (1), the rhythmic groups of the model are unambiguous, beginning-accented trochees;[23] the groups in the complement are more doubtful. For the harmony suggests that the groups are beginning-accented dactyls, but the repeated notes in the first measure of each pattern tend to become anacrustic, creating latent (⌐⎯⎯⌐) end-accented groups. On the second level (2) the contrast between model and complement is clear. The rhythm of the model is beginning-accented; that of the complement is end-accented. On the third level (3)—where pitch symmetries are most apparent—the rhythmic organization is trochaic in both parts, so that the impression

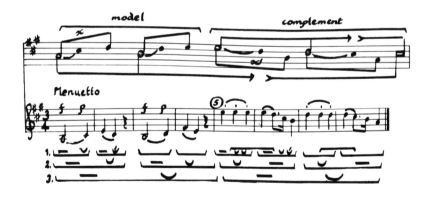

Example 96

[22] This symmetry is preserved even if the next lower level is included—i.e., if the notes given without stems in the analysis are counted.

[23] For a discussion of the basis for this analysis, see Meyer, *Emotion and Meaning in Music*, p. 107.

of complementary structure is certainly felt, if not consciously recognized.

There is another difference between this linear, complementary melody and the one from Brahms' First Symphony. In Brahms' melody the phrases imply alternative goals: the model moves conjunctly toward the lower Ab, while the complement moves toward the Ab an octave higher. In such cases —and the melody from the "Linz" Symphony is similar in this respect— the complementary motions may be *divergent* in the sense that they imply no common melodic meeting point. In the melody from Mozart's String Quartet, on the other hand, model and complement do imply a common meeting tone, the C♯—assuming that for the moment we may disregard the fact that the linear motions occur in different octaves. Such complementary melodies might be called *convergence* types.

The similarity between this convergence melody and one analyzed earlier—the theme which begins the exposition section of the first movement of Beethoven's Seventh Symphony (Example 70)—will not have escaped the reader. Not only are the high-level patterns very similar, but even the keys are the same. The obvious difference is that in Mozart's melody the ascending conjunct motion (A—B) precedes the descending motion (E—D), while in Beethoven's theme the opposite order (E—D, A—B) prevails.

In Mozart's Menuetto, as in Beethoven's movement, the arrival of the implied C♯ is considerably delayed. No satisfactory, stable C♯ occurs either in the remainder of the first part of the rounded-binary form or in the second part—the recapitulation. Only at the beginning of the codetta, after the return of the melody has regenerated the implicative process, does C♯ occur as a structural tone (Example 97).

Example 97

Because the model and complement are presented in different octaves, there is a question whether the C♯ in measure 65 is a satisfactory realization of the implications generated by the immediately preceding patterning and by the original presentation. Three considerations suggest that it is satisfactory. First, the relationship between the end of the model and the beginning of the complement involves a transposition to the upper octave which the change of register at measure 65 appropriately mirrors. Second, because the recapitulation of the melody, beginning in measure 55, is an octave higher than the initial presentation, the register of the C♯ is medial, linking earlier and later statements of the melody. The C♯ is in the proper register in relation both to the complementary pattern (E—D) of the initial statement of the melody and to the model pattern (A—B) of the recapitulation version. Finally, and most important of all, the diminished-seventh chord in measures 63 and 64, coming as the end of a relatively uniform sequence, is both unstable and strongly goal-directed.[24] Consequently, when it moves to tonic harmony in the following measure, the satisfaction of resolution makes registral matters seem of slight importance, and the ability of the C♯ to function as a stable goal is considerably enhanced.

That the C♯ is a satisfactory realization of the implications generated by the preceding statements of the melody is also indicated by the way in which the harmony is treated. For the diminished-seventh chord implies not a root-position triad, but one in the second inversion. The tonic harmony which follows is not, however, in the six-four position. In other words, Mozart is careful to arrange the harmony so that the C♯ can function as a relatively stable, structural goal before it becomes part of the implied and mobile $^{6\text{-}5}_{4\text{-}3}$ progression, moving through B to the tonic, A.

Disjunct as well as conjunct complementary patterns may be convergent. The antecedent-consequent melody which begins the first movement of Haydn's String Quartet in B♭ Major, Opus 55 No. 3, has this kind of organization. The theme is structurally complex, and an adequate analysis of its implicative processes would entail a discussion of the whole movement. Only the immediate and essential complementary and implicative relationships will be considered here (Example 98).

The antecedent phrase consists of two parts: the model and its complement. As the graphs 1b and 2b show, both are predominantly triadic, and in both the direction of motion changes toward the end of the pattern. At this point, too, both model and complement become more linear. This parallel

[24] The C in these measures is basically part of the complement pattern: coming from D, it acts as a lower neighbor to the following C♯. At the same time, there is a slight sense that it acts as a chromatic passing-tone between B and C♯ in the model.

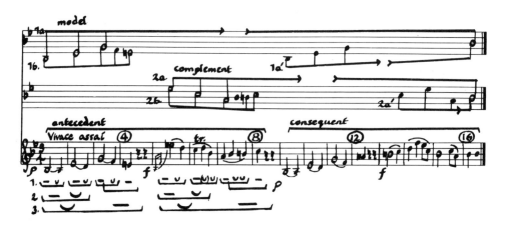

Example 98

change helps to make the structure audible and evident.[25] In addition, as the analysis under the example shows, the rhythmic structure of the two parts of the phrase is virtually identical. As a result, the complementary relationship between the pitch patterns is patent and palpable.

Because the root of the triad does not begin the patterning of the model, continuation to the stability of octave identity on the upper B♭ is probable. But instead of moving directly on to the upper B♭, the pattern is deflected down to E.[26] As the analysis indicates, the implied B♭ is realized only at the end of the consequent phrase—after the generating triadic pattern has been repeated (graph 1a′). The triadic structure of the complement, suggesting dominant-seventh harmony, also implies B♭ (graph 2b). The tonic follows

[25] Though it is obviously more conjunct than the model, the complement is written so that the disjunct aspects of the first two measures are emphasized. The E♭ at the beginning of the complement is strongly stressed by the large skip, the grace-notes, and the *forte* dynamics. As a result, the trochaic group in measure 5 is closed: the D is understood as coming *from* the E♭ rather than as moving *to* the C, and the impression of linearity is thereby minimized. The rhythmic group of the next measure is similarly closed. Not only is the C stressed by the trill, but the potential linear flow is broken by the *échappée*, D.

[26] The E is equivocal. On the one hand, the linear motion leading to it implies continuation and, after an octave transfer, E♭ and conjunct foreground motion follow. The chromaticism latent in this relationship (and explicit in measure 7) has consequences later in the movement. On the other hand, the impression that E is the leading tone of a secondary dominant (V/V) suggests that it will move up to F—as it does provisionally through the grace-note at the beginning of measure 5. This possibility, too, plays a part in subsequent events.

as the consequent phrase begins, but in the "wrong" register. The realization is only provisional. A satisfactory realization is delayed until the end of the consequent phrase, in which the version of the complement also implies the tonic. For, though their order is changed and they come on weak beats, the tones of the complement are nonetheless present and emphasized in measures 13–15—two of the tones, C and E♭, are resolutions of secondary dominants, and the A resolves the dissonance of a $^{6\text{-}5}_{4\text{-}3}$ progression (graph 2a′). Thus the implications of both model and complement converge in, and are realized by, the B♭ which closes the melody in measure 16.[27]

Axial melodies

Axial melodies, as the name indicates, consist of a main or axis-tone embellished by neighbor-notes above and below.[28] They do not, as a rule, occur on high structural levels. Like complementary melodies, they have two parts: a model and its inversion or "mirror." Both the model and the mirror move from the axis-tone (A) to the neighbor-note (N) and back:

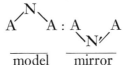

model   mirror

Though the foreground patterning of the axis-tone and its neighbors may suggest probable continuations, the relationship between model and mirror is, as the diagram shows, primarily formal—that of repetition by inversion— rather than processive.[29] The articulation of the parts of an axial melody is partly the result of the low-level closure which takes place as each neighbor-note returns to the stability of the axis.

On the highest level, however, closure is weak and implication absent. Implication is absent because, since axial melodies are essentially prolongations of a single tone, no high-level processive relationships are possible. Closure is weak because, without implicative processes, there are no goals to act as points of stability and completion. In short, continuation is likely, because of the lack of established points of closure rather than because of the generation of specific implicative relationships. Axial melodies, then, are

[27] Much more might be said about this melody. But the continuity of the general discussion must take precedence over more detailed analysis.

[28] I am indebted to Professor Eugene Narmour both for calling my attention to this kind of organization and for the term "axial."

[29] See Chapter IV, pp. 93–94.

relatively stable—even static—patternings, yet, at the same time, more or
less open-ended.[30]

The first theme of the last movement of Dvořák's "New World" Symphony is an axial melody (Example 99). The essential elements of the pattern are established in the first four measures. As graph 1 makes clear, the
tonic, E, is embellished by an upper neighbor, F♯, and a lower neighbor, D.
Each of these is in turn embellished by a neighbor-tone on a lower hierarchic level: the F♯ by G, and the D by B. The melody is repeated in measures 14–17, but the penultimate measure is varied, emphasizing closure.
The whole eight-measure period is then restated. A single two-measure motive has thus become the basis for a double period of sixteen measures. And
there is more to come. But before going on, let us consider the implicative
relationships within this period.

The melody is not markedly processive. Not only does each phrase
begin and end on a tonally stable tonic, but, as the harmony in the other
instruments of the orchestra (see score) makes clear, the notes in between
are essentially ornamental. This is obvious in the first two measures, for the
F♯ and G are both nonchord tones, and it is also clear in measure 12. Because they are understood as mirroring, and functionally analogical to, the

---

[30] Unequivocal instances of axial melodies do not, as far as I have been able to
discover, occur in the repertory of tonal music before the middle of the nineteenth
century. Without pretending to account for this in an adequate way, the following
observations seem pertinent.

During the nineteenth century, the size and make-up of the concert audience
changed considerably. Individual concerts tended to have larger, but rather more
heterogeneous, audiences than did those of the eighteenth century. This change, complemented by the literary predilections, philosophical inclinations, and aesthetic taste
of both composers and their audiences, led to a growth in scale and length of "public"
compositions. (Composers continued to write shorter, more intimate works for "home
consumption.") The larger instrumental forms (such as sonata-form movements)
tended to become, if not more complex, quite a bit longer. Probably, as the size and
heterogeneity of the audience increased, the general level of musical training and
sophistication declined. Greater length coupled with less musical experience created
the need, mentioned in Chapter III, for striking and easily remembered themes.

Axial melodies have the advantage of combining length and memorability. Because they are not decisively closed, they are easily repeated—either at the same or
at a new pitch level. In this way four measures of music can be extended to eight,
sixteen, or even more. Yet the amount of material—the number of different relationships—to be perceived and remembered is relatively small. Not only is the relationship
between statements of the melody redundant, but so are the relationships within statements. For on a high level, the pattern is reducible to a single tone, and on the lower
one, the second part of the melody is understood as an inverted repetition of the first
part.

Example 99

F♯ and G, we take the D and B to be ornamental. Moreover, though the D and B are chord tones, the harmony which accompanies them is itself an embellishing chord which immediately returns (at the beginning of measure 13) to the tonic harmony and the sonority which preceded it. Even in measure 16, where more patent implications are generated, the sense of motion to different goals is, so to speak, overshadowed by the cadential progression.

The predominant ethos is one of assertive and assured stability. And the impression that change will follow the second statement of the period is as much a result of the feeling that further repetition would be supererogatory as of the strength of specific implicative processes generated by the patterning itself.

Yet specific implicative relationships are not entirely absent. As graph 2 indicates, the linear patterning of the foreground in measures 10 and 14 implies continuation—though not with such urgency that the varied repetition of the pattern and the restatement of the period create any real tension. Only after being restated and reinforced in measures 26 and 34 is this implicative relationship realized, when the melody moves conjunctly from E up to B in measures 38 and 39.

The patterning of measure 16 is more patently implicative. Emphasized by the novelty of disjunct motion and the greater speed of the triplet figure, both the foreground triadic pattern and the second-level pentachordal relationship imply continuation to the high E (graph 3). There is, in addition, as graph 4 indicates, some sense that the potential of the B—which is prominent in itself and stressed by the preceding disjunct-triplet motion—has not been fully actualized. It is actualized after the repetition of the first period, when it becomes the axis-tone in a slightly varied version of the melody. And this creates a still higher level of motion, a motion of eight-measure units, in which the pentachordal relationship between the axis-tones E (in measures 10–17, and their repetition) and B (in measures 26–33) imply continuation to the high E (graph 6).

The statement of the axis melody on the high E is clearly the culmination of the passage, for a number of reasons. The implications of the high-level, period motion (graph 6), of the middle-level pentachordal and low-level triadic patterns (graph 3), and even of the foreground linear motion of measure 26 (graph 2) are all realized when the octave is reached. Both as the goal of preceding motion and as a point of octave definition, the E is particularly stable. The sense of arrival is heightened and signaled by a change in sonority and texture. Violins and woodwinds play the melody in unison, while the lower strings enrich the texture with figuration. The role of the brass instruments is initially harmonic and rhythmic. But just when the linear continuation implied in the first period is realized—when the melody moves beyond G to A and B (measure 39, see graph 2)—the first horn and trumpet, accompanied by the other brass instruments, join in playing the melody, and in so doing, they emphasize the continuation implied at the beginning of the passage. The high B can act as a stable goal not only because it is the fifth of the scale and part of a closed trochaic rhythm, but because, as the note an octave above the upbeat which begins this consummatory statement, it defines the limits of melodic motion.[31] To balance the greater motion of this version of the melody and to emphasize the closure of the whole section, the cadential pattern which follows the B is extended for three measures. But the E to which it moves, though harmonized correctly, is in the wrong register. Not until the coda of the movement is a cadentially satisfactory E presented in the right register.

One final point. Despite the symmetry of the patterning, in which motion above the axis is balanced by motion below it, whatever implications there are seem to be those generated by the patterning above, rather than below, the axis tones. Three reasons help to explain this. First, because the axis-tone is the tonic, the neighbor-note below is understood as part of a cadential pattern. Even though the D in measure 12 is a whole-step, rather than a half-step, below the tonic, its leading-tone function (emphasized and strengthened by its own motion to the dominant, B) is clear and unequivocal. Second, because the model is neither strongly shaped nor clearly closed, the mirror is understood as a dependent reflection—completing and balancing the pattern—rather than as an entity in its own right. And third, the psychology of pattern perception may be such that, generally speaking, motion above a point of reference—for instance, an axis-tone—seems more important, more marked for consciousness, than motion below it. The significance of these *ad hoc* reasons will become apparent in the analysis which follows.

The main melody of the second key area (A♭ major) of the first movement of Franck's Quintet in F Minor for Piano and Strings is also an axial melody (Example 100). It consists of a pair of similar eight-measure periods, each made up of two four-measure phrases. These are related by axial symmetry. In the model, the fifth of the scale, E♭ is embellished by a succession of upper neighbors—a half-step, F♭; a whole-step, F♮; and a diminished

[31] In this connection, see Example 84.

fourth, A♭♭ (see graph 1). As the analysis below the example shows, the rhythmic group is an anapest (⌣⌣¯). From a formal point of view, the pattern is a bar-form (m—m′—n). In the mirror phrase, the E♭ is embellished by lower neighbors at the same intervallic distances. It, too, is an anapest/bar-form structure. The second period (measures 132–139) is like the first, except that the third neighbor-note (C♭) in the model phrase is noticeably further away from the axis-tone—a minor sixth, rather than a diminished fourth—than was previously the case (in measure 126). Both because it is markedly separated from the axis-tone, and because the large skip stresses it (a fact reflected in Franck's dynamic markings), the C♭, though structurally ornamental, is melodically prominent.

This prominence calls attention to the chief basis for implication in the theme as a whole: the neighbor-notes are all potential structural tones. In both model and mirror the first two neighbor-notes (the F♭ and F♮ in the model, and the D and D♭ in the mirror) are stressed weak beats, emphasized by their relative duration and by the anticipation which precedes them. Melodically, they are prominent because they come at the end of a rhythmic pattern. The melodic salience of the third neighbor-notes (the A♭♭ in the model, and the C♭ in the mirror) is even more patent. For they are more noticeably separated from the axis-tone and, because they are approached by disjunct motion, receive additional stress. But what makes the neighbor-notes the continuing focus of aural attention is that, since the structural, axis-tone does no more than persist, they create the only melodic motion, and that motion takes the form of a strongly shaped and rhythmically regular linear pattern. Yet, though the patterning is pronounced, we are aware that it is made of ornamental tones. And this discrepancy between audible prominence and syntactic function implies continuation to an actual structural tone.

At this point, two differences between this melody and the one from Dvořák's "New World" Symphony should be noted. In this melody the axis-tone is not the tonic, but the less stable fifth of the scale. Consequently, motion to the tonic is implied by the tonal organization of the pattern. Secondly, in Franck's melody, both model and mirror are rhythmically closed and clearly structured from a formal point of view. As a result, though the mirror is related to the model by inversion, it is relatively autonomous. For both these reasons, motion below the axis, as well as motion above it, should be implicative.

Example 100

However, though the descending pattern of neighbor-notes may be implicative, it is not forcefully so. Probably this is because motion below an axis
tone is always less pronounced than motion above it. Possibly, too, because
descending patterns tend to have less urgency—to seem less goal-directed—
than ascending ones. Nevertheless, the C in measure 139, and the C♭ which
follows in measure 140, can be considered actualizations of the implications
generated by the preceding pattern of ornamental tones (graph 2b) [32] for
a number of reasons. First, and most important, the linear patterning of
potential tones is so patent that almost any structural tone which fits into
the conjunct patterning will be interpreted as an actualization. As the first
structural tone below the axis-line which has more than an auxiliary function,
the C fulfills this condition. And even though it enters below the whole-note
E♭, which ends the repetition of the mirror, the C is prominent because it
begins both a new voice and a new patterning—a dialogue, through inversion, between the first and second violin (supported by the cello and viola
respectively). Second, the foreground motion of the viola in measure 141,
which condenses and summarizes the pattern of ornamental tones, leads to a
structural C♭. And finally, the higher-level motion from structural C to
structural C♭ can be understood as part of the descending linear pattern.

[32] If a succession of potential tones creates a pattern implying a more or less
specific continuation, then arrival at a structural tone congruent with that pattern
will constitute a satisfactory actualization of *all* the preceding tones. See p. 197.

After a varied repetition of the dialogue between first and second violin, the linear patterning is apparently continued as the piano moves conjunctly down to the A♭ (measures 143–145). But the connection is tenuous at best. For a decisive change in sonority, texture, and even melodic structure [33] mark this as the beginning of a new section. In short, though the descending ornamental tones of the mirror are actualized by a structural tone, the implicative relationships are not forceful, and the arrival at the goal is not striking.

Just the reverse is the case with the ascending pattern of potential structural tones in the model (graph 2). But actualization is delayed. And though linear motion to structural tones does occur in the development section at measures 234 and 238, the most sustained and impressive instance is that which occurs at what I take to be the beginning of the coda. There, as

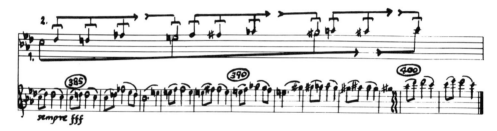

Example 101

Example 101 shows, the final note of the pattern of potential tones becomes the structural axis-tone for the next statement of the model (graphs 1 and 2). This relationship is made explicit at the end of each pattern, where the preceding axis-tone moves by a slurred skip to an anticipation of the next one—for instance, in measure 387. As the sequence continues, a higher-level pattern of disjunct motion by major thirds, C—E—G♯, is established, and continuation is implied (graph 1). Consequently, even though the third statement of the model is broken off after measure 393, we recognize that the implications of the patterning have been realized when the beginning of the pattern is presented on the high C in measure 400.

The stability of the high C is dependent upon the interruption of the patterning which implied it. Because it is completely uniform, the motion by major thirds establishes no point of syntactic closure and stability. It is

[33] Though not in rhythm, or even in register, because the piano part is in the same register as the viola and cello.

circular and might continue indefinitely. Consequently, differentiation is needed if the high C is to function as a goal and point of completion. The interruption creates tension through delay and digression, so that when the C is presented, it is understood to be a point of realization and completion. And it is also for this reason that the restatement of the neighbor-note figure is understood as a return and a closure, rather than as a continuation of the uniform patterning.

Changing-note melodies

Changing-note melodies are superficially similar to axial ones. Like axial ones, they begin and end on the same pitch, which is "surrounded" by upper and lower neighbor-notes. But syntactically they are very different. Instead of being foreground, nonchord tones, the upper and lower neighbors are relatively high-level, structural tones. Consequently, changing-note melodies are not prolongations of a single tone, but involve motion away from and back to stability. Thus they combine high-level, and at times foreground, symmetry with implicative, goal-directed motion. For this reason, they are generally closed in contrast to axial melodies.[34]

The subject of Bach's Fugue in C♯ Minor from Book I of the Well-Tempered Clavier is a clear and unadorned changing-note melody (Example 102). Though the symmetry is one of parallelism rather than inversion, a motion from tonic to leading-tone is balanced by one from supertonic to tonic. Both neighbor-notes are structural tones. The harmony suggested, though not always the harmony presented, is I—V: V—I. Both the explicit

Example 102

[34] Although axial melodies are relatively common in the music of the nineteenth century, changing-note melodies are not. Maybe, because they are closed, they were not compatible with the flowing lyricism favored at the time. On the other hand, changing-note melodies are frequent in the music of the eighteenth and early nineteenth centuries. This is not, I suspect, because of a desire for symmetrical elegance, but because the drama of tension and surprise, of delay and variation, can best be realized when implications are clear and strong.

melodic pattern and the latent harmonic progression imply return to the tonic. As indicated in the graph, the sense of goal-directed motion is strengthened by the gap from B♯ to E, which implies conjunct fill moving to the tonic.[35]

The first movement of Mozart's Oboe Quartet in F Major (K.307) begins with a simple, unpretentions melody which can be comprehended and remembered without difficulty. Its tonal materials are commonplace, its form is regular, and its processes archetypal and familiar. Yet behind this almost folklike facade lie relationships which are both intricate and subtle. It is not the organization of any particular level of patterning that is complex, however, but the relationships among the several levels (Example 103).

The opening eight measures—the melody proper—consist of two phrases: a model and its parallel (graph 1 and 1a). The first phrase begins on F and closes on G; the second, which is sequentially related, begins on E and closes on F. On this level the tune is a symmetrical changing-note pattern. Indeed, it is an exact inversion (or a retrograde) of Bach's fugue subject (Example 102). Its harmonic structure, like that of Bach's fugue subject though different in detail, is both unambiguous and implicative: I—II—V—I. The melody is patently an instance of a changing-note organization.

Each phrase of the larger changing-note organization is in its turn made up of two parts: a model and its complement. In the first phrase, the model consists of a rising third from F to A, and the complement reverses this motion, falling a third from B♭ to G (graph 2). In the second phrase, the model moves from E up to G, and the complement descends a third—from A to F. However, because it can be understood as a continuation of the descending triadic pattern of the first phrase, the E in measure 5 belongs to both phrases of the melody—functioning as the end of the preceding complementary phrase (B♭—G—E) and as the beginning of the model part of the second phrase. Moreover, though they are on a lower hierarchic level, the C in measure 2 and the B♭ in measure 6 so easily fit into this scheme that they too form part of the patterning—making the complementary relationships fully triadic (graph 2a).

If the E belongs to the patterning of the first as well as the second phrase, then, though the high-level changing-note relationship and the partial complementary organization (graph 2) are completed in measure 8, the larger complementary structure (graph 2a) is not. Just as the descending third,

[35] Because the E is not a harmonic tone in relation to B♯, continued disjunct motion is not implied.

B♭—G, was continued to E, so the descending third, A—F, of the second phrase, implies continuation to D. The D is presented in measure 9 (graph 2b), and though it is the resolution of a long appoggiatura, C♯, it is structurally equivalent and temporally parallel to the E in measure 5.[36] This is another instance of the bifurcation of form and process. The melody proper reaches closure in measure 8, but the implicative processes generated by the larger complementary patterning of the second phrase continue beyond this point of cadential articulation.

It is now apparent—though perhaps largely in retrospect—that a still higher-level melodic process is involved: a linear patterning from F to E to D (graph 3). This linear motion also implies continuation. Though the linear motion is more rapid in the following measures, there is no hierarchic discrepancy because the sequential pattern makes clear that the C in measure 10 is equivalent to the preceding D. An unequivocal octave transfer through

Example 103

[36] The parallelism is made more palpable by the conformant relationship between these two points in the melody—that is, because the motion from the F at the end of measure 8 to the C♯ and D is analogous to the higher-level patterning from G(m.4) to E(m.5) to F(m.8).

the tonic triad is followed by continued conjunct motion through B♭ to A.[37] Then, after a delay of five measures (during which the appoggiatura pattern of measures 9 and 10 is repeated an octave higher),[38] the melody moves, as though recapitulating and summarizing the motion of measure 11, to a strong, embellished G, which moves to a cadential F in measure 20. Here the melodic processes generated by the highest level of motion reach closure.

This melody is as clear an example as one could wish for of a strongly-shaped hierarchic structure. On the highest level, the motion is that of a complete and relatively regular descending F-major scale (graph 3); on the next level, the patterning consists of a symmetrical changing-note relationship (graph 1 and 1a); and on the level of the half-phrase, the organization is patently complementary (graph 2a and 2b). Each of these structures is an instance of a well-known, traditional schema. Yet their combination is complex and elegant. The whole is said to be strongly-shaped because the several levels of structure support and reinforce one another.

What about the lower levels of organization? The note-to-note foreground of the first phrase consists of ascending conjunct motion from F to D, followed by descending conjunct motion back to G. But the predominant patterning is clearly triadic. The G in measure 1, the B♭ in measure 2, and so on, are passing-tones. This patterning is begun and emphasized by the upbeat skip of a fourth. Normally there would be little question about the implicative relationships of this sort of patterning. Particularly when preceded by an upbeat in the lower octave, the fifth would tend to function as the relatively stable upper limit of melodic motion (see Examples 76, 84, 85 and 98). In this case, however, linear and triadic continuation to the octave above the tonic, F, is more probable.

It is so largely because of the melodic and rhythmic position of the D in measure 2. Because the parameters do not move congruently, the function of the D is equivocal belonging partly to preceding and partly to following events. Harmonically, it groups with the events which follow, for it is accompanied by a secondary dominant chord (V/II) which moves to a G-minor triad in measure 3. Melodically it is syntactically ambiguous. For, though the sixth degree of the scale in the minor mode clearly implies motion to the fifth, in the major mode conjunct continuation up to the

---

[37] That the B♭ in measure 11 and the A in measure 12 are structural tones is clear from the harmony, which is sketched in below the example.

[38] These measures are not given in Example 103.

tonic is almost equally probable.[39] Though the D can be understood as part of the following triadic pattern (D—Bb—G), it is more patently part of the preceding conjunct motion—following *from* the C, rather than moving toward the next structural tone, Bb. Temporal relationships, however, are the crucial parameter. As the analysis under Example 104 shows, the prevailing rhythm of the first two measures is that of an eighth-note followed by a longer note—basically a dotted quarter-note. Had this pattern been continued, so that the D came as the last eighth-note of measure 2, then the D would have been a relatively inconsequential ornamental tone (an upper neighbor) which, for reasons of proximity, would have been grouped as an upbeat with the following pattern. Because it enters too soon, breaking the established iambic rhythm, the D is not only emphasized, but connected with the preceding C. As a result an impression of linear motion is, so to speak, left hanging in mid air—without satisfactory continuation. Moreover, because the D is a weak afterbeat coming from the C, the C itself is made mobile. Instead of being the goal of an end-accented iamb, it is also the beginning of a trochaic group. The resulting mobility raises the possibility of triadic continuation.

It would be a mistake to exaggerate the forcefulness of this implication or to suggest that it is accompanied by a noticeable sense of incompleteness. The strength of the higher levels of patterning is such that the melody is felt to be satisfactorily closed in measure 20. Nevertheless, the listener is, I believe, somehow aware of the possibility of linear, and perhaps triadic, continuation to the high F. And it seems clear that Mozart was too. For though long delayed, the high F does occur just before the final cadence of the movement— and it is reached by explicit and unequivocal conjunct motion from the D (example 104).[40]

[39] This difference is probably a result of proximity relationships. In the minor mode, the sixth is only a semitone away from the fifth and is separated from the seventh by a whole step in the "melodic" minor and by an augmented second in the "harmonic" minor. In the major mode, on the other hand, the sixth is equally distant from both fifth and seventh.

[40] This example suggests that in the Viennese classical style foreground simplicity tends to be complemented by hierarchic and implicative complexity. In the style of nineteenth-century romanticism the opposite is the case: foreground complexity— chromaticism, extensive use of nonchord tones, and nuances of temporal organization and harmonic color—is frequently coupled with hierarchic simplicity.

Example 104

CONTEXTUAL DISCREPANCY

Context was not an important consideration in the melodies analyzed in the preceding sections. Attention was directed to the implications generated by an order in the pattern itself. What was implied was the continuation of a process until some relatively stable goal was reached—even though arrival at such a goal was at times deflected or delayed. In this section we will be concerned, though all too briefly, with a different kind of implicative relationship—one in which a discrepancy between the structure of an event and its syntactical or formal context suggests that a change of function is probable. Implications are generated not because a pattern suggests continuation to an internal goal, but rather because an event is felt to have a potential function which has not been satisfactorily actualized.

Potential tones and rhythms

A potential structural tone, to repeat the definition given earlier, is one whose melodic prominence is not matched by its structural importance. More specifically, it is a weakbeat marked for consciousness in some way—often because it is approached and left by disjunct motion, and generally speaking, the larger the disjunction, the more prominent and more strongly implicative the note. Potential structural tones may occur singly or in a patterned series. In the former case, the melodically prominent weakbeat is actualized when the same pitch subsequently occurs as an accented structural tone. In the latter case, the whole series is "resolved" when a subsequent note understood as part of the pattern is an accented structural tone. Because several potential structural tones have already been discussed,[41] only two will be analyzed here.

[41] See Chapter IV, Examples 50 and 53; and Chapter V, Examples 66, 95, and 100–101.

The Burlesca from Bach's Partita No. 3 for Harpsichord contains a clear example of a series of potential structural tones (Example 105). The melody of the soprano voice, before the cadence that closes the first part of the movement, is a bilevel structure. The primary level consists of a conjunct pattern moving from C through D to E (graph 2). This pattern is embellished by a subsidiary line of potential tones a sixth above. The A and B in measures 10 and 12 are aurally prominent but are structurally unimportant weakbeats (graph 1). Continuation to C is implied not only because the secondary level is itself a clearly patterned conjunct motion, but because it parallels the primary line. Consequently, when the E occurs in measure 13, its sixth, C, is implied. Instead of coming on the third beat of measure 14 (the previous metric position of the secondary line), the C comes on the accent. It is a structural tone, actualizing the implications latent in the preceding series of potential tones. Both for this reason, and because it is an octave above the C in measure 9 which began the melodic process,[42] the C in measure 14 is an important goal.

Indeed, the rising line of eighth-notes in measure 13 suggests the C as the goal of the primary level of patterning also. But this is not the case. The implicative relationships are more complex. In the first place, the patterning of the primary level of motion has been in two-measure units; and the eighth-note "continuation" is obviously on a much lower level. If the hierarchic levels are kept straight, the motion from E to C must be analyzed as disjunct, and the C would not be a goal, but part of an implicative gap of a minor sixth. Though this relationship undoubtedly helps to define the

Example 105

[42] That both C's are harmonized by subdominant chords in root position emphasizes this relationship.

direction of motion in measures 14 and 15, the E, reinforced by its occurrence in the alto voice, continues in the aural imagination of the listener and,
picked up in measure 15, moves to D♯ and then back to E in measure 16.
In other words, E is, and remains, the main melodic goal because its occurrence in measure 13 is unsatisfactory—primarily for harmonic reasons: it is
accompanied by an unstable, first-inversion triad, and the triad itself is part
of a uniform chromatic bass-line which lacks syntactic articulation.

While the motion of the primary level is thus suspended, a degree of
bilevel patterning nevertheless continues. For the descending, conjunct
motion from C to E also contains a subsidiary level (graph 3), though one
that is much less obtrusive than that created by the line of potential structural
tones. And this subsidiary, perhaps tertiary level, seems to derive in part from
the rising eighth-notes in measure 13.[43] As the analysis indicates, all these
levels converge to the E which closes this part of the Burlesca.

Though the actualization of potential structural tones is, as a rule,
proximate, it may be remote—it may take place after the closure of the
main melodic pattern. Such remote actualization occurs in the Minuetto
movement of Haydn's "London" Symphony (No. 104) (Example 106).
Consequently, to explain how the implications generated by the potential
structural tones are actualized, later parts of the movement, as well as the
opening melody, must be considered.

The main melody, which opens the movement, is an interesting mixture
of different kinds of structural relationships. The first phrase is essentially
axial—an A embellished by neighbor-notes which are stressed by *sforzandi*
(graph 2).[44] The first two neighbor-notes, though stressed, are not melodically prominent, but the third, D, is—even though it is connected through
the B to the axial A. For not only is it separated from the axial tone by disjunct motion, but it is both the upper tonic to which the fifth, A, might
have moved, and it is an octave above the upbeat which begins the melody.
Because at the same time it is also rhythmically unstable and structurally
weak, the D is a potential structural tone (graph 1).

Because its melodic position and rhythmic function is like that of the
D, *in retrospect* the B in measure 1 seems possibly to have been more than a
mere embellishment. And this possibility is given support by the relationship

[43] It is related by conformance to the previous sixteenth-note figures.

[44] The role of the *sforzandi* in the articulation of rhythmic groups is discussed in
Grosvenor W. Cooper and Leonard B. Meyer, *The Rhythmic Structure of Music*
(Chicago: University of Chicago Press, 1960), pp. 26 and 140–141.

between these pitches in measure 3. But the function of the B as a potential structural tone is not unequivocal and explicit until measure 6. There, though it remains rhythmically unstable and structurally weak, it is melodically prominent (graph 1a), for it is both stressed by a *sforzando* (relating it to the earlier D) and above and separated from the main conjunct patterning of the melody.

The B is also important because it strengthens the closure of the first part of the Minuetto. Let us consider why. The axial A is implicative not only because for tonal reasons the fifth of the scale tends to move toward the tonic, but also because it is preceded by an auxiliary gap—the upbeat from D. After a renewal of the gap at the beginning of the second phrase, the implied fill is realized by descending conjunct motion to the D in measure 8 (graph 3). The realization, however, is so regular and "easy" that a reversal is needed to articulate satisfactory closure. The skip from B down to C♯ does this: by creating a marked gap, it implies conjunct motion in the opposite direction—and it is followed by rising motion to the tonic, D.

The B is also important, and hence emphasized, rhythmically. For though the last group in the first section, like the preceding ones, is an amphibrach, it is twice as long as the others. As a result, the second phrase is an end-accented anapest (level 2, in the analysis under the example), and the whole melody is an end-accented iamb (level 3). The melody is closed rhythmically as well as melodically.

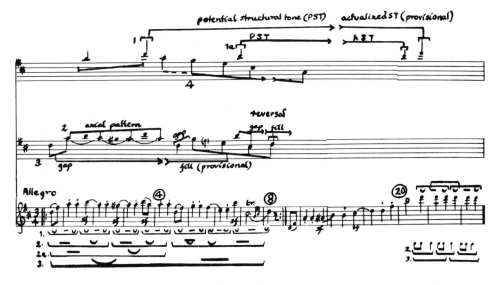

Example 106

Yet closure is by no means definitive. Most important, there has been no tonal departure and only minimal structural tension in relation to which return and stability would create strong closure. But there are other reasons as well, and these are effective precisely because no high-level processes have been generated. The first is a matter of hierarchic equivalence. The established unit of melodic-rhythmic motion in the first six measures is three quarter-notes long. But the F♯ in measure 5 is only a quarter-note; it is not a structural tone on this level of motion. Consequently, the conjunct fill implied by the initial gap is only provisionally realized. Indeed, this aspect of the patterning of the second phrase implies, not the D which follows, but continuation to A—which proves to be the first structural note after the double bar (graph 4). Not until after the melody is repeated in the second part of the movement—as the reader will discover if he turns back to Example 58—does the F♯ occur as a structural tone. There the pattern is so striking and the octave displacement so clear that the change in register does not obscure the realization of implications: the conjunct motion from G to F♯ in measures 41 and 42, and from E to D from measure 48 to 49 is both explicit and hierarchically satisfactory.

Another reason why closure is not definitive, and our main concern here, is that the potential structural tones remain to be actualized. They are so—or at least partly so—at the beginning of the second part of the form. The triadic upbeat which begins this part of the movement does two things: it leads to the A implied by the motion of the second phrase of the melody (graph 4); and it implies continuation to a structural D in a higher octave —as did the upbeat which begins the movement. The A is realized immediately, and the B and D follow without delay. Though the B occurs in measure 18, the potential tone implied earlier is realized in measure 20 (graph 1a), where the B comes in the proper register, as the goal of a cadential progression (V/VI—VI), and as the final note of an end-accented rhythmic group. The D occurs as an accented note in the proper register in measure 21 (graph 1). But as the seventh of a secondary dominant (V⁷/V), rather than the root of a tonic chord, it lacks stability. It is only a provisional actualization.

The stability of the D is also weakened by the temporal organization. The D is not the goal of a closed, end-accented group, because repetition precludes the possibility of unequivocal patterning. All that remains is meter, and even that is threatened. For while the repeated D's are still presumably grouped in threes, the accompaniment, indicated by the sketch under the staff, is in twos.

The kind of implicative relationship involved here is not, strictly speaking, an aspect of melody: it is what I have called the weakening of shape.[45] Not only is the metric organization weakened by the cross meter, but melodic patterning disappears in the succession of repeated D's. The lack of distinct and regular patterning creates a sense of tension and uncertainty, itself implicative of a return to the psychic security of stable, unambiguous shapes.[46]

The implications of the D, provisionally actualized in measure 21, are more than regenerated when the melody is repeated in the second part of the Minuetto. For there the D's are, if anything, both more prominent and less structurally important than in the original statement of the melody. But the function of the D as a potential structural tone is even more striking in measures 42 and 44 (Example 58). In both measures, the D is markedly separated from the main melodic motion, and in the second, it is followed by a grand pause—left without immediate continuation. Its continuation and its actualization—and that of all the preceding potentially structural D's— takes place at the very end of the movement, when the final D occurs as the goal of an end-accented rhythm, with tonic harmony, and in the right register.[47]

Though potential rhythms are considerably less common than potential structural tones, the last movement of this same Haydn Symphony contains a clear example of this kind of implicative process. It occurs in the passage which begins in measure 19, following the second statement of the main melody of the movement (Example 107). The melodic-rhythmic pattern of the passage is derived from the penultimate measure of the melody (measure 17). The second half of that measure (the E) acts as a pivot linking it to measure 18. It also groups with the preceding A for both harmonic and rhythmic reasons: harmonically, because the E and A belong to and are harmonized by the same triad; rhythmically, because the trochaic grouping established in the first two measures of the phrase tend to be continued (level 1). The E and F♯ are also grouped with the following downbeat both because of their melodic proximity to the D, and because the more rapid motion of the final eighth-notes make both the subprimary (¹) and primary level (1) trochees mobile and anacrustic.

[45] See *Emotion and Meaning in Music*, Chapter 5.

[46] Harmony which is patently patterned is specifically implicative, and it gives direction to the implications generated by the weakening of the other parameters.

[47] Perhaps because of its prominence, Haydn actualizes the B as a structural tone in measure 44—even though its previous actualization in measure 18 should have sufficed.

In measures 19–21, however, the second half of the measure does not act as an upbeat to the following measure, for two main reasons. First, as noted in Chapter IV, repetition does not make for cohesion but for separation. The rhythmic identity and intervallic similarity between these measures is such that each is perceived as an individual entity. Secondly, the marked pitch disjunction between the end of one pattern and the beginning of the next prevents the eighth-notes from functioning as upbeats. The two parts of each measure cohere not only because they belong to the same harmony, but because they are patently trochaic.

The trochaic pattern is strongly reinforced by the orchestration. As the abstraction of the accompaniment rhythm (graph 4) shows, the brass and tympani (stems down) play a half-note on the first part of each measure. By thus stressing the accent, they help to create beginning-accented trochees on level one (1). The woodwinds and lower strings (stems up) reinforce this organization and, in addition, create trochaic groups on the subprimary level (i). Nevertheless, despite all the aspects of the patterning which make us perceive the groups as trochees, we are aware, both because of their relative speed and because of their previous function as pivots, that the final eighth-notes in these measures *should* be upbeats (graph 1). These potential rhythms imply a pattern in which the final quarter-note of each measure will be grouped with the following downbeat in an end-accented rhythm.

Example 107

The implications generated by the rhythmic organization are complemented and strengthened by the melodic patterning. For though the rhythm
of the paired measures is identical, making for separation, there is melodic
motion between them. Because register is conspicuous and melodic-rhythmic
activity is greater, the second half of each of these measures captures attention. From a melodic point of view, they are much like potential structural
tones. As a result, we are specially aware of the relationship between the
G and B of measure 19 and the F♯ and A of measure 20,[48] and the linear
pattern thus established implies continuation to a point of relative stability.
And the final eighth-notes of each measure create a gap which implies that
conjunct motion in the opposite direction, filling the gap, will follow
(graph 3).

All these implications are realized in the following measures. The final
eighth-notes of measure 22 become actualized upbeats, perceived as connected with—moving to—the accent in measure 23. This patterning is supported by a change in orchestration. For the first time, the accompanying
instruments play a pattern which moves from the last beat of one measure to
the first beat of the following one. The flutes play such a rhythm from the
last beat of measure 22 to the first beats of measure 23, and then all the
instruments play the rhythm from measure 23 to measure 24. The foreground gap is filled as the A at the end of measure 22 moves to G, and the
higher-level linear patterning continues to E—and beyond.[49] The resolution
of the pent-up tension, caused by the delay of goal-directed melodic and
rhythmic processes, requires time and the compensatory emphasis of reiteration.[50] Not only are both the upbeat rhythm and the gap-fill figure repeated
as the higher-level pattern continues, but measures 23 and 24 are themselves
twice repeated before the impetus is sufficiently dissipated, allowing the
passage to move to temporary closure on the D in measure 29.

Closely related to potential rhythms are those which can be character-

[48] The motion between first beats (from B to A) seems somehow subsidiary—
almost as though the temporal order of an "oompah" bass pattern had been reversed,
with the repeated notes of the accompaniment figure coming on the accent instead of
on the weak beat.

[49] Because the E cannot act as a goal, the linear motion continues and, after two
repetitions of measures 23 and 24, reaches temporary stability on D. This continuation
is indicated by the arrow at the end of graph-line 2.

[50] Because this is the beginning of a transition passage, the marked closure of a
reversal would be out of place. The accumulated momentum of preceding events
must be allowed to slow down of its own accord.

ized as incomplete. Rhythmic incompleteness is not only implicative in its own right, but qualifies and complements the implications generated by more specifically melodic relationships. However, since this kind of patterning is discussed elsewhere,[51] a brief account and a single example will suffice here.

The existence of similarity and difference is, as noted earlier,[52] an essential condition for patterning. This is as true of temporal patterns—rhythms—as it is of melodic or harmonic events. If a series of events is so uniform that it provides no basis for distinguishing accents from weakbeats, then the rhythmic structure will be incomplete.[53] And because it is incomplete, it is implicative, implying the probability—even the necessity—of a differentiation to which the succession of like events can be related. Because the repeated note or pattern is in this sense goal-directed, the series is generally understood to be anacrustic—a succession of weakbeats moving toward an organizing, differentiating accent.[54]

An incomplete rhythm may arise on the lowest hierarchic level, when a single tone or chord is repeated without change in duration, dynamics, or timbre; or it may occur on a higher level, when a pattern, itself internally structured, is repeated exactly. The higher-level incompleteness is the more effective and, hence, the more common. For a differentiated foreground structure provides the satisfaction of orderly patterning and at the same time makes it difficult for the listener to impose subjective differentiation on the higher-level uniformity—as he can easily do when, say, a single note is repeated.

Because they are unstable and goal-directed, incomplete rhythms are most frequently encountered in conjunction with the melodic mobility and harmonic tension characteristic of transition passages and development sections. But they occur elsewhere as well: even within primarily thematic

[51] Cooper and Meyer, *The Rhythmic Structure of Music*, pp. 85f., 149f., and passim.

[52] P. 260.

[53] Temporal uniformity must be complemented by uniformity in other parameters, for changes in pitch, dynamics, harmony, and timbre can become the basis for rhythmic differentiation. Indeed, changes in other parameters will tend to be specially noticeable precisely because temporal relationships are unchanged.

[54] Anapest rhythms, frequently the basis for phrase structure in the examples in this book (see Examples 79, 86, and 100), are nascent incomplete rhythms. For when a pattern is repeated, even at a different pitch level, the similarity between events tends to weaken temporal patterning and is taken to imply motion to a larger group that serves as an organizing accent and goal.

statements—though not as part of stable, cadential ones, such as closing themes. This kind of implicative relationship is much more common in the dramatic style of classicism and romanticism than in the Baroque style, for exact repetition, which rhythmic incompleteness requires, is not consonant with the flow of contrapuntal voice-leading favored in the earlier period. Thus incomplete rhythms are characteristic of Beethoven's music—for instance in the first movement of the "Eroica" Symphony (measures 128–131 and 272–279)—but not of Bach's.

The Scherzo of Bruckner's Seventh Symphony begins with an incomplete rhythm—four measures which are exactly alike (Example 108). The lowest level (i) is clearly and strongly structured. Accent and weak beats create a relatively closed dactylic grouping: the initial eighth-notes make the second beat seem stressed and thereby diminish the tendency of the last quarter-note to act as an anacrusis to the following measure. On the next level (1), however, there is no differentiation and, consequently, no basis for grouping.

Because beginnings are generally marked for consciousness, the first measure is assumed to be accented—but only momentarily. When exact repetition follows, our understanding of the first measure is changed. In retrospect it is understood, together with the next three measures, as anacrustic and goal-directed. An event with which the unpatterned repetition can be patterned, and which will serve as an accent for the series of first-level (1) weak beats is implied. The motto melody, played by the trumpet in measures 5–8, provides the necessary differentiation and is the goal of the preceding measures.

Example 108

The first four measures are implicative melodically, as well as rhythmically, in two ways. Negatively, we are sure that this is not the "real" musical substance—a theme or melody—but only an ostinatolike introduction. We feel this both because, taken as a whole, the relationships are additive and formal rather than syntactic and processive, and because our experience with tonal music tells us that this kind of structure does not normally constitute the main basis for melodic organization.

On the positive side, the relationships within the repeated motive are syntactic, and they generate specific implications. Though these relationships may seem minimal—almost lost in the insistent repetition and overshadowed by the entrance of the motto melody—they are not inconsequential. Since the smallest unit of regular motion is a quarter-note, the eighth-note B is only a passing-tone. Consequently, the first melodic relationship is the third from A to C. The third implies disjunct continuation—to the fifth, and perhaps the octave as well—and, functioning as a gap, conjunct motion in the opposite direction. The second of these possibilities is realized within the motive: the B on the third beat fills the gap. The linear pattern (from B to C) which results is itself implicative—suggesting continuation to A, and perhaps beyond (graph 2). Both the disjunct continuation through E to A and the conjunct descending motion to A and beyond are provisionally realized in measures 6 and 7.[55] Even this provisional realization is, however, overshadowed by the entrance of the motto melody in the trumpet. Satisfactory realizations of both implicative relationships occur later in the movement, but in a key other than the tonic. But in the coda of the Scherzo, realization takes place in the tonic: first, the continuation of the conjunct pattern leads to the lower A (graphs 2 and 2a); then, the continuation of the disjunct motion leads through E to an octave A—and there the movement ends (graphs 1 and 1a).[56]

Melodic gesture and potentiality

Earlier in this chapter, melodies were grouped according to the kind of patterning which generated implicative relationships—that is, as being linear, triadic, gap-fill, complementary, and so on. But other modes of classification are also possible. Not surprisingly, melodies which perform the same general function in a particular kind of composition often have

[55] The E is only a provisional realization because it comes on a weak eighth-note; the linear continuation is so, because it does not follow from the generating conjunct motion.

[56] Because violas, celli and basses play these patterns one, two, and three octaves below the pitches played by the violins (which are the ones given in the Example), registral implications are satisfactorily realized.

common characteristics, a kind of family resemblance. Some melodies seem typical of the beginning of sonata-form movements; others are members of the class of closing themes. Some melodies are characteristic fugue subjects; others seem like themes upon which a set of variations might be built. A good number of melodies cannot be classified in this way because they are more or less neutral with respect to function.

At present there is, to the best of my knowledge, no adequate typology of the compositional gestures of tonal music—though a number of scholars are, I believe, doing work in this field.[57] Such a typology is sorely needed in analytic criticism. Creating it will require the close cooperation of the disciplines of style analysis and music theory. The account given here does not pretend to be even a beginning. Rather, after a number of preliminary remarks—based, unfortunately, upon too small a sample and too little study— it seeks merely to illustrate how this sort of implication works.

Typical compositional gestures do not appear to be defined primarily by internal melodic structure. One kind of melodic patterning—say, a gap-fill structure—can evidently be the basis for a number of different kinds of compositional gestures: a fugue subject, a sonata-allegro theme, or the melody of a nocturne. Special rhythms, usually in combination with a particular kind of intervallic structure, often serves as a sign of a type of gesture: for instance, a fanfarelike melody or a march tune. Harmony, too, may play an important role in specifying the function of a melody. Formal organization, however, appears to be most important of all, defining and limiting compositional possibility. For instance, an antecedent-consequent structure can function as the opening melody of a sonata-form movement or as the first part of a theme upon which variations will be based, but it is too patently divided into phrases and too closed to serve as the subject of a fugue.

To a considerable extent, then, our understanding of the function of a compositional gesture depends upon its own characteristic features and internal structure. But it also depends upon convention and practice—and the implications generated by gestures are no less influential because this is the case. A typical melodic gesture is as much a component of a musical style as are tonal syntax and archetypal melodic or rhythmic patterns. A competent listener understands not only the implications generated by tonal, melodic, and rhythmic relationships within a pattern, but the functional potential of the pattern as a whole. This is partly the result of his having learned, through

---

[57] Because gesture and ethos are intimately connected, Frank Kirby's study of the "Characteristic Symphony" may also be important. See Chapter III, pp. 68f.

experience as a listener and perhaps performer, how different kinds of gestures tend to behave.

Characteristic melodic gestures usually occur in appropriate and familiar contexts. When they do, a more or less specific compositional procedure is implied, and perhaps formal organization as well. Such implications may be realized directly, or they may be delayed for a time. In some cases, however, there is a discrepancy between the normal function of a gesture and its actual use in a composition. When this occurs, what is implied is that the gesture will probably be presented in a context consonant with its customary and characteristic function.

The Finale of Schumann's Piano Quartet in E♭ Major, Opus 47, begins with a melodic gesture which anyone familiar with the style of tonal music will immediately recognize as calling for contrapuntal development—probably as a fugue or fugato (Example 109). However, polyphonic textures and contrapuntal procedures are not common in compositions of the period. The question is: what is the basis for this recognition of melodic potential?

Example 109

First of all, it is *not* primarily a matter of texture. The first three notes are accompanied by full, sonorous chords. But even had the movement begun with a monophonic or unison texture, this would have been only a contributory clue, not a sufficient condition for the recognition of gestural potential. Many melodies in both eighteenth- and nineteenth-century compositions are for solo instrument or ensemble playing in unison or octaves. But polyphonic treatment is by no means implied. Three examples come to mind: the opening melody of Mozart's Sonata for Violin and Piano in E Minor (K.304); the beginning of the first movement of Brahms' Quintet in F Minor for Piano and Strings; and the main melody, played by a solo flute, of Debussy's *Prélude à l'Après-Midi d'un Faune*.

The gesture suggests polyphonic texture because this kind of patterning—with its assertive gap and contrasting, running fill—is the basis for countless fugue subjects and contrapuntal compositions of the Baroque period: for instance, the subject of the C-Major Fugue from Book II of the

Well-Tempered Clavier (Example 110A). And in our own time, Stravinsky employs this kind of structure in the first movement of the Octet for Winds, when he wants to create a Baroquelike contrapuntal texture (Example 110B). But prevalent conventions and persuasive traditions are not as a rule arbitrary. Repeated use indicates that the gesture is especially suited to—indeed, calls for—contrapuntal treatment.

Example 110

The melody is a gap-fill structure (Example 109). The parts, the gap and the fill, are distinct, so that they can be used separately as well as together; and each has a distinctive profile, so that it will be recognizable even when the texture becomes complex. Moreover, the parts are different not only in function, but in rate of foreground motion: the gap consists primarily of quarter-notes, the fill of sixteenths. As a result, gap and fill can be contrapuntally combined, yet retain their identity (Example 113).

The marked motivic contrast has another virtue. It allows the parts to be clearly defined without the need for internal closure. The pattern is a single process whose momentum is not diminished by cadential articulation. The structure is potentially continuous—a desideratum in polyphonic music—in other ways too.

The fill part of the melody consists of a series of thirds, C—A♭—F—D—B♭, which ends when a reversal creates—almost forces—temporary closure on E♭ (Example 109). Following this, the viola begins the fill part of the pattern and extends it sequentially (Example 111). Though the pattern is modified, both by the skip of a sixth and by a change in the rate at which thirds succeed one another, the underlying organization remains a continuous triadic motion (graph 1). The sequential patterning of the second-level structure which is also triadic (graph 2), enhances the sense of on-going flow. And this is true of the highest level as well: there, the melody is linear, implying continuation to E♭ which is realized a measure later—first in the viola and then in the piano (graph 3).

Example 111

The gap part of the melody also initiates a linear pattern—from B♭ to C. When the F comes on the accent at the beginning of the third measure, the possibility of sequential continuation, a falling fifth followed by a rising sixth, is evident (Example 112). This possibility is actualized in the passage

Example 112

given in Example 113, where the essential components of the melody are presented as part of a sequence, and in imitation at the octave and fifth.[58]

Example 113

[58] Sequential imitation of a somewhat different sort occurs earlier in the movement —beginning at the end of measure 72.

But Schumann reserves what he clearly considers to be the culmination
—the ultimate actualization of the melody's potential—for the beginning of

Example 114

the coda. There the gap part of the pattern, extended by sequence and by a rhythmic motive from a transition passage, becomes the subject in a canonic-fugal exposition which is accompanied by the sixteenth-note fill pattern (Example 114).

The phrase given in Example 115 is unmistakably a cadential gesture. The harmonic pattern, ending I_4^6—V^7—I, is a traditionally established closing progression. The rise to the tonic in the second measure is a common penultimate motion in closing themes—for instance, the one which comes at the end of the slow movement of Mozart's String Quartet in D Major (Example 132). The remainder of the phrase, a descending motion from fifth to tonic, is equally characteristic: a similar pattern brings the slow movement of Mozart's Haffner Symphony to its final cadence (Example 89). Yet this is the *opening* phrase of the slow introduction which begins Haydn's Symphony No. 97 in C Major.

Example 115

Clearly there is a discrepancy between the customary, cadential function of this characteristic gesture and the use Haydn makes of it here. It should come not at the beginning of an event, but at the end. And it does: it closes the slow introduction. But the discrepancy is so striking that it is not fully resolved by this preliminary closure. As the eighteenth-century theorist, Johann Mattheson, wrote: "One can make use of many ordinary and well-known devices. Cadences, for example, are quite common . . . and may be found in every piece. When, however, they are used at the beginning of a piece, they become something *special*, since they normally belong at the end." [59]

That Haydn, too, considers such use "something *special*" is shown in the fact that this melody returns as the closing theme of the sonata-form

[59] From Hans Lenneberg's translation of portions of *Der vollkommene Capellmeister* (1739) in his article, "Johann Mattheson on Affect and Rhetoric in Music," *Journal of Music Theory*, II, 1 (April 1958), 70.

structure. At the end of the exposition section it is transformed into an even more obviously cadential pattern—a kind of dancelike figure (Example 116). In the recapitulation (measures 240–262) its importance is emphasized when it becomes the basis for a passage which moves through a series of keys to the first dominant harmony of the coda.

Example 116

ARCHETYPAL SCHEMATA

From time to time throughout this book reference has been made to archetypal patterns and to traditional schemata. Though not so labeled, all the melodic types analyzed in this chapter might be thought of as archetypal patterns, and the compositional gestures discussed just above might be regarded as traditional schemata. The subject is so significant that it merits a section of its own.

To recognize this significance, recall an observation made in the first chapter: particular events are invariably understood as members of some class. Archetypal patterns and traditional schemata are the classes—"the rules of the game," in Koestler's phrase—in terms of which particular musical events are perceived and comprehended. No melody, however original and inventive, is an exception to this principle. Indeed, the concepts of originality and invention—as distinguished from the eccentric and the bizarre—presume relationship between a particular instance and the class or norm to which it belongs. Furthermore, as I have argued elsewhere,[60] the delight of intelligent mental play and the excitement of its complement, affective experience, are significantly dependent upon the deviation of a particular musical event from the archetype or schema of which it is an instance.

Such norms are abstractions. One cannot find an archetypal gap-fill melody or an ideal cadential schema in the literature of tonal music. But

[60] *Emotion and Meaning in Music,* Chapter 1 and passim.

it does not follow that they are remote or detached from actual musical experience. Just as the speaker of a language understands and responds to verbal utterances according to the types to which they belong—prose or poetry, emotive exclamation or reasoned argument, declarative assertion or interrogative alternative—so the competent listener understands and responds to the melody from Strauss' *Till Eulenspiegel* (Example 85) partly in terms of its triadic structure, to the subject of Bach's D-Minor Fugue (Example 77) in terms of its gap-fill and triadic organization, and to the theme of Schumann's Piano Quartet (Example 109) in terms of its potential for contrapunal treatment. To take the analogy to language still further beginning the movement of a symphony with a cadential gesture, as Haydn does, is like beginning a story with the words: "and they lived happily ever after."

In theory it is possible to distinguish between archetypal patterns and schemata. The former would be those patterns which arise as the result of physiological and psychological constants presumed innate in human behavior. The latter would be those norms which were the result of learning. But the distinction breaks down in practice. For most traditionally established norms have some basis in innate constants, and, on the other hand, patterns derived from innate constants become parts of tradition. This being the case, the terms will be used more or less interchangeably, and the phrase "archetypal schema" will be used to refer to the general class of stylistic norms.

The difficulty of distinguishing between learned and innate patternings is illustrated by the main, and opening, melody of the slow movement of Brahms' Sonata for Violin and Piano in G Major (Example 117). Like the beginning of Haydn's Symphony No. 97 (Example 115), it is a cadential gesture. But whereas Haydn's gesture reaches its close without significant delay, implying change of function but not further melodic motion, Brahms' gesture does not. Consequently, both continuation to realization and change of function are implied.

Presumably innate modes of perception and patterning tend to characterize the gesture. The melody begins on the third of the scale, G. From a tonal point of view, therefore, descending motion to the tonic is probable (Example 117, graph 1). The actual patterning begins with a gap of a third, G—B♭, which implies conjunct fill moving toward the tonic (graph 2).[61] Moreover, because upbeats are seldom longer than downbeats in this style,

---

[61] Triadic continuation to the high E♭ is not implied because the B♭ is relatively stable—the goal of an end-accented rhythm—rather than weak and mobile. In this connection, see the discussions of Examples 62 and 63, above.

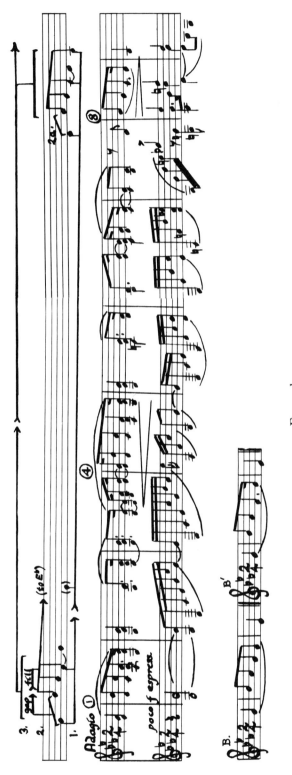

Example 117

once the A♭ follows within the first quarter-note of the measure, we suspect (in retrospect) that the B♭ should be understood as an "unconsummated" appoggiatura—a surmise confirmed when the motive is repeated in measures 4 and 18 (Example 118).

The most regular and "normal" continuation would have been conjunct motion directly down to the tonic, as shown in part B of Example 117. Avoiding this obvious and dull possibility, however, the motive skips down to the F, creating a complementary gap which is filled by the following G. For both rhythmic and harmonic reasons, the G is understood to be an *échappée* implying motion directly to the tonic, E♭. In short, the motive *should* have been like that in part B′ of Example 117. But the G proves (again, in retrospect) to be an anticipation: G, rather than E♭, follows on the first beat of measure 2.[62]

The first part of the melody is repeated in syncopated rhythm in measures 4 and 5, and then the linear motion is continued to the D, where the motive is stated on the dominant. This time it is properly continued, as the *échapée* (D) moves to an accented B♭ (graph 2a). Though this actualization reassures the listener that his understanding of the pattern is correct, he also knows, for tonal reasons, that it is only provisional.[63]

After an eight-measure melodic and harmonic development, the melody returns (Example 118). The implied E♭ is again avoided. Then a sequence based upon the first three notes of the motive moves the pattern up a third. This enlarged motion makes the repetition of the F—G pattern in measure 21 particularly prominent. Once more, however, G is substituted for the probable E♭. Actualization finally takes place in the next measures: preceded by an anacrusis (D—C), F leads through an *échapée* G to E♭. The rhythmic augmentation—doubling the duration of the F and G—not only emphasizes their cadential character, but seems an appropriate compensation for the continued delay of motion to E♭. This cadence ends the first part of the movement and, as it does so, realizes the implied goal of the opening motive and its potential function as a closing gesture.

[62] Because they come on weak beats, are not preceded by dominants, and are the beginnings of motives, the E♭'s in measures 2 and 3 are not goals. Consequently, they cannot act as even provisional realizations of the implications generated by the opening motive.

[63] The arrival at an accented B♭ is important not only because it confirms the listener's idea of how the motive should end, but because, as the octave below the first accent, it is understood as defining the main area of melodic activity. As a result, it seems unlikely that the high E♭ will be the goal of this melody.

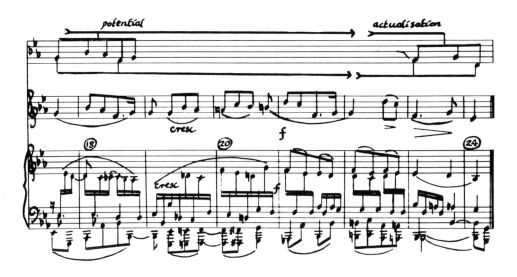

Example 118

However natural or innate the implicative relationships generated by the structure of the melody, their force and specificity is also, and significantly, the result of learning. The implied continuation and the motivic actualization can be avoided again and again because our repeated encounters with this sort of patterning makes us confident that it is cadential—that it will sooner or later reach closure more or less as expected. Two examples, chosen because they are in the same key and the same tempo, indicate that this is a familiar and traditional cadential gesture (Example 119A and B).

Example 119

The first (A) is the closing figure from the slow movement of Mozart's String Quartet in B♭ Major (K.458). No explication is needed: it is self-evident that the bracketed figure (m) belongs to the same family as Brahms' gesture—indeed, it lacks only the *échapée*, G. The second example (B) is taken from the Cavatina of Beethoven's String Quartet in B♭ Major, opus 130 —to my mind, one of the most exquisite and moving movements in the repertory of Western music. The four measures (8–11) given at the beginning of the example bring the first melodic pattern to a close. Measures 8 and 9 belong to what might be called the family of cadential-*échapée* gestures (as does Brahms' melody)—except that the *échapée* functions as an anticipation until the cadence at the end of the first part of the movement. The motive (m′) in measures 10 and 11 is a member of the same fifth-to-tonic class as Mozart's cadential figure and as Brahms' melody. Both kinds of closing gestures—the fifth-to-tonic and the cadential *échapée*—are joined together in measures 63 and 64, where they form the melody of the last authentic cadence of Beethoven's Cavatina.

Archetypal schemata need not, of course, be cadential gestures. The last movement of Beethoven's Fourth Symphony, which Sir George Grove characterized as a "*perpetuum mobile*," [64] begins with a gesture whose infectious verve and piquant wit suggest continuation, contrast, and development. To appreciate the complex and subtle relationships among events within the melody, one must consider the implications of the initial sixteenth-note motive, m (Example 120A). The motive consists of the tonic, B♭, ornamented by a lower neighbor-note and followed by the skip of a third to D. Thus reduced to essentials, it is a major third (120B) which can be understood either as part of a triadic pattern implying continuation to F, and perhaps the upper tonic as well (120C); or as the disjunct part of a gap-fill pattern implying C, and perhaps sequential motion to D and beyond (120D). Such sequential motion is probable because, once the C is reached, a higher-level linear pattern arises, and it in turn implies continuation to a point of relative stability or closure. Moreover, to the extent that it is more than ornamental, the neighbor-note pattern from A to B♭ seems to imply linear continuation, for this sort of pattern occurs in various guises throughout the period of tonal music (120E). Finally the implicative openness of the motive comes in no small measure from the D's rhythmic weakness and functional mobility (120B). Had the neighbor-note figure been an upbeat and the D an accented goal (120F), triadic continuation, especially, would have been considerably less probable.

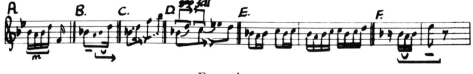

Example 120

[64] *Beethoven and His Nine Symphonies* (New York: Dover Publications, n.d.), p. 122.

Here the implicative inferences of a competent listener may be based upon the patterning *per se*. But once again, it is impossible in practice to separate whatever innate processes may be involved, from our familiarity with the behavior of this traditional schema. For the motive, and others belonging to the same family of gestures, is common in the repertory of tonal music. Let us consider some examples.

First, triadic continuations. In the first movement of Haydn's String Quartet in B♭ Major, Opus 76 No. 4 (Example 121A), the motive (m) occurs within a triadic pattern and is continued immediately to the implied fifth, F, and then in measure 4 to the octave, B♭. Here, as in other Classical period examples, the motive is set off and called to the listener's attention by the grace notes which embellish its beginning. The motive also occurs in the second measure of the fourth movement of Schubert's Octet for Strings and Winds (Example 121B).[65] The continuation is triadic—to G—but in the wrong register. The realization is, therefore, only provisional (Pr.). The triadic implications of the motive are satisfactorily realized, however, when the melody returns in the second part of the rounded-binary form (measure 21). But instead of the probable G, A follows—as part of the dominant of D minor (V/II). Schubert "acknowledges" the special, deviant character of the A with a *forte-piano* marking. The poignancy of the A is the result not only of its deviant character and its harmonic context, but of the fact that the larger interval—a sixth, rather than a fifth—acts both as a triadic continuation and as a gap implying descending motion toward closure.

Example 121

[65] I have purposely chosen a work written *after* Beethoven's Fourth Symphony to emphasize that our understanding of schemata is atemporal. Schubert's use of this traditional pattern influences our understanding of its implications in Beethoven's music, just as its use in Beethoven's music modifies our comprehension of Schubert's. Similarly, Stravinsky's use of the contrapuntal potential of a fuguelike gap-fill pattern (Example 110B) affects our understanding of similar patterns in the music of preceeding composers. In this connection, see the discussion in Meyer, *Music, the Arts and Ideas*, p. 47f.

Gap-fill, sequential continuations are also common in the literature. The motive occurs near the beginning of the first movement of Mozart's Piano Sonata in C Major, K. 279 (Example 122). In this case, instead of moving triadically to the G, the third (C—E) functions as a gap and is followed by D, which is the fill (graph 1). Sequential continuation is implied not only by higher-level linear motion from C to D, but by the foreground third, D to F, which pairs with the preceding C to E. This, however, proves to be part of a cadential figure leading to a repetition of the first two measures. The implied linear continuation does not occur until twelve measures later, where the motive moves in conjunct motion from C to G (graph 2a). This passage not only represents the realization of the implied conjunct continuation, but, when G is reached, the triadic potential latent in the motive (and regenerated by its repetition at the beginning of the sequence) is also actualized (graph 3a). In addition, as the motive moves on strong beats (3 and 1) from C to E to G, a still higher-level triadic motion is generated which carries both patternings beyond G to the octave-defining stability of the high C. The same motive, embodied in a somewhat more elaborate figure, is the basis of a

Example 122

sequential, gap-fill pattern in the Gigue from Bach's Partita No. 5 for Harpsichord in G Major (Example 123). Partly because the whole pattern includes a complete triad and partly because the triple meter weakens the mobility of

Example 123

the second beat, there is evidently little implication of triadic continuation.

Opening melodies generally establish the character or ethos of a movement. This is certainly true of the last movement of Beethoven's Fourth Symphony. From the first measure, the affective tone is one of pert, yet not hostile, verve and caprice. For the most part this is the result of syntactic relationships—the sudden changes in register and dynamics, and the sharp breaks in implicative process. But the nature and customary use of the motive itself also contribute to character. For, as the preceding examples indicate, the motive usually occurs within a melody which is already under way, or is included as part of a transition process. Here, however, it is the first gesture. Without benefit of polite preparation or customary introduction, the beginning seems brusquely witty and genially willful (Example 124).

The opening motive (m) implies triadic motion to the fifth, and perhaps to the upper octave of the tonic (graph 1). The fifth, F, follows, but not in the implied register, so the realization is only provisional (indicated by parentheses in the analysis). The F is also implied by the linear pattern of potential structural tones (graph 2): because the D in measure 1 and the E♭ in measure 2 are melodically prominent weakbeats, not effectively connected with the following low-level accents, continuation to an accent is called for. As the analysis indicates, the F's thus implied are not realized until measure 20.

But the most important aspect of the triadic patterning is harmonic. When the tonic (I) and supertonic (II) triads follow one another in root position (as they do in this case), the syntax of tonal harmony makes it highly probable that, if the linear patterning of first notes is continued, the next chord will be the tonic triad in the first inversion, not the improbable triad on the mediant (III). The opening measures of Schubert's Sonata for Violin and Piano in D Major are a clear illustration of this typical progression (part B of Example 124). For these reasons, the latent triadic motion of the first two measures of Beethoven's theme imply the patterning in measures 19–21—continuation to B♭ (graph 3).

The second implicative relationship generated by the opening motion —the gap-fill pattern—is provisionally realized when the motive is repeated on C (graph 5). The realization is not entirely satisfactory because the fill should follow the gap directly—as in Mozart's Piano Sonata (Example 122, measure 14f.). The gap and fill are brought together in the proper register in measure 19 (graph 6), and here, too, the D implied by the second foreground gap, C—E♭, is realized (graph 5a).

Example 124

The relationship between the motive (m) and its repetition (m′) creates
a higher-level conjunct pattern which implies continuation to D. After two
measures, D arrives. But, once again, register is wrong. A satisfactory D is presented in measure 19 (graph 4), where it also functions as the beginning of
the implied first-inversion triad (graph 3).

In the preceding discussion, the triadic implications of the second statement of the motive were not fully considered. Because the G, implied by the
foreground patterning of the motive (C–E♭), comes in the lower octave in
measure 2, its realization is only provisional. Though it tends to pass unnoticed because the triad to which it belongs is part of a higher-level process
leading to measures 19–21 (graph 3), no explicit realization of the G occurs in
the exposition section statement of the main theme. In this respect the
G is unlike the corresponding F, which is satisfactorily realized in measure
20. These roles are reversed in the recapitulation, where a satisfactory G
is realized both explicitly and without delay (see Example 125, m. 186).

Not only is the G in measure 2 in the wrong register, but the following
sixteenths move in the wrong direction: they do not parallel the equivalent
patterning in the first measure. Had they done so, a rising line would have

led to D on the first beat of measure 3, and the previously established linear and triadic patternings would then have been continued. Instead, as if heedless of preceding events, the line seems to plunge downward into an unrelated and unexplored register. Though this headlong descent continues in the lower strings (as the reader will find if he consults the score), the listener's attention is peremptorily engaged by the entrance of a new gesture—played *forte* by the whole orchestra—whose even-paced emphasis and rising conjunct motion sets off and counterbalances the downward rush of sixteenth-notes.

Before considering this new gesture and its implication, a word about its character and kind. The impression of melody—only three notes in conjunct succession—is too minimal to be characteristic. But the three clipped chords played by the full orchestra (with violins playing double and triple stops) and the V-I-V harmony have a familiar sound and sonority. We have heard this configuration countless times in this music—sometimes as introductory gestures, but more often as codas to symphonic movements. Its use here, in the middle of a melodiously processive first theme, is unusual and surprising.

In comparison with the previous breaks between the motive and its continuations, the entrance of this assertive gesture seems abrupt—an almost arbitrary interpolation of an alien idea, contrasting with the preceding pattern in almost every way. This sense of anomaly is both confirmed and heightened when, after only three beats, the original motive, orchestration, and soft dynamics return. Yet, like earlier breaks, this one is connected with what went before. For the new gesture can be understood as the palpable and explicit continuation of the incipient pattern of provisional realizations—the motion from F to G. Had the triadic continuations of the motive not been displaced in register, the relationships between the F—G motion and the conjunct motion of the gesture would be obvious, not only because of the continuity of conjunct pitches, but because the metric position of the A is the same as that of the F and G (graph 7).[66]

Even discounting this connection with earlier patterning, the conjunct motion of what I shall call the coda figure—to distinguish it from the motive (m)—implies continuation to D. But precisely because of its chordal, cadential character, return to B♭ is a possible alternative. The D which

[66] That this suggestion is not so farfetched as might at first appear is shown in the recapitulation. There, because the G is not displaced down, the connection seems clear and more explicit.

follows in measure 5 is not, however, a satisfactory continuation of the coda figure: not only its register, but its dynamic level, orchestration, and, above all, its motivic content prevent it from being grouped with the coda figure. Nor, for the same reasons, can the D in measure 19 act as a realization of the implications generated by the pattern in measures 3 and 4.[67] Instead of moving on to the D, the coda figure returns to B♭ in measure 21. There its motion and that generated by the motive converge as the melody reaches closure.

Continuation to D remains to be realized. It is so, but at the very end of the movement. Before discussing this, however, let me summarize what takes place in the recapitulation (Example 125). First, the G implied by the triadic motion of the second statement of the motive occurs in the right register throughout the recapitulation (graph 1)—except for the last presentation of the melody. Consequently, not only is this implication realized (as it was not in the exposition), but the connection between the motive and the coda figure is made explicit (graph 2). Next, the theme is not completed as it

Example 125

[67] Measures 7–18 have been omitted from Example 124. In those measures, first the motive continues the sequential pattern begun in measure 5. Then, in measure 12, a lyrical melody, which contrasts with both the pert verve of the motive and the assertive force of the coda figure, is presented over a dominant pedal. The repeated F's which end this tune are picked up in measure 20, where they lead to a resolution on the tonic.

was in the exposition. Instead of leading to a sequence based on the motive, as it did in measure 5 (Example 124), the coda figure continually returns to the beginning of the melody. For instance, in the first statement of the melody in the recapitulation (m. 185f.), the motive part is played by the bassoon; the coda figure, performed pizzicato by the violins (m.187–88), leads to a *forte* repetition of the same music an octave higher (m.189). This change has a number of important consequences.

1) The motion of the coda figure to the tonic (with A and C acting as neighbor-notes), which was inferred in the exposition, is here made explicit.

2) Because the passage which would have repeated measures 5–21 is missing, neither the sequential continuation in which the gap of a third was followed directly by fill nor the F implied by the opening motive occur within the theme. These implications and potentialities are first realized at the beginning of the coda, where a chromatic sequence, slowed by internal repetition, leads from B♭ to F (Example 125, part B; measures 281–294). Subsequently (measures 335–343), a compressed version of this sequence leads to an even more emphatic and stable F. In the course of both these sequences, the D implied by the motion of the opening motives is realized.

3) But the D implied by the coda figure is not. For to realize the implications generated by that pattern satisfactorily, the D must occur in the proper register (which it does not do in the sequences), be the resolution of dominant harmony (with root progression in the bass), come on an accent, and, ideally, follow the generating figure directly. These conditions occur twice in the coda. Following the statement of the theme which begins in measure 302, the coda figure moves conjunctly from A to high G, as shown in the sketch at the end of Example 125A. That this is a version of the coda figure is clear not only from its relationship to the opening motives and its own melodic pattern, but from the harmony and bass motion.

Nevertheless, the realization leaves something to be desired, partly because the clipped chords associated with the figure have been replaced by a smoother, more continuous succession of pitches. Mostly, however, because the D occurs within a larger motion, the fact of arrival and realization lacks appropriate emphasis. The D is, however, appropriately conspicuous and emphatic when it occurs as part of the final cadence of the movement (Example 126). For it is the goal and end of the quarter-note rhythm of the coda figure and of the sixteenth-note motion of the bass. And in these chords, too, the potential inherent in the character of the gesture is unequivocally actualized.

Example 126

I conclude this section with a final example, a question, and an observation.

The example, from the beginning of the transition passage from the Haydn Quartet movement quoted earlier (Example 121A), is:

Example 127

The question: If Beethoven's music can be characterized as original, what is the basis for this quality?

The observation: Given the prevalence and central importance of archetypal schemata in tonal music, originality in musical art, at least until recently, consisted not in the invention of novel means and syntactic relationships, but in the inventive use of established relationships and shared conventions.

PROLONGATIONS

Not all melodic relationships are implicative. Most nonimplicative events are what are commonly called prolongations. There are important differences among kinds of prolongation, though they are often treated as a single, monolithic class. Some prolongations contain clearly defined implicative processes; others do not. Some are implicative rhythmically or harmonically, but not melodically. Some serve to create balanced morphological lengths; others stretch established lengths and thereby heighten the effectiveness of implications already generated. Most prolongations are related to preceding events by conformance, but some—for instance, what will be called parentheses—are not. The following discussion is an attempt to distinguish a few broad subclasses.

Declarative prolongations

The basic motive or thematic idea of a melody or composition may itself be a prolongation. The first four measures of the first prelude in Book I of the Well-Tempered Clavier, for instance, are a prolongation of a tonic—C Major—triad (Example 128A). Because the melody begins on the third, motion to the tonic is probable. But this implied tonal motion is not reinforced by the patterning of the parameters. The second and third measures imply closure and return, rather·than continuation and mobility. Melodically, the F's in measures 2 and 3 function as the upper neighbor of E. Harmonically, the progression is cadential, I—II^4_2—V^6_5—I. For this reason, rhythm appears to be end-accented on the phrase-level. In short, these measures are understood to be a stable, closed shape—a statement of motivic materials, texture, and tonal center. The implicative processes which shape the motion of the Prelude are not generated until measure 5.

Example 128

The first theme of Beethoven's Third Symphony is essentially a stable, axial melody (Example 128B). E♭ is prolonged, and the other notes of the triad revolve around it. Because the B♭ implied by the initial third (E♭—G) is realized within the melody (the third beat of measure 5), implication is internal. The tendency of the triad in measure 5 to be continued is not strong: not only is B♭ the relatively stable fifth of the triad and the goal of the patterning in measure 3, but it is defined as the probable upper limit of melodic activity by the B♭ in measure 4. Rhythmically, however, the theme is open and mobile, as the analysis under the example shows. Nevertheless, like the Bach example, this theme is understood primarily as a statement of the main "stuff" of the composition, rather than as a pattern generative of specific implications. It is a declarative prolongation.

Although they are not specifically implicative, declarative prolongations usually have an aura of latency about them—if only because they are beginning events, and we believe there will be more music. This feeling of anticipatory tension is specially strong when the declarative event does not itself contain strong internal processes: when harmonic, rhythmic, and melodic relationships do not articulate marked closure. Partly for this reason, Beethoven's theme seems so much more fraught with potential than does Bach's.

Because the music we are concerned with is hierarchic, what is implicative on one level may be a stable prolongation on the next—and vice versa. Though implicative processes are generated within it, a whole melody may be considered a prolongation—an essentially formal entity—if it is a complete, closed and stable shape. Since our interest has been in implication, few such melodies have been considered: probably the melody from Smetana's *Vltava* (*The Moldau;* Example 84) or the one from Mahler's Fourth Symphony (Example 88) are the clearest cases of such declarative prolongations. Finally, many, but not all, melodies which are the basis for theme-and-variations movements are also examples of complete, stable events.

Normalizing prolongations

Prolongations frequently occur in conjunction with implicative processes. When this is the case, they may perform a number of somewhat different functions. One of these is to make the phrase or period fit with a previously established or stylistically normal morphological length. Often the normalization of length is achieved through simple repetition.

The melody of the second movement of Schubert's Trio in B♭ Major, Opus 99, is an antecedent-consequent structure, though the consequent phrase is two measures longer than the antecedent (Example 129). The first phrase begins on the third, G (measure 3), and from a tonal point of view, motion to the tonic is probable. Melodic patterning begins with conjunct descending motion which also implies continuation to E♭ (graph 2).

This implication is reinforced when, after a gap of a third, the melody again descends conjunctly, from Ab to G in measure 4, and then continues to F in measure 5 (graph 2a). At the same time, the second level pattern from G to Ab implies, and moves to, Bb, the relatively stable fifth of the scale (graph 1).

The foreground patterning of the melody is partially closed at the end of measure 5. Harmonically, the progression from I to V $_5^6$ is a semicadence. Rhythmically, the change from shorter to longer note values—from a sixteenth-note to an eighth, and from eighth to quarter-note—creates a clearly closed, trochaic grouping on lower levels. Melodically, the G and F constitute a return to the opening pitches, and the sense of closure is enhanced by the gap from Eb to G, which is filled by the F.

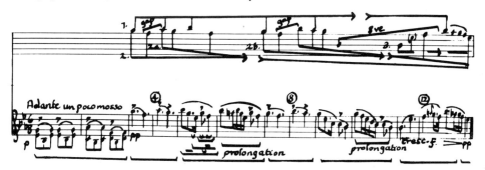

Example 129

But more music is needed. Two-measure lengths have been established as the norm—in the melody itself, and in the introductory measures as well. The varied repetition in measure 6 does not change or even noticeably reinforce implication.[68] Rather, the sixth measure serves to create a normal, regular phrase length. This is an instance of the bifurcation of form and process discussed at the end of Chapter IV. Here, as in the Dumka from Dvořák's Piano Quintet (Example 57), process reaches closure before morphological length is complete. The normalizing prolongation completes the morphological length.

The construction of the second phrase is similar to that of the first. Like measure 6, measure 10 is a normalizing prolongation. But there are interesting differences. The implication of descending motion is somewhat stronger

[68] It does, however, emphasize closure by somewhat intensifying the rhythmic motion toward G, and by suggesting more complete linear patterning, Bb—A—G, down to F.

at the beginning of the consequent phrase because the gap from F to B♭ is larger than the corresponding gap from F to A♭ in the first phrase, and because the B♭ functions like an appoggiatura. On the other hand, the low-level patterning at the end of the phrase (measures 9 and 10) does not imply direct conjunct motion to the tonic, as the G—F motion at the end of the first phrase did. Instead, the melody descends to B♭ which defines the area of melodic activity and thereby stabilizes the upper fifth, making linear or triadic continuation above it less likely, and implies disjunct motion to the tonic (graph 3).[69] As a result, F is delayed, and so is the closure of the phrase. Because the melody fails to reach the tonic in measure 10, two cadential measures are necessary. In these, the several strands of melodic patterning, indicated in the analytic graphs, converge to the E♭.

To balance the length of the six-measure consequent phrase, Schubert begins the movement with a two-measure introduction. These measures might be regarded as a kind of normalizing prolongation *before* the phrase. However, because they are obviously a ground—an archetypal accompaniment figure, rather than a well-patterned melody—the measures are implicative. We expect that a strongly shaped melody will be presented shortly. Though the regularity of the rhythm and the simplicity of the harmony, dynamics, and tempo, suggest that what follows will be lyrical, we have no way of knowing what the melody will be. Implication is not specific.

That this introduction is implicative indicates that the effect of a normalizing prolongation depends in part upon where it occurs in a melody. When it occurs at the end of a phrase, as in measure 6 and 10 of Schubert's melody, a prolongation will not as a rule be implicative. But when it occurs at the beginning or in the middle of a phrase, it will tend to be so—though perhaps for rhythmic rather than melodic reasons.

The melody which begins the second movement of Mozart's String Quartet in D Major (K.575) illustrates this point (Example 130). Like the melody of Schubert's Trio, it consists of an antecedent and a consequent phrase, each divided into two parts. The implicative relationships within the antecedent phrase merit attention—both because the effect of the prolongation depends in part upon them and because they are of interest in their own right.

---

[69] Because it is conspicuous through its absence, D is implied as a probable goal. The skip from B♭ to E♭ in measure 11 in particular implies D as a fill. And when the melody is repeated, the D (measure 22) follows the E♭ and moves toward a cadence on the dominant.

The antecedent phrase (Example 130A) begins with a four-measure prolongation of the third of the scale, C♯ (graph 1). For tonal reasons, motion through B to the tonic, A, is probable. This implication is reinforced by a surprisingly subtle, yet basically simple, melodic structure. In the foreground, two descending conjunct patterns, each preceded by a gap, imply continuation to the tonic: the first moves down from E *not* F♯, an appoggiatura (graph 2); the second, from A (graph 3). On the next level, the structural tones are those of the tonic triad, and the second part of the phrase (measures 5–8) is included in this pattern (graph 4). Again, the lower tonic is implied, not only because by measure 4 (and more patently by measure 5) the triad is complete except for the lower tonic, but because the gap-fill structures suggest descending motion. Consequently the probability of triadic continuation to the upper C♯ is low.

Once again seemingly slight differences have implicative significance. In the consequent phrase, the first measure is varied so that the relationship between C♯ and E implies continuation to the upper octave (Example 130B): in measure 9, a weak, mobile eighth-note, E, follows C♯ directly, so that further triadic motion is probable. And, after the A in measure 11, the second part of the phrase begins on the high C♯.[70] (See graph above and rhythmic analysis below in Example 130 B.)

In the second part of the antecedent phrase (Example 130), C♯ is prolonged until measure 8, where it becomes an appoggiatura in a semicadence moving to B. The motive in measures 5 and 6 is a linear rise to E, but further motion is not implied. The E is the end of a relatively closed group: rhythmically, it is preceded by a sixteenth-note which acts as a "micro-level" upbeat, and, consequently, the higher-level dactyl is closed; melodically, the skip from B to E (in a II—V harmonic context) makes the E sound like the completion of a group. The interesting conformant relationship between this motive and the patterning of measures 1 and 2 is shown in graph 5.

Turning now to our chief concern—prolongation. Whatever the melodic implications of the patterning through measure 5, they are in no way changed by the repetition that takes place in measure 6. From a melodic point of view, measure 6 contributes nothing. Its contribution is formal and

---

[70] This calls attention to an important point in critical method. A specific change cannot be adequately explained on the grounds that it provides *variety*. Certainly, there is a need for variety, but there are innumerable ways of achieving it. What is required is an explanation which suggests why this particular way of achieving variety is appropriate or what its formal or implicative consequences are.

Example 130

rhythmic. From a formal point of view, it normalizes the morphological length of the second part of the phrase—so that like the first it will be four measures long.

Rhythmically, the repetition is processive and implicative. Because they are identical and come at the beginning of the second part of the antecedent, measure 5 and its normalizing prolongation, measure 6, make it probable that the whole subphrase will be an anapest, 3 + 3 + 6 beats, on the second level. And this implication is realized in measures 7 and 8, which form a pivoted rhythmic group. The sense of goal-directed motion created by the rhythmic structure depends in part upon the context of strong melodic implication. At the same time, rhythmic implication compensates for the temporary suspension of melodic motion toward the tonic.

Extensions

The consequent phrase of Mozart's melody is given in Example 131. If the changes in melody and register already considered and those in the closing measures (16 and 17) are disregarded, the phrase is regular and typical, reaching the expected cadence on the tonic in measure 16. Just when stability and closure seem assured, however, the viola and cello begin a repetition of part B of the phrase. The violins are, so to speak, obliged to follow along, elaborating a new counterpoint. The resulting lack of closure is emphasized by the fact that the tonic triad is in the first inversion, rather than root position.

This repetition, too, is a prolongation. But instead of being normalized, the morphological length is stretched. In other words, measures 16–19 belong to the class of prolongation known as *extensions*. Not only is the morphological length stretched, but the extension begins before the consequent phrase has finished—reached its normal length. There is an *elision*: measure 16 is both the end of the main melody and the beginning of the extension. The "morphological dissonance" which results from this overlapping creates a tension whose resolution enhances the sense of satisfaction and closure when an undisturbed cadence is reached at measure 19. Indeed, the tension is such that some of the accumulated energy spills over into the bridge passage which follows.

Most extensions at the end of a phrase do not, however, involve elisions. They occur after the morphological length is complete. The coda of the Mozart movement we have been analyzing provides a clear illustration (Example 132). After the theme presented in the two preceding examples, a modulation to the dominant leads to the statement of a secondary melody. This leads back with virtually no delay to a restatement of the antecedent-consequent melody. Though details are varied, the music is basically the same. But now no bridge passage follows to absorb the tension of the elision and to arrest the momentum built up by the delays in the melody. The coda of the movement accomplishes these ends. It is, so to speak, a composed *ritardando*.

As Example 132 shows, the coda begins after a full cadence in the tonic at measure 61. It is an extension consisting of a four-measure pattern (A), I—II^6—I$^6_4$—V^7—I, which is repeated (A′). This is followed by a further extension—a two-measure authentic cadence (B), which is also repeated (B′) closing the movement. Since the extension is essentially a melodic prolongation

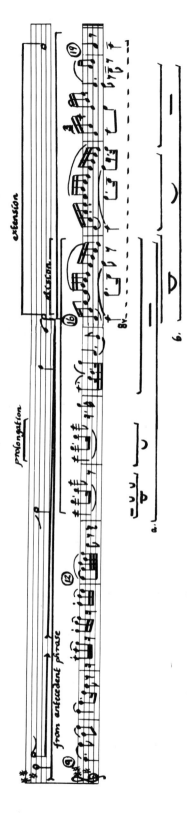

Example 131

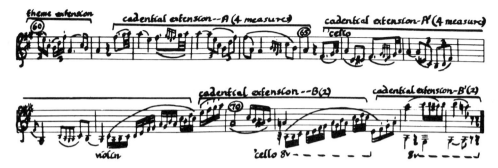

Example 132

of the tonic, A, moving through three octaves, no implicative relationships are generated.[71]

Extensions also occur within phrases. Though they do not influence the direction of the implicative process, such internal extensions often heighten the listener's sense of implication by delaying arrival at implied goals. A striking instance of an internal extension which intensifies the feeling of goal-directed motion occurs in the first section (measures 1–17) of the Prelude to *Tristan und Isolde*. The larger structure and harmony of these measures have been expertly analyzed by William J. Mitchell.[72] My concern will be the complex relationships within the prolongation, which occur between measures 12 and 16 (Example 133A).

The passage is forcefully implicative—harmonically and melodically. Harmonically, each element of the sequence consists of the "Tristan" chord, which functions as a secondary dominant and resolves to an unambiguous dominant-seventh chord. As indicated under graph 4, the first element ends on the dominant seventh of A minor (V^7); the second, on the dominant of C major (V^7/III), the relative major of A minor; and the third, on the dominant-of-the-dominant (V^7/V). Each is therefore internally processive and implies continuation. The sense of goal-directed motion generated by this foreground patterning is enhanced by a higher-level triadic structure created by the roots of the chords of resolution, E—G♯—B. This structure implies continuation to E (graph 3).

[71] The closure in different octaves at measures 71 and 73 is one of the results of the motion of the consequent phrase to the upper C♯. Other results may be found in the middle section of the movement.

[72] "The Tristan Prelude: Technique and Structure," in William J. Mitchell and Felix Salzer, eds. *The Music Forum*, Vol. I (New York: Columbia University Press, 1967), pp. 162–203.

The melodic patterning, which complements this harmonic structure, is no less implicative. On the lowest, note-to-note level, it consists of a chromatic scale which rises from G♯ to F♯ (measures 2–11). On the next level, eliminating those tones which are obviously appoggiaturas or passing tones, the melody is a diatonic scale in A minor. As shown in graph 1, both these motions imply continuation to the upper G♯—and, because the processes are quite uniform, perhaps beyond.[73] On a still higher level, the passage consists of a series of thirds, G♯—B—D—F♯; continuation of this patterning would lead to the high A.

Rhythmic organization supports and enhances the goal-directed processes generated by melody and harmony. On the primary level (1), each phrase ends on the weak part of the rhythmic group. Hence, even though the lowest level is a partially closed trochee, the basic structure is mobile. As a result, the appoggiatura pattern which ends each phrase remains mobile and goal-directed, even when it is detached and begins an impulse, as it does in measures 14 and 15. On the next level (2a), that of phrases, the varied repetition of a single pattern weakens the impression of structure and suggests that the ultimate organization of the whole section will be some sort of anapest group. As a result, the second and third groups—and the first in retrospect—are perceived as on-going and implicative.

These strongly goal-directed processes "get stuck" after measure 11. Instead of continuation, there is obstinate repetition. Not only is the realization of the processes generated by the patterning of the first eleven measures delayed, but morphological lengths are stretched and metric continuity is disturbed.

The analysis of these measures is somewhat problematic: are they all extension, or partly extension and partly normalizing prolongation? They might be considered a complex extension, for had the melody continued to the cadence in measure 17 without any repetition whatsoever, the result would have been regular: if measure 10 had been immediately followed by measures 16 and 17, then the passage would have consisted of three four-measure phrases. This is shown in part B of Example 133, where the slight elision in measure 8 has been removed to show the potential regularity of the phrase structure. Seen from the perspective of melody alone, the extension runs from measure 12 through measure 15.

---

[73] Because the chromatic pattern is uniform and undifferentiated, a clear reversal is needed if closure is to take place. The gap from G♯ to B (measures 16–17), filled by the tonic (A), creates the required reversal.

Nevertheless, for rhythmic reasons, and harmonic ones as well, these measures also seem to involve normalization. The organization suggested as basic in part B of the example is far from satisfactory; it is too regular and reaches the cadence too quickly. Not only does the melodic motion, which heretofore moved with intense deliberation, now speed with unwarranted ease, but the articulation of the crucial cadential harmonies is cursory and casual. Above all, the equal, four-measure phrase lengths and sequential uniformity create no higher-level structure. For all these reasons, closure at the end of such a twelve-measure pattern would have been abrupt and weak.

Though these measures are best analyzed as part extension and part normalizing prolongation, it is not easy to determine which is which. The analysis given in the example is based on a number of considerations. Because they function as upbeats to the closing cadence, measures 14 and 15 create a strongly end-accented anapest grouping on the primary level (1). This patterning supports the melodic closure at measure 17 and emphasizes the harmonic articulation of the deceptive cadence. In addition, they reestablish the four-measure phrase lengths with which the passage began. For these reasons, measure 15 seems to be a normalizing prolongation.

Though measures 14 and 15 are similar in structure and function to measures 5 and 6 of Mozart's String Quartet (Example 130A), they are much more patently implicative, for four reasons. First, in Wagner's Prelude, the half-step motive, E♯—F♯, is part of, and by reiteration reinforces, the implications previously generated by the melodic patterning. In the Mozart, on the other hand, the comparable measures are not derived from, and do not support, the basic descending melodic motion. Second, harmonically these measures are implicative because of their previous association with goal-directed processes—the dominant-seventh of the dominant (V^7/V) in measure 11. In Mozart's movement, however, the comparable measures are part of stable, tonic harmony. Third, when first presented in measures 11 and 13, this motive was a weak, mobile part of the rhythmic group. Because it retains the function that it was originally understood to have (even in the absence of the accent in relation to which it was a weak element), the repeated motive is rhythmically implicative. In the Mozart, measure 5 is initially understood as accented and stable, and is rhythmically implicative only in retrospect. Finally these rhythmic and melodic implications are affirmed and underlined by the crescendo (within each measure) which "points to" (acts as a sign of) an organizing accent.

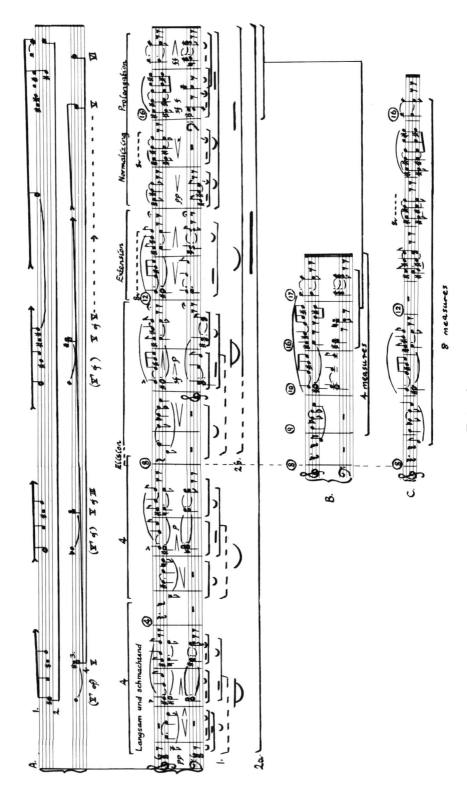

Example 133

Measures 12 and 13, then, are an extension. This is evident if the third element in the sequence is "normalized" as in part C of Example 133. Now each phrase begins on the last eighth-note of the measure, and the final four measures "fit" perfectly into the regular pattern of four-times-four measures. And this is precisely what is wrong with the structure: not only is it tedious, but no higher-level rhythmic structure arises. It is so uniform that closure would be weak and anticlimatic. A longer, complementary patterning is needed, and such patterning has already been potential in the basically equal morphological lengths of the first two elements of the sequence. The elision welds the third element of the sequence to the last four measures so that, in a broad sense, the structure of the whole section is a bar-form, with an extension, both on the middle level (2b) and on the highest level (2a).

Parentheses

Internal extensions, like the one in Wagner's Prelude, take place within, and are continuations of, processes generated by the preceding melodic-rhythmic patterning. By stretching morphological lengths and delaying motion to implied goals, they disturb continuity, but they do not interrupt it. Consequently, they are understood as intensifications of the existing patterning. But there are internal prolongations which, while not affecting established implications, interrupt the musical structure, usually after arrival at some point of provisional stability. Because they do not really "belong" to the preceding and following patterning, such internal interruptions have been called *parentheses*.[74]

This kind of discontinuity is discussed in *The Rhythmic Structure of Music*, and, rather than paraphrase what was said there, I take the liberty of quoting one paragraph:

> A case of interrupted continuity that comes readily to mind is found in the classical concerto, in which the resolution of a I_4^6 chord onto a V chord may be delayed for several minutes by the insertion of a cadenza. The effect of this kind of interruption (and of similar kinds) is perhaps even more surprising than are the effects of links and overlappings. For two things happen. First, suspense results, and suspense intensifies whatever continuity there may be. It may be several seconds

[74] Earlier theorists such as Mattheson (see footnote 59, p. 212), who took language as a model, used this term. But I am not sure where the modern use comes from. I have, however, frequently discussed these matters with, and learned much from, Professor Lawrence Bernstein.

after the lightning flash that the sound of thunder reaches our ears, but when we see the lightning we know the thunder will follow. Second, there is a certain unreality about the interruption. It is not part of the "real" piece, which will resume as though nothing had happened whenever it is allowed to. In one sense, of course, the cadenza is part of the piece because we expect it to be there; in another very real sense, however, it is not. There are somewhat analogous cases in both art and literature. A painting is supposed to have a frame; the frame is not part of the painting—but it is. A story with a frame—for example, a play within a play or a novel with a flashback—includes and does not include the frame. Extraneous comic interludes are and are not part of a serious play. A ballet in an opera does and does not belong to that opera. And so on.[75]

The melody which begins the last movement of Haydn's String Quartet in E♭ Major, Opus 50 No. 3, contains an unequivocal example of a parenthesis. The theme is an antecedent-consequent structure. The antecedent phrase and the last two measures of the consequent are given in Example 134.

The patterning of the highest level is linear, moving up from E♭ to G and then returning to F in the antecedent phrase and to the tonic, E♭, in the consequent (graph 1). Because of the patterning of the lower levels, the G which continues the processes generated in the first four measures is clearly not the one in measure 5, but the one in measure 9. The middle-level pattern (graph 2) consists of a series of thirds, E♭—G, F—A♭, which should continue with G—B♭. But B♭ does not follow in measure 6, as it should. Instead, the direction of motion is reversed—moves down to the D. The failure of the implied patterning to continue is emphasized by the repetition of the parenthesis figure. The melody continues in measures 9 and 10, where the tension built up by the delay carries the motion to the high E♭ for an instant.[76] The main area of melodic activity is, however, defined by the octave from the opening upbeat B♭ to the B♭ in measure 9.

The lowest level (graph 3) is also linear. And again the patterning is broken in measures 5–8. The continuation in measure 9 is not in doubt. And the momentum of the linear motion carries the melody to the sixth degree of

[75] p. 149.

[76] Although the high E♭ is harmonized by a subdominant triad, it is also part of the tonic melodic triad (graph 2). For the triadic motion latent in each of the first two thirds suggests tonic and supertonic patterns in root position, and, according to the probabilities of tonal syntax, the next member of the series would be the first inversion tonic triad. (See the discussion of Example 124A, graph 3, and 124B.)

the scale (C) which, moving to the second degree in the antecedent phrase and to the tonic (harmonized by a $_4^6$ chord) in the consequent, creates a traditional closing gesture—much like that of the cadential extension in Example 132.

From a rhythmic point of view, the goal of the first four measures is clearly the last four, not the middle ones. Measures 1–4 are made up of two similar rhythmic patterns. A four-measure unit in relation to which these two events can be grouped is implied. But measures 5–8 are even more patently divided into two identical events which form no higher-level rhythmic structure. The implications of the first four measures are, as the analysis under the example shows, realized in the last four.

Example 134

For all these reasons, we recognize at once that measures 5–8 are not part of the "real" melody. And such recognition is facilitated by the character of the pattern and by its lack of motivic (conformant) relationship to the opening pattern. For the opening melody is emphatically conjunct, but the motive of the parenthesis is primarily disjunct—almost like a thumping bass, marking time. And the real melody is characterized by goal-directed motion; but the parenthesis is static. It is as though a person purposefully striding toward some objective should suddenly pause, perform a dancelike caper, and then continue to his objective.

The need for the parenthesis is not hard to understand. The motion of the first four measures is so apparent and palpable that had the goal been reached without delay—had measure 9 followed measure 4, as it could have done—the result would have been obvious and uninteresting. If the second phrase of the *real* melody is to be felt as an achieved and worthwhile goal, there must be delay. This the parenthesis provides.

CHAPTER VIII

A Summary Example

By way of reviewing some of the theoretical concepts and analytic methods developed in these Essays and Explorations, let us consider the first twenty-one measures of the first movement of Beethoven's Piano Sonata in E♭ Major, Opus 81a—"Les Adieux." Our concern will be primarily with implicative relationships and hierarchic organization, but other kinds of relationships—ethetic and conformant ones—are also important in our understanding and experience of music. A brief discussion of these will act as a preface to the main analysis.

I.

A competent listener perceives and responds to music with his total being. As tonal stimuli, filtered and processed by a selective auditory nervous system, are related to one another by the patterning proclivities and habits of the human mind, every facet of behavior—physiological and psychological, motor and mental—becomes attuned to and congruent with the process and structure of musical events. Through such empathetic identification, music is quite literally *felt,* and it can be felt without the mediation of extramusical concepts or images. Such kinesthetic sensing of the ethos or character of a musical event is what the term *ethetic* refers to.

Because human experience is not compartmentalized into musical and nonmusical, aesthetic and nonaesthetic, the ethos of a musical event will often seem similar to and suggest some aspect of the extramusical world. The musical event is felt to be sad or joyful, restrained or exuberant, calm or agitated, and the like. And such characteristic states of being may in turn be associated with more specific circumstances and ideas: a summer evening's calm, the gaiety and bustle of a social gathering. Moreover, when it explicitly imitates extramusical sounds—as in birdcalls, wind and thunder, and the like—or is established as part of the tradition of Western musical iconography,[1] a musical pattern may denote quite specific kinds of events, actions, and ideas in the extramusical world.

Although they can perhaps be differentiated in theory, in practice ethetic relationships are inseparable from implicative and hierarchic ones. The ethos of a musical event, based in part upon the more constant parameters of music such as tempo, dynamics, register, mode, and the like, influences and qualifies the listener's sense of how the event will probably proceed syntactically and formally. Conversely, the syntactic processes and formal structure of an event—whether regular or sporadic, balanced or asymmetrical, predictable or capricious—play a crucial role in defining its ethos. And just as our preliminary opinion of an individual is revised and modified in the light of his subsequent behavior, so our impression and understanding of the character of a musical event is often modified by its use and variation later in the work.

The beginning of the Sonata "Les Adieux" is a case in point. The first event—the "Lebewohl" motto which plays a central role in the movement—has a very special savor and feeling-tone (Example 136A). That words cannot adequately express the simple and unpretentious, yet touching, sense of wistful regret and resignation does not gainsay the importance of the ethos of the motto.

Its particular ethos is the result of a combination of factors. Register and sonority, tempo and dynamics are obviously crucial. Had the same pitch-time relationships been presented in a high register, at a fast tempo, and with *forte* dynamics, character would have been very different. The action of these parameters is complemented by the patent and regular melodic, rhythmic, and harmonic structure of the motto—despite the deceptive cadence closing the event. This cadence further defines the ethos of the motto, bringing "the eternal note of sadness in"—and perhaps suggesting that the parting is not final.

Feeling-tone is also the result of the deviant use of an archetypal schema, horn fifths: a conventional patterning—virtually a formula—used in the eighteenth century by natural brass instruments (without valves) to play authentic cadences. Their occurrence just before the end of the fourth movement of Mozart's Symphony No. 39 in E♭ Major is typical. As Example 135 shows, they follow a harmonic progression, II^6_5—V^7, which

[1] See pp. 64f.

strongly implies motion to the tonic. The horn fifths are the resolution of this progression, and they prolong and emphasize the cadential character of the passage through an alternation of tonic and dominant-seventh chords.

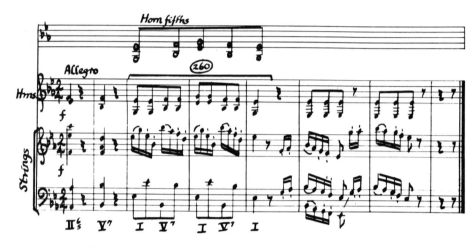

Example 135

Because they are melodically and harmonically cadential, horn-fifth patterns normally occur in closing sections or codas of fast movements and, as in Mozart's symphony, they are frequently played *forte*. As a rule, however, they are not the main melodic substance, but support and reinforce the cadential use of motives taken from first or second theme groups. In so doing they act as signs of impending closure.

The use of horn fifths in the first measures of Beethoven's "Les Adieux" Sonata is unusual in almost every way. Instead of coming at the end of a fast movement, they are the beginning of a slow introduction; instead of being accompanimental, they are the main substance; and instead of reaching emphatic closure on the tonic, they end in a deceptive cadence which is mobile and on-going. The deviant use of this traditional pattern not only emphasizes the importance of the motto, but contributes considerably to its peculiar poignancy.

The ethos of the "Lebewohl" motto, characterized in part by its internal relationships, suggests something of the probable course of subsequent events in the movement: it establishes an ambience inimical to towering developments, heroic contrasts, and capricious surprises. The almost aphoristic specificity and palpability of the motto (Example 136A), taken together with the fact that it is deflected from its tonic goal, makes its subsequent

ubiquity both appropriate and convincing. As it returns in new contexts
and different guises, the various facets of its character are revealed. It functions in varied form as the forceful, driving first theme of the Allegro
(136B), as the beginning of the second key area (136C), as the basis for the
flowing themes of the closing group (136D),[2] as the source for the ambiguous, almost hesitant linear motion of the development section (136E),
and as the main material of the coda, where it occurs in its pure archetypal
form, first in its closing theme (136F) and then in canonic imitation (136G).

Ethetic relationships are unquestionably important—particularly in

Example 136

[2] For the sake of comparison, these are given as they occur in the recapitulation,
where they are in the tonic.

some styles and in some compositions. And the "Les Adieux" Sonata is, I think, one of these. However, though they are notoriously easy to discuss in casual, plausible fashion, ethos and affect are hard to analyze with rigor and precision. Partly, this is because language cannot adequately distinguish between and delineate subtle shades of character and nuances of feeling-tone. A more basic problem is that, in the absence of an adequate theory of ethetic change and transformation or without a text or program explicitly connecting the character of earlier events to later ones, it is difficult to explain the succession of characteristic gestures or the sequence of different sorts of feeling-tone.[3]

Conformant relationships, too, are important in this movement. As Example 136 makes clear, all the main materials of the movement are related by conformance to the "Lebewohl" motto. The various and varied returns of the motto mark important points of structural articulation. At the same time they create a coherence which tends to lessen the sense of explicit contrast in what is a basically dramatic form. But the main reasons for the pervasiveness of the motto are syntactical and implicative.

2.

The horn fifths which open this movement are as clear an example of a strongly established schema as one can hope to find. The pattern is specified melodically and intervallically, harmonically and, with somewhat more latitude, rhythmically. We have no doubt as to how it should sound. Consequently, we are acutely aware that the low C used to harmonize the minor sixth (G—Eb) at the beginning of measure 2 is an aberrant imposition, and we presume that the correct, archetypal version of the formula will occur later in the movement. However, though it appears in a myriad of variants, the schema is not presented in its pure, horn-fifths form until the middle of the coda. Appropriately this archetypal version occurs immediately following what can be considered the "solution" of the C-minor problem, the deceptive cadence, which gave rise to the implicative relationship in the first place.

---

[3] In music, and particularly in instrumental compositions, the connection between successive ethetic states is probably largely conventional. This does not mean, however, that characterization and feeling-tone are less persuasive and captivating. But it does mean that important work must be done in the area of style analysis before such relationships can be satisfactorily explained.

Because the schema is so well known and specific in its pattern, the effect of the alien, C-minor harmony is particularly powerful. This is no mere deceptive cadence; it strikes us as expressly anomalous.[4] For this reason, we sense, though perhaps only intuitively, that it is significant. And so it is. The implications of the intrusive C-minor harmony reverberate throughout the movement. Let us begin by considering some of these.

1) C-minor harmony has an important effect upon the melodic tendency of the E♭ which it harmonizes. For the linear motion generated by the descent from G now has less tendency to stop on the E♭. What the listener "knows" ought to have been a stable tonic is experienced as a mobile third, possibly implying motion within submediant harmony to C, or implying motion to the leading-tone, D. The first of these possibilities is realized in the closing theme version of the pattern, where the "Lebewohl" motto is followed by a skip to the note (C) a third below (Example 137).

Example 137

The tendency of the E♭ to move to D is the result of harmonic as well as melodic relationships. The syntax of tonal harmony makes it probable that a I—V—VI progression such as this will move to the leading tone, harmonized by a dominant chord, and then back to the tonic. Such a progression is shown in Example 138.

[4] Here an interesting psychological paradox arises—one which I can describe, but not really explain. While we *know* that the deceptive cadence is aberrant and in this sense unexpected, we would be at least as surprised—even taken aback—if the first beat of measure 2 were an unembellished tonic triad. In other words, though we are conscious of how the schema should go, we are also aware that an obvious and predictable authentic cadence is improbable at the very beginning of a composition. In the same way, we both expect and don't expect that the cadential pattern which begins the slow movement of Brahms' Violin Sonata in G Major (Example 117) will move to the tonic at the beginning of the second measure.

Example 138

The implied motion from E♭ to D and back to E♭ is realized provisionally when the prolonged E♭ (see below) moves to D and back to E♭ in measure 12 (Example 139A), and more forcefully in the third measure of the Allegro theme (Example 139B) which is a varied version of the earlier patterning.

Example 139

But the implied cadential progression does not occur in the proper register and with an unequivocally end-accented rhythm until the penultimate cadence of the coda (Example 140). For implications are specific, not only with respect to schema, but also to register, harmony and rhythm.

Example 140

2) The proximate consequence of the imposition of submediate (C-minor) harmony at the end of the horn-fifths formula is the prolongation which follows. The prolongation is important both because in this case it is itself implicative and because it proves to be a basis for the Allegro theme which begins the exposition section of the sonata.

The prolongation begins with the skip from E♭ to A♭. When this gap is followed by G, conjunct continuation to the tonic is implied (Example 141, graph 1). The fill does not follow directly, however, but comes in measures 7 and 8. That this analysis is not fantasy is shown by the harmonization of the G in measure 7 (graph 1a) and by the fact that it, too, is preceded by an A♭ upbeat: Beethoven specifically connects the G at the beginning of measure 3 to the one at the beginning of measure 7 by using essentially the same harmony in both places.[5] Though the G in measure 7 does move to E♭ as implied, the cadence is again deceptive—and in the wrong mode as well. Consequently the realization is only provisional.[6]

Instead of motion to E♭ following the G in measure 3, the gap figure (x) is repeated (x′) beginning on G. This repetition generates further implications. Like the first statement of the figure, the second also implies descending fill. And this implication is realized when the C moves to B in measure 4, and through B♭ and A♭ to the G in measure 7 (graph 2).[7] Once the C in measure 3 is reached, the melodic motion is clearly triadic on a somewhat higher level (graph 3). The high E♭ implied by this patterning is realized almost immediately. The E♭ closes out the triadic motion both because of the satisfaction of octave completion and because, as the analysis under Example 141 shows, it is the accented goal of both lower and higher rhythmic groupings.

Because it involves disjunct motion, the triadic patterning is also implicative. The first gaps, which are filled as shown in graphs 1 and 2, have

[5] Because this harmony is unusual, the conformant relationship seems to be intentional.

[6] The fourth, E♭ to A♭, might be thought to imply triadic continuation to the C in measure 3. However, though the C does follow, the implication is weak. Because the C-minor harmony is strong and the A♭ is only a sixteenth-note, the A♭ tends to be understood as an ornamental tone, leading to the G and implying conjunct fill rather than triadic continuation.

[7] That originality in art does not entail the discovery of novel, let alone unique, syntactical means or even archetypes is indicated by the fact that a sequential gap-fill pattern very similar to the one Beethoven employs here occurs in the first measures of Schubert's song, "Das Wandern" (Example 79).

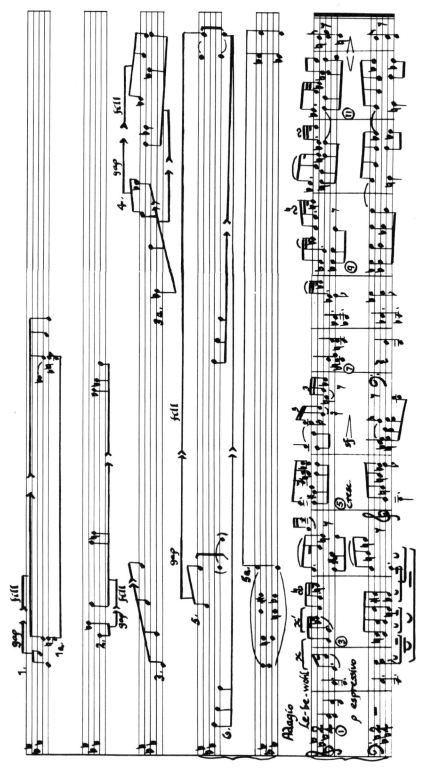

Example 141

already been discussed. The third one, from C to E♮, implies descending
motion to D (graph 5) and is particularly important not only because E♮
is a melodic and rhythmic goal, but because it reinforces, though an octave
higher, the implications generated by the linear motion and deceptive
cadence of the first two measures (graph 6). These melodic implications
are strongly supported by the harmony. Because the E♮ comes on a six-four
chord whose appoggiatura tones normally resolve by step, the most probable
note to follow is D.

The implied D could have followed directly, as shown in Example 142,
or could have been realized in some other way. One of these Beethoven employs when the triadic motion is repeated a third higher in measures 8–11
(Example 141). He makes the continuation sequential, so the gap from E♮
to G♭ is filled by the F♮ in the next measure, and then moves through E♭
to D (graph 4).[8] Both the earlier triadic motion (graphs 3 and 5) and the
later one (graphs 3a and 4) converge on the E♭ and move together to the
D in measure 12.

$$\text{IV}^{6\natural}_{3} \quad \text{I}^{6}_{4} \quad \text{V}$$

Example 142

Descending motion does in fact follow the E♮ in measure 4. But it is
not by step. The D is conspicuous by its absence. The gap patterning is
emphasized again by the skip of a sixth at the beginning of the echo—and
again the D is avoided. The implied motion from E♭ to D is not realized until
the close of this section of the introduction—in the movement from measure
11 to 12 (Example 141, graph 5). Not only are the registral relationships—
the octave E♭—the same in measure 11 as in measure 4, but the intervallic
relationships are similar: in both places E♭ is a sixth above the bass, first as
part of a C-minor six-four chord and then as part of an E♭-minor triad in
the first inversion (graph 5a). The octave E♭ in measure 11 is the result of

[8] The earlier, less important gap from B♭ to E♭ is filled by the secondary voice
shown in graph 4a.

Example 143

the division of the melodic line which is created by the triadic motion in measures 2–4. The lower E♭ which closes the motto (and its varied repetition in measures 7 and 8) is not really displaced into the upper octave, but persists, moving to the D in measure 12 (graph 6).

Like the patterns which generate them, implications are hierarchic. For example, the implications generated by the gap-fill patterns x and x′, though not immediately realized, are essentially low-level—in the foreground (graphs 1 and 2). Their main pitches give rise to a higher level triadic structure (graph 3). On a still higher structural level, the prolonged E♭ and G♭, which are structurally equivalent, combine to form a long-range triadic pattern implying a B♭, actualized in measures 21 and 22 (Example 143). Supporting this supposition is the manifest octave motion that was implicit in the lower-level triadic motion.

3) One of the most characteristic sequences of sounds in the first movement of the "Les Adieux" Sonata is that which begins the Allegro theme (Example 144A)—a chord progression from an A♭-major triad to a G-major one (n). The relationship is striking both because it is the only common harmonic progression in which two major triads are connected by half-step motion in all voices, and because in this case all the voices actually move in parallel fashion.

As it occurs at the beginning of the Allegro, the progression is equivocal. Usually it is understood as a progression from VI to V in the minor mode. Here it would be in C minor (144B). Or less frequently, the first chord might function as a Neapolitan sixth. In the latter case, the bass would move up a whole step so that the following chord (G major) would be in the six-four position (144C). As it occurs in measure 17, however, the A♭-major chord has been so firmly established by preceding events as the subdominant of E♭ major that a "reading" in C minor seems out of the question—particularly since such an analysis is not supported by what follows.

Example 144

This ambiguity is supported by the fact that melodic and rhythmic processes are not congruent. The melodic connection between the two chords is strong—the stepwise parallel motion is unmistakable and is reinforced by its subsequent continuation in measure 18. In the foreground, there seems to be patent linear motion from A♭ (m. 17) to D (m. 19), and back to A♭ (m. 20). But the rhythmic connection between the two chords is tenuous. For the fourth beat of measure 17 is unquestionably the beginning of an anapest rhythm which reaches temporary closure in measure 19, as the analysis under Example 144A shows. However, though the fourth beat of measure 17 is marked because it is the beginning of a rhythmic group, its metric position is weak. Consequently, from a melodic point of view, the bass (B) seems like a passing-tone between C and the B♭ at the beginning of measure 18.

The proximate consequence of this set of relationships is, as we shall see, that the A♭ chord is primarily related not to the phrase which immediately follows, but to the dominant-tonic progression at the end of the theme, in measures 20 and 21. The more remote consequences are to be found at the beginning of the development section and in the coda.

After a chord on the dominant of E♭ major, the development section continues with the A♭-major to G-major relationship (Example 145A). But

Example 145

now the progression moves to, and is understood as being in, C minor—which appropriately enough is the main key of the development. But here too, the motion is quite uniform and continuous rather than cadential. What seems to be called for is a cadence involving the A♭ to G chord progression which can be unequivocally interpreted in the tonic, E♭ major; and ideally one which moves through a I$_4^6$—V chord progression.

And this is precisely what occurs at the crucial cadence of the coda (Example 145B). There, the G-major triad is treated as a passing chord—a possibility in the Allegro theme—which moves to I$_4^6$ in E♭ major. The great importance of the cadence is shown in the fact that following it, the "Lebewohl" motto is presented for the first time in its archetypal, horn-fifths form (measures 197–199). With this cadence the "problem" generated by the deceptive cadence in measure 2 is literally resolved.

4) The development section begins and ends in C minor and in this respect is related to the deceptive close of the horn-fifths pattern in measure 2 (Example 141). But the second deceptive cadence—V⁷ to VI in E♭—from measure 7 to 8 also has consequences in the development. After a number of measures which are melodically, rhythmically, and harmonically ambiguous, a harmony which we realize (in retrospect) was an augmented-sixth chord—IV$_5^{6\sharp}$ in E♭ minor—leads to a clear dominant-seventh chord in measure 87 (Example 146).

Example 146

Here, for a brief moment, the relationship between the deceptive cadence in minor and the half-step progression of the Allegro seems to be made explicit. The motion of the dominant of E♭ minor to C♭ major in measure 90 is the same as that of the deceptive cadence at measure 8 (Example 147, graph 1), and the reverse motion, from the C♭-major triad to the B♭-major one is the same as the half-step progression of the Allegro theme (graph 2).

Example 147

3.

There is a contemplative, improvisatory quality about the slow introduction. The "quasi fantasia" feeling is the result of a lack of strongly processive relationships between successive foreground events. (Note again the intimate connection between ethetic and implicative relationships—and hierarchic ones as well.) Patterns tend to be quite closed, or, if they are not so, the syntactic connections between them are significantly attenuated. Consequently, though there is hierarchic structuring within low-level patternings, there is little between them. In a sense the Adagio is a *potential* hierarchy rather than an actualized one. Yet the over-all motion is goal-directed, not desultory.

The "Lebewohl" motto with which the introduction begins is, as emphasized earlier, a palpable, well-defined pattern. The melodic motion from third to tonic, the harmonic plan from tonic to dominant to (possible) tonic, and the limits specified by the schema itself—all make us aware that the pattern is at least provisionally complete. Though not forcefully closed, the pivoted rhythmic pattern, 𝅘𝅥 𝅘𝅥 | 𝅘𝅥 , is end-accented and not markedly on-going (Example 148A, level 1). The group is mobile and implicative because of the powerful effect of the deceptive cadence, and because at the beginning of the movement we naturally look forward to more music.

Many of the consequences of the deceptive cadence have already been considered. One more will concern us here. The deflection from a clearly implied tonic establishes a particularly powerful harmonic goal—one regenerated in measures 7 and 8 by a second deceptive cadence: an unequivocal authentic cadence in the tonic, E♭ major. The "need" for such a cadence acts like a magnetic pole, giving direction to the Adagio even as it appears

to be curiously inconclusive and hesitant. The tonic goal creates the ambience within which the ensuing events are understood; the first twenty
measures have an authentic cadence in E♭ as their primary and principal goal.[9]

Because the patterning of the motto is quite closed and because no harmonic, melodic, or rhythmic process connects it to the prolongation, the
relationship between them is essentially additive. The prolongation follows
the motto but is not implied by and does not follow *from* the motto. For
these reasons, the motto tends to be understood as a discrete entity, connected
not so much with the measures which come directly after it as with its own
varied repetition in measures 7 and 8.

The first two measures of the prolongation create a clearly end-accented,
anapest rhythmic group on the primary (1) level (Example 148A). Both
because the B is implied by the second gap-fill patterning (graph 3) and
because the dominant harmony is the goal of the preceding harmonic progression (C minor: V_7^9/IV—IV^6—$IV_5^{6\sharp}$—I_4^6—V) closure is strong. But this
point of relative stability and arrival is immediately weakened by the echo
repetition of the accented part of the pattern; the masculine ending is made
feminine (level 1, measures 4–5).

Example 148

[9] Going further, one might reasonably suggest that the whole movement has as its
goal an authentic cadence with the E♭ above middle C in the soprano, reached on a
clearly articulated end-accented rhythm. And such a cadence occurs only at measure
243, twelve measures before the end of the movement. See Example 140.

The echo "opens up" the rhythmic structure of the prolongation, but mobility is achieved at the expense of implicative connection. Melodically, the echo separates the end of the main part of the prolongation (measure 4) from its implied continuation in measures 6 and 7 (graphs 2 and 3). Rhythmically and harmonically, the echo is only weakly connected to what follows. Register helps to relate the two events, as does the *crescendo* which Beethoven calls for. Nevertheless, the pattern beginning on the last eighth-note of measure 5 is not a goal of the preceding measures. Consequently, despite the *sforzando*, it is weak on the second rhythmic level (2), but as another afterbeat, not as an anacrusis.

The return to the lower octave in measure 6 is not markedly processive, any more than the preceding rise to the echo was. The lower B♭ is not implied by, and is not strongly connected with, the high B♭. The end of measure 6 relates back to the earlier gap-fill patterns and to the first statement of the motto, connecting it with its repetition in measure 7. Although the melodic motion in measure 6 is toward the following G, the rhythmic group is not strongly anacrustic. For the *crescendo* to and the *sforzando* on the first beat of measure 6 tend to tie the following weak beats to the accent, making the group into a fused trochee (level i). In other words, melodic organization and rhythmic structure are not congruent at this point.

If this analysis is correct, it would seem that, from a melodic point of view, the high B♭ is left hanging in mid air—without connection with what directly follows. Its connection is not with the motion through A♭ to G in the lower octave, though this acts as a kind of provisional realization and a clue to its probable motion. Its patterning is register-specific: it is connected with the B♭ in measure 20 (graph 4), where it moves to the G, which is even more strongly implied by the A♭ in measure 17.

In the first six measures, processive bonds appear, for the most part, attenuated. The nonimplicative connection between the motto and the prolongation which comes after it, the additive relationship between the cadence on G and its echo, the weak progression from the echo to the harmonies which follow it, and the ambiguity of motion back to the motto—these are related to, and complemented by, what might be called a *counter-cumulative* hierarchic structure. In a cumulative structure, cohesive, strongly bonded, hierarchic structures are created when units of equal length (e.g., 4 + 4, as in an antecedent-consequent phrase) are combined, or when shorter groups precede a longer one (e.g., 1+1+2, as in a bar-form). These measures exhibit the opposite kind of structure, moving from longer to shorter lengths (Example 148B).

The second six measures are similar to the first in basic phrase structure. Yet near the end, these measures are much more markedly processive than their earlier counterparts, because of the strong sense of goal-directed motion created by the sequence in measures 9–12. The passage is subtly complex and worth analyzing in some detail (Example 149).

Harmonically, the main sequential motion, which employs a version of fourth-species counterpoint, begins with the upbeat to measure 10 (graph 1), but this progression can be traced back to measure 9, where the applied dominant (V/VI—VI) relationship is first presented. Melodically, the sequence contains three interrelated patterings. The first, defined by the harmonic and rhythmic structure, consists of three varied statements of a foreground motive (graph 2). But this pattern is bilevel—made up of the two linear strands shown in graph 3 and 3a. At the same time, the upbeat skip of a third suggests the possibility of a gap-fill patterning (graph 4). Each of these patterings moves through E♭ to the downbeat of measure 12, making the D an emphatic point of arrival.

Though the sequence does continue, in another sense it ends with the third eighth-note of measure 11, where a reversal takes place. Harmonically, the first inversion E♭-minor triad breaks the previously established pattern—even though the bass continues as before. Melodically, there is an interesting paradox: because the intervallic relationships are continued (as the C♭ moves to E♭ at the end of measure 11), we are confident that the sequence is over. For instead of coming on an accent as it would have done had the pattern been rhythmically regular, the E♭ comes on the last eighth-note of the measure. As a result, the C♭ is understood in retrospect as an elision: it acts both as the end of the previous motive and as the beginning of a new one. Because it "should" have been an accented note, the E♭ receives special psychological emphasis. Beethoven "acknowledges" this change of placement and of function by stipulating that the E♭ be played louder than the preceding and following notes. Thus stressed, the E♭ is a particularly strong upbeat. Both for this reason and because it is the goal of much of the previous melodic patterning (also see Example 141, graphs 5 and 6), the D is a particularly heavy downbeat.

Though it is an emphatic downbeat, the D in measure 12 is very mobile, for a number of reasons. Rhythmically, the motion from measure 11 to 12 is end-accented on the lowest level—as the motion from measure 6 to 7 was not. But on the next level (2), the iambic group, taken as a whole, is weak: a high-level afterbeat. To a considerable extent this is because the accent is harmonized by an unstable second-inversion dominant-seventh chord. Finally, though the melodic-rhythmic organization of the upper voices is subtly, but significantly changed, the bass line moves as before; and, since its motion is quite uniform (graph 5), continuation is implied—and occurs.

Example 149

If the motion at the end of this section is more patently processive than that of the preceding one (measures 1–6), the motion at the beginning is, if anything, less so. Because of the B♭ upbeat in the bass in measure 7, the full dominant-seventh harmony, and the contrary motion in the outer voices,

closure at the end of this variant of the motto is considerably more forceful
than it was in the first version of the "Lebewohl" motive. Moreover, the
separation between the motto and its prolongation is emphasized by parallel
skips in all voices. Despite the dominant harmony which precedes it, the
second statement of the motto has the aura of a fresh beginning—partly because the striking diminished-seventh chord which harmonizes the first note
does not follow from the dominant chord, but is connected with the harmony at the beginning of measure 3. As a result, there is a feeling that the
"Lebewohl" motto returns not because it is implied by the prolongation that
precedes it, but because the previous statement of the motto was deflected
from its goal. It was only a provisional realization. The repetition in measures 7 and 8 is, so to speak, a second "try" at reaching a cadence in E♭; and
it too is abortive.

Even though the prolongation in measures 3–6 intervenes, the second
statement of the motto is understood as being related to, even subliminally
grouped with, the first. It is this relationship of varied repetition at the same
pitch-level which gives rise to what I earlier referred to as potential hierarchy. For, to the extent that the two statements of the motto group together—are felt to constitute a single event—they imply the possibility of a
bar-form organization: 2+2+4. This type of structure suggests itself because, as we have seen time and time again in the course of this study, like
patterns tend to imply a more extensive event to which both can be related.
The possibility of such grouping is indicated by the dotted lines of level 2
in the rhythmic analysis of Examples 148 and 149.

The two prolongations are also related to one another, so that their
combined high-level motion, E♭ to G♭, implies the B♭ so prominent in measures 21 and 22 (Example 143). It also follows from this analysis that the
motto's main motion, doubled at the octave by motion through the triad
(Example 141), is to the passage beginning with the D in measure 12.
And this hypothesis is supported by the construction of the Allegro theme
which combines the two events.

Measures 12–16 are quite straightforward and, in contrast to what precedes them, manifestly goal-directed (Example 150). Melodically, the middle-level motion is a diminished fifth, from D to A♭, which implies the G
realized in measure 17 (graph 1). The foreground scale-line implies continuation to B♭, because conjunct motion begun on a weakbeat tends to continue on to the next downbeat. Thus the F's in measure 13 and 14 are con-

tinuations of, and appropriate goals for, the linear patterns which lead to them. But because they do not continue the preceding linear motions, the Ab's in measures 15 and 16 are not satisfactory goals. In measures 19 and 20 a compressed version of this linear motion (graph 3) leads to the implied Bb (graph 2). In addition to the convergence of these conjunct patternings, the Bb "left hanging" in measure 6 also was analyzed as implying the Bb in measure 20. Thus three implicative patternings converge on the penultimate note of the Allegro theme.

Example 150

Rhythmically measures 12–16 function as an anacrusis to the Allegro—both on the highest level and, in the last two measures, on lower levels as well. Here the pattern of repetition latent in the "Lebewohl" motto and its restatement seem to be made manifest. A two-beat motive (x) which is almost an inversion of the motto is repeated (x′)—implying that a longer, four-beat event will follow. Instead, however, a varied version of the motive (y) is stated a third higher and then repeated (y′). The two pairs combine to form a higher-level repetition, $(1 + 1) + (1 + 1)$, which tends to imply a four-measure group. "Tends," because when the Ab's in measure 16 come on weak beats, the pattern is prevented from reaching satisfactory closure. The weakbeats become upbeats which lead to the Ab that begins the Allegro. In short, like the repetition of the motto, though more explicitly, this passage is a potential bar-form, and the compelling force of the Allegro theme arises in part out of the fact that it is the realization of the need for a cohesive four-measure melodic-rhythmic-harmonic event.

4.

The driving energy of the Allegro theme is also a result of the compression and unification of elements that were previously only loosely connected. The "Lebewohl" motto and the last section of the Adagio are welded together to form a single event—the Allegro theme. As Example 151 shows, there is a clear conformant relationship between the motto, together with its extension to measure 12, and the descending motion of the Allegro theme. The similarity between the end of the slow introduction (measures 12–16) and the last part of the theme is no less striking.

Example 151

The patterning of the bass-lines is also similar. The relationship between the bass-line at the end of the slow introduction and the end of the Allegro theme is obvious (Example 151). The conformant relationship between the bass-line at the beginning of the Adagio and that at the beginning of the Allegro is somewhat less so, but, as Example 152 shows, it exists. It is not primarily that both patterns are chromatic descending lines, but that in each case the main point of structural articulation (measures 12 and 19) occurs on a dominant-seventh chord in second inversion, with D in the soprano. The compacting synthesis is not merely within the bass and soprano separately, but between them. In the Adagio the descending bass-line accompanied the

Example 152

prolongation, not the motto. In the Allegro theme, the bass-line derived from the prolongation pattern is, as it were, fused with, almost imposed upon, the melodic line of the motto. The intensity of the opening of the Allegro is thereby increased considerably.

Rhythmically the Allegro theme is a single event on the highest structural level (Example 153, level 3). The dotted half-note, A♭, is both the goal of the rhythmic events which immediately precede it and the accented beginning of the new patterning. It is separated out, however, as an accent on the highest level: that is, it is related not to the iambic group, [musical notation] ,

which directly follows it, or even to the varied version of the motto, but to the whole weak group that unites it to the accented G at the end of the theme (measure 21).

Example 153

In the second rhythmic level (2), the next event is a cohesive, bar-form version of the "Lebewohl" motto. But the clear articulation and closure potential at the end of the group does not take place. The extra stress of the *sforzando* on the downbeat E♭ compels it to function as the beginning of a rhythmic group as well as the end of one. Beethoven makes this relationship clear by putting a phrase mark from the E♭ to the B♭. The rising scale is anacrustic to the G in measure 21, and its fusion, through the pivotal E♭ and D, with the earlier bar-form pattern makes the whole middle part of the theme functions as a weak group connecting two high-level accents (level 3).

This analysis of the rhythmic structure of the Allegro theme helps to make the larger melodic and harmonic patterning clear. It indicates that the over-all melodic motion is from the A♭ in measure 17 to the G in measure 21, and that the basic harmonic progression is an authentic cadence in the tonic (Example 154).

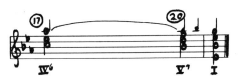

Example 154

Since, as we have seen, the Allegro theme is a synthesis of the main patternings of the Adagio, it is not unreasonable to consider the whole passage—the first twenty-one measures—as a single event: more specifically, as an extended prolongation of tonic harmony with the third in the soprano voice. Though the prolongations in the Adagio ultimately lead the motto to the D in measure 12 and are important because of the long-range implication which they generate, they do not play a decisive role in shaping the process of the highest level. Nor is the arrival of the D—either in measure 12 or in measure 19—an event on the highest level. Both in the Adagio and the Allegro, whatever structural importance the D might have had is undermined by the six-four position of the dominant chord and by the on-going motion of the bass-line.

The harmonic-melodic processes generated in the Adagio are not closed or even decisively articulated at the beginning of the Allegro. They continue to the cadence in measure 21—at which point a new impulse carries the music forward. One indication that these measures constitute a single process is that the bass-line moves in an essentially continuous linear manner from the C in measure 2, through the C in measure 17, and to the B♭ in measure 20—at which point the first disjunct, root progression of the movement takes place (see the bass-line in Example 151). If this analysis has merit, then, melodically, the first twenty-one measures of the movement may be considered to be an extended neighbor-note figure: G—A♭—G; and, harmonically, they constitute a high-level cadence in E♭ major (Example 155).

Example 155

The first twenty-one measures of this movement are a single *process*, but they are differentiated in terms of *form*. From a formal point of view, the sonata-form structure begins in measure 17. This beginning is made clear by the change in tempo, by the abrupt *forte* on the repeated A♭, and by the contrasting character of the Allegro theme, which, though derived from the patterns presented in the Adagio, is significantly new. There is, in short, a bifurcation of form and process which can be diagrammed as follows:

PROCESS:	(melody)	G. . . . . .A♭– A♭– G
	(harmony)	I. . . . . .IV⁶–V⁷ – I
FORM:		Introduction Sonata form
		a(1–6) — a′(7–12) — b(13–16) A (17–21)
		first theme group

Though the implicative processes generated in the Adagio transcend this formal articulation and have important consequences in the sonata-form proper, it is nevertheless a distinct and separate formal entity—as is shown by the placement of the repeat marks. Beethoven does not return to the tempo and pace of the Adagio, including it as part of the sonata-form structure, as he does in the first movement of the String Quarter in B♭ Major, Opus 130.

The formal articulation which marks the beginning of the Allegro was attributed not only to the marked change in dynamics and tempo, but also to the evident contrast between the ethos of the Adagio and that of the first Allegro theme. The ethos of the Adagio has already been considered. The character and feeling-tone of the Allegro theme is not merely the result of the faster tempo and louder dynamic level, but of syntactic processes—melody, rhythm, and harmony. It is not just tempo which changes, pace changes; and it is not just dynamics which change, but the level of psychological intensity. And these, of course, complement one another.

Melodically, the separate events of the Adagio are compacted into a single kinetic gesture. Here there are no introspective pauses, no contemplative repetitions. The chromatic motion of the bass is emphatically goal-directed, and because each note of the motto is accompanied by two harmonies instead of one, pace and psychological intensity are increased. Moreover, beneath the ambiguity of the chromatic bass motion lies the the latent possibility of a rapidly moving cycle of fifths—a possibility that contributes something to the urgency of the first part of the theme.

Rhythm, too, is important. On the lowest level (1) (Example 153), the end-accented groups—emphasized by the melodic-harmonic repetition across the barline—are incisive. Their combination, on the next level, creates a potentially end-accented bar-form. But the final notes of this pattern function as the beginning of a new rhythmic impulse as well. This restructuring not only prevents the relaxation of tension which would have occurred had the phrase closed on D, but the elision of the two patterings increases the force of the melodic-rhythmic motion. The kinetic character of the theme, thus reinforced, is carried forward by the contrary motion between soprano and bass.

Like other relationships—implicative, hierarchic, and conformant—generated during the first twenty measures of the "Les Adieux" Sonata, the contrast between the contemplative melancholy of the Adagio and the fervent intensity of the Allegro theme has consequences through the movement. But the analysis must end here—not only because the reader's interest must be flagging and his patience exhausted, but because, as mentioned earlier, the rigorous analysis of ethetic relationships is beyond my knowledge and skill.

Much work needs to be done, both in this aspect of analysis and in the study of implicative processes and hierarchic structures. There will be disagreements about these matters. Sometimes different explanations of a passage or composition will really conflict: for instance, when they stem from fundamental differences in theory. At other times, disagreement will be more apparent than real, and explanations will be complementary, not conflicting: for instance, when different hierarchic levels or different parameters are made the chief focus of attention; or when different kinds of relationships—conformant, implicative, hierarchic, or ethetic ones—are the basis for the analysis of a particular work.

Whatever the reasons for such disagreements, they should encourage, rather than discourage, critical analysis, not only because the task itself is challenging and fascinating, but because there is no escape. For our devotion to music ultimately stems from our delight in, and love for, particular compositions. And everything we do—all of our study and research—seeks in the end to illuminate as fully as possible the source and basis of their power to engage and entrance us.

Index of Subjects and Names

Abraham, Gerald, 56 n.

Abstraction. *See* Patterning; Understanding

Accompaniment: absence of, permits ambiguity, 169; structure clarified by, 161, 170, 175, 184

Actualization. *See* Realization

Ad hoc hypotheses. *See* Hypotheses

Aeschylus, 16

Aesthetic experience. *See* Experience

Affective experience: depends on cognition, 6, 113; deviation and, 213; intellectual experience and, 6, 113, 213. *See also* Ethos; Kinaesthetic experience

Alternatives: awareness of, affects understanding, 19, 111–113; composer's, considered by critic, 18 f. (*see also* Composers); awareness of, depends on patterning, 111 f. *See also* Criticism; Implicative relationships

Analysis. *See* Criticism; Style analysis

Anomaly: discussion and explanation of, 20, 118, 223, 247; possibility of, 20 f.

Antecedent-consequent patterns (A-A'): discussion of, 10–11, 14, 19 f. [Ex. 1], 35, 40, 86, 95, 144 [Ex. 17], 52 f. [Ex. 29], 81, 86, 89 f., 96, 98 [Ex. 47], 102 f. [Ex. 54], 103, 147 [Ex. 56], 142–144 [Ex. 70], 178 [Ex. 95], 181 f. [Ex. 98], 228–230 [Ex. 129], 230–234 [Ex. 130–131], 240 f. [Ex. 134]; equivocal case of, 132 f.; high-level, 96; rhythm does not structure, 86

Archetypal schemata. *See* Schemata

Aristotle, 26

Avant-garde, music of, 66

Axial melodies, 94, 183–191: additive and formal, 94; discussion of, 94, 175 [Ex. 52], 184–187 [Ex. 99], 187–191 [Ex. 100–101], 186 f. [Ex. 106]

Bach, J. S., 16, 21, 22 f., 23, 31, 50, 67, 89, 97, 110, 205 *

Bar-form patterns (a-a-b): anapest rhythms equivalent to, 85 (*see also* Rhythm); discussion of, 39 f. [Ex. 17], 85–98 *passim* [Ex. 47], 188 [Ex. 100], 239 [Ex. 133], 261 [Ex. 148–149], 262 [Ex. 150], 265–267 [Ex. 153]; other instances, but not discussed as bar forms, Examples 21, 29, 63, 66, 85–87, 134; sonata-form not, 96

Baroque music, 209: incomplete rhythms uncommon in, 205

Barth, John, 5

Beardsley, M. C., 73 n.

* References to particular compositions are given in the Index of Music.

ble, 76–78; intention and (*see* Intentionality); masking of, 45–48, 75; memory aided by, 58, 70, 97; methodology and (*see* Method, exigetic; Reti, R.); motivic individuality enhances, 48 f.; in nineteenth and twentieth centuries, 55–59; parameters and (*see* Parameters); processive, 48 f., 53 f., 61; psychic parsimony and (*see* Parsimony); in prolongations, 227, 241; Reti's analysis of, 59–65, 70 f. (*see also* Reti, R.); rhythm and (*see* Rhythm); significance of, between movements, 57 f., 70–72, 97; significance of, between works, 71–73; strength of, 46–49, 54, 74 f.; style and, 74–75; thematic transformation and, 55–59; unity and, 64–67 (*see also* Unity)

Conjunct patterns, 131–144. *See also* Linear melodies

Contextual discrepancy, 123, 196–213; basis for implication, 196, 218, 244. *See also* Potentiality

Continuation, principle of, 33, 130

Convergence: discussions of, 100 [Ex. 53], 141 [Ex. 68], 142–144 [Ex. 70–74], 147 f. [Ex. 76], 149 [Ex. 77], 157 [Ex. 82], 163 f., 165 [Ex. 86], 170 [Ex. 90], 173 [Ex. 92], 180 [Ex. 96–97], 198 [Ex. 105], 224 [Ex. 124], 262 [Ex. 150]

Cooke, Deryck, 69 n.

Counterfactuals: psychological significance of, 112; understanding and, 112

Counterpoint: fourth species, 141 f., 168, 259; gesture and, 208 f.; probabilistic, 7; pure process and, 92 n.; sixteenth-century, 8

Critical analysis. *See* Criticism

Criticism: *ad hoc* hypotheses used in, 12–14 (*see also* Hypotheses); affective experience and, 6; alternatives considered in, 18 f., 116; composer's choices and, 18 f., 22 f.; conscientious, 34; description and, 9; disagreements about, 121, 268; documentation and, 21 f.; not exhaustive or definitive, 24 f., 105; explanation and, 4, 9–12, 14, 130 (*see also* Explanation); knowledge necessary for, 17; length of, 14 f.; limits of, 4 f., 14,

24 f., 110; methods used in, 17 f., 24, Chapter VI *passim*, 231 n. (*see also* Methodology; Methods); need for, 25, 268; objections to, 4–6; particulars explained by, 6 f., 12–15 (*see also* Hypotheses); and performance (*see* Performance); relevance of sketches for, 23, 77–79; style analysis and (*see* Style analysis); theory and, 9, 12, 14; views of composers and theorists and, 21 f.; individual responses not explained by, 4

Deflections: alternative goals created by, 119, 130; definition, 118 f.; discussion, 102 [Ex. 54], 118 [Ex. 59], 124 [Ex. 61], 154 [Ex. 80], 160 [Ex. 83], 177 [Ex. 95]; gap creates, 124 (*see also* Gaps, structural); reversal a special case of, 119 (*see also* Reversal)

Determinism, mistaken applied to music, 20

Dialectical change, music as, 56–59, 64 f.

Digression: need for, 10–12 [Ex. 1 & 4], 27, 241. *See also* Instability

Disjunct patterns, 144–174. *See also* Gap-fill melodies; Gaps, structural; Triadic melodies

Dray, William, 19

Dynamics: ethos and, 35, 40 f., 128–130, 166, 221, 243; psychological intensity and, 267; structure clarified by, 102, 144, 155, 223, 267; syntactic function of, 35 f. (*see also* Stress)

Echo: morphology normalized by, 104 [Ex. 57]; potential realized by, 155 [Ex. 79]; stability weakened by, 257 f. [Ex. 148]

Eliot, T. S., 6

Elision: bifurcation of form and process creates, 100; emphasis created by, 259 [Ex. 149]; morphological dissonance created by, 233 [Ex. 131], 236 [Ex. 133]; sequence welded by, 239 [Ex. 133]

Ethetic relationships. *See* Ethos

Ethos: compression affects, 263, 267; deviation and, 219, 221, 222, 243; implication inseparable from, 218, 223,

Index of Music

DATE DUE